中国人民银行

THE PEOPLE'S BANK OF CHINA QUAR

2020-1

总第 97 期

VOLUME XCVII

| 1 | 主要经济指标概览 | **4-8** |
|---|---|---|
| 2 | 金融机构货币统计 | **9-55** |
| 2.1 | 主要金融指标 | 9 |
| 2.2 | 主要金融指标（消除季节因素） | 10 |
| 2.3 | 社会融资规模增量统计表 | 11 |
| 2.4 | 社会融资规模存量统计表 | 15 |
| 2.5 | 金融机构信贷收支表（人民币） | 16 |
| 2.6 | 存款性公司概览 | 20 |
| 2.7 | 货币当局资产负债表 | 24 |
| 2.8 | 其他存款性公司资产负债表 | 28 |
| 2.9 | 中资大型银行资产负债表 | 32 |
| 2.10 | 中资中型银行资产负债表 | 36 |
| 2.11 | 中资小型银行资产负债表 | 40 |
| 2.12 | 外资银行资产负债表 | 44 |
| 2.13 | 农村信用社资产负债表 | 48 |
| 2.14 | 财务公司资产负债表 | 52 |
| 3 | 宏观经济金融运行监测 | **56-59** |
| 3.1 | 金融统计数据报告 | 56 |
| 3.2 | 景气状况分析: 2019 年四季度 | 58 |
| 3.3 | 宏观经济 | 59 |
| 4 | 金融市场统计 | **60-72** |
| 4.1 | 全国银行间同业拆借交易统计表 | 60 |
| 4.2 | 全国银行间质押式回购交易统计表 | 64 |
| 4.3 | 国内各类债券发行统计表 | 68 |
| 4.4 | 国内各类债券余额统计表 | 69 |
| 4.5 | 人民币汇率统计表 | 70 |
| 4.6 | 国内股票市场统计表 | 72 |
| 5 | 利率 | **73-75** |
| 5.1 | 中央银行基准利率 | 73 |
| 5.2 | 金融机构: 人民币法定存款基准利率 | 74 |
| 5.3 | 金融机构: 人民币法定贷款基准利率 | 75 |
| 6 | 资金流量表（金融交易账户） | **76-77** |
| 6.1 | 2018 年资金流量表（金融交易账户） | 76 |
| 7 | 经济调查 | **78-81** |
| 7.1 | 5000 户企业主要财务指标 | 78 |
| 7.2 | 5000 户企业主要财务分析指标 | 80 |
| 7.3 | 5000 户企业景气扩散指数 | 81 |
| 8 | 物价统计 | **82-83** |
| 8.1 | 主要物价指数 | 82 |
| 8.2 | 企业商品价格指数 | 83 |
| 9 | 主要经济金融指标图 | **84-90** |
| 10 | 主要指标的概念及定义 | **91-109** |

目 录

Contents

# 目录
# 录

Contents

| 1 | Survey of Major Economic Indicators | 4-8 |
|---|---|---|
| 2 | Monetary Statistics of Financial Institutions | 9-55 |
| 2.1 | Major Financial Indicators | 9 |
| 2.2 | Major Financial Indicators (Seasonally Adjusted) | 10 |
| 2.3 | Aggregate Financing to the Real Economy (Flow) | 11 |
| 2.4 | Aggregate Financing to the Real Economy (Stock) | 15 |
| 2.5 | Sources and Uses of Credit Funds of Financial Institutions (RMB) | 16 |
| 2.6 | Depository Corporations Survey | 20 |
| 2.7 | Balance Sheet of Monetary Authority | 24 |
| 2.8 | Balance Sheet of Other Depository Corporations | 28 |
| 2.9 | Balance Sheet of Large-sized Domestic Banks | 32 |
| 2.10 | Balance Sheet of Medium-sized Domestic Banks | 36 |
| 2.11 | Balance Sheet of Small-sized Domestic Banks | 40 |
| 2.12 | Balance Sheet of Foreign-funded Banks | 44 |
| 2.13 | Balance Sheet of Rural Credit Cooperatives | 48 |
| 2.14 | Balance Sheet of Finance Companies | 52 |
| 3 | Macroeconomic & Financial Situation | 56-59 |
| 3.1 | Financial Statistics Data Report | 57 |
| 3.2 | Business Climate Analysis: 2019 Q4 | 58 |
| 3.3 | Macroeconomics | 59 |
| 4 | Financial Market Statistics | 60-72 |
| 4.1 | Statistics of Interbank Lending | 60 |
| 4.2 | Statistics of Interbank Pledged Repo | 64 |
| 4.3 | Statistics of Debt Securities Issue | 68 |
| 4.4 | Statistics of Debt Securities Outstanding | 69 |
| 4.5 | Statistics of Exchange Rate | 70 |
| 4.6 | Statistics of Stock Market | 72 |
| 5 | Interest Rates | 73-75 |
| 5.1 | Benchmark Interest Rates of Central Bank | 73 |
| 5.2 | Financial Institutions: Official Benchmark Rates of RMB Deposits | 74 |
| 5.3 | Financial Institutions: Official Benchmark Rates of RMB Loans | 75 |
| 6 | Flow of Funds Statement(Financial Transactions Accounts) | 76-77 |
| 6.1 | Flow of Funds Statement, 2018(Financial Transactions Accounts) | 76 |
| 7 | Economic Research | 78-81 |
| 7.1 | Major Financial Indicators of 5000 Principal Enterprises | 78 |
| 7.2 | Major Financial Analytical Indicators of 5000 Principal Enterprises | 80 |
| 7.3 | Diffusion Indices of Business Survey of 5000 Principal Enterprises | 81 |
| 8 | Price Statistics | 82-83 |
| 8.1 | Major Price Indices | 82 |
| 8.2 | Corporate Goods Price Indices(CGPI) | 83 |
| 9 | Charts of Major Economic & Financial Indicators | 84-90 |
| 10 | Concepts and Definitions for Major Indicators | 91-109 |

## 1 1 主要经济指标
## Major Economic Indicators

单位：亿元
Unit:100 Million Yuan

| 时间<br>Time | 国内生产总值 *<br>（现价）<br>Gross<br>Domestic<br>Product*<br>(Current Price) | 第一产业<br>Primary<br>Industry | 第二产业<br>Secondary<br>Industry | 第三产业<br>Tertiary<br>Industry |
|---|---|---|---|---|
| 2012 | 538580 | 49085 | 244643 | 244852 |
| 2013 | 592963 | 53028 | 261956 | 277979 |
| 2014 | 641281 | 55626 | 277572 | 308083 |
| 2015 | 685993 | 57775 | 282040 | 346178 |
| 2016 | 740061 | 60139 | 296548 | 383374 |
| 2017.01 | | | | |
| 2017.02 | | | | |
| 2017.03 | 179403 | 8206 | 69704 | 101493 |
| 2017.04 | | | | |
| 2017.05 | | | | |
| 2017.06 | 378581 | 20851 | 152358 | 205372 |
| 2017.07 | | | | |
| 2017.08 | | | | |
| 2017.09 | 588405 | 39107 | 237116 | 312183 |
| 2017.10 | | | | |
| 2017.11 | | | | |
| 2017.12 | 820754 | 62100 | 332743 | 425912 |
| 2018.01 | | | | |
| 2018.02 | | | | |
| 2018.03 | 197920 | 8574 | 77117 | 112229 |
| 2018.04 | | | | |
| 2018.05 | | | | |
| 2018.06 | 417215 | 21576 | 168558 | 227081 |
| 2018.07 | | | | |
| 2018.08 | | | | |
| 2018.09 | 646711 | 39800 | 261823 | 345088 |
| 2018.10 | | | | |
| 2018.11 | | | | |
| 2018.12 | 919281 | 64745 | 364835 | 489701 |
| 2019.01 | | | | |
| 2019.02 | | | | |
| 2019.03 | 213433 | 8769 | 82347 | 122317 |
| 2019.04 | | | | |
| 2019.05 | | | | |
| 2019.06 | 450933 | 23207 | 179984 | 247743 |
| 2019.07 | | | | |
| 2019.08 | | | | |
| 2019.09 | 697798 | 43005 | 277869 | 376925 |
| 2019.10 | | | | |
| 2019.11 | | | | |
| 2019.12 | 990865 | 70467 | 386165 | 534233 |

* 季度国内生产总值为当年累计数。
* The quarterly data for GDP are grand totals of current year.

## 1-2 主要经济指标
## Major Economic Indicators

单位：%<br>Unit: %

| 时间<br>Time | 国内生产总值 *<br>Gross Domestic Product* | 第一产业<br>Primary Industry | 第二产业<br>Secondary Industry | 第三产业<br>Tertiary Industry | 工业增加值 **<br>Industrial Value-added** | 国有及国有控股企业<br>State-owned and State-holding Enterprises | 集体企业<br>Collective Enterprises | 外商及港澳台投资企业<br>Foreign-funded Enterprises |
|---|---|---|---|---|---|---|---|---|
| 2011 | 9.60 | 4.20 | 10.70 | 9.50 | 13.90 | 9.90 | 9.30 | 10.40 |
| 2012 | 7.90 | 4.50 | 8.40 | 8.00 | 10.00 | 6.40 | 7.10 | 6.30 |
| 2013 | 7.80 | 3.80 | 8.00 | 8.30 | 9.70 | 6.90 | 4.30 | 8.30 |
| 2014 | 7.30 | 4.10 | 7.40 | 7.80 | 8.30 | 4.90 | 1.70 | 6.30 |
| 2015 | 6.90 | 3.90 | 6.20 | 8.20 | 6.10 | 1.40 | 1.20 | 3.70 |
| 2016 | 6.70 | 3.30 | 6.30 | 7.70 | 6.00 | 2.00 | -1.30 | 4.50 |
| | | | | | | | | |
| 2017.01 | | | | | | | | |
| 2017.02 | | | | | | | | |
| 2017.03 | 6.8 | 3.0 | 6.2 | 7.7 | 7.6 | 7.7 | 1.5 | 7.1 |
| 2017.04 | | | | | 6.5 | 5.6 | 1.9 | 5.5 |
| 2017.05 | | | | | 6.5 | 6.2 | 3.2 | 5.9 |
| 2017.06 | 6.8 | 3.5 | 6.2 | 7.7 | 7.6 | 6.8 | 3.9 | 8.0 |
| 2017.07 | | | | | 6.4 | 6.7 | -3.6 | 6.7 |
| 2017.08 | | | | | 6.0 | 7.8 | -2.1 | 7.9 |
| 2017.09 | 6.8 | 3.7 | 6.1 | 7.8 | 6.6 | 9.0 | -2.6 | 8.9 |
| 2017.10 | | | | | 6.2 | 6.6 | 3.6 | 6.5 |
| 2017.11 | | | | | 6.1 | 6.3 | -0.7 | 6.8 |
| 2017.12 | 6.8 | 4.0 | 5.9 | 7.9 | 6.2 | 5.0 | 0.5 | 5.7 |
| | | | | | | | | |
| 2018.01 | | | | | | | | |
| 2018.02 | | | | | | | | |
| 2018.03 | 6.8 | 3.2 | 6.3 | 7.5 | 6.0 | 5.7 | 3.9 | 4.9 |
| 2018.04 | | | | | 7.0 | 7.7 | -6.4 | 6.8 |
| 2018.05 | | | | | 6.8 | 8.1 | -2.9 | 8.4 |
| 2018.06 | 6.8 | 3.3 | 6.1 | 7.6 | 6.0 | 6.1 | -1.9 | 5.4 |
| 2018.07 | | | | | 6.0 | 6.2 | -2.8 | 6.1 |
| 2018.08 | | | | | 6.1 | 5.6 | -1.2 | 4.9 |
| 2018.09 | 6.7 | 3.4 | 5.9 | 7.7 | 5.8 | 5.6 | 2.0 | 3.2 |
| 2018.10 | | | | | 5.9 | 4.6 | -3.6 | 3.9 |
| 2018.11 | | | | | 5.4 | 3.9 | 2.0 | 1.9 |
| 2018.12 | 6.6 | 3.5 | 5.8 | 7.6 | 5.7 | 3.6 | -1.4 | 1.7 |
| | | | | | | | | |
| 2019.01 | | | | | 6.8 | | | |
| 2019.02 | | | | | 3.4 | | | |
| 2019.03 | 6.4 | 2.7 | 6.1 | 7.0 | 8.5 | 4.7 | | 4.2 |
| 2019.04 | | | | | 5.4 | 6.0 | | 2.5 |
| 2019.05 | | | | | 5.0 | 3.7 | | -0.3 |
| 2019.06 | 6.3 | 3.0 | 5.8 | 7.0 | 6.3 | 6.2 | | 1.8 |
| 2019.07 | | | | | 4.8 | 3.7 | | -0.2 |
| 2019.08 | | | | | 4.4 | 4.1 | | 1.3 |
| 2019.09 | 6.2 | 2.9 | 5.6 | 7.0 | 5.8 | 4.9 | | 2.9 |
| 2019.10 | | | | | 4.7 | 4.8 | | 2.1 |
| 2019.11 | | | | | 6.2 | 3.7 | | 3.2 |
| 2019.12 | 6.1 | 3.1 | 5.7 | 6.9 | 6.9 | 7.0 | | 4.8 |

\* 国内生产总值累计增长率和工业增加值当月增长率按可比价格计算。

\* The growth rates of accumulative GDP and the growth rates of monthly industrial value-added are calculated on the basis of comparable price.

\*\* 工业增加值口径自 2011 年起改为年主营业务收入 2000 万元及以上的工业企业。

\*\* The industrial value-added has been adjusted to industrial enterprises with the annual sales income from main business over 20 million yuan since 2011.

1 3 主要经济指标
## Major Economic Indicators

单位：亿元<br>Unit: 100 Million Yuan

| 时间<br>Time | 固定资产投资（不含农户）*<br>Fixed Assets<br>Investment<br>（Excluding Rural Households）* | 国有及国有控股<br>State-owned and<br>State-holding Units | 房地产开发<br>Real Estate<br>Development | 消费品零售额 **<br>Total Retail Sales<br>of Consumer<br>Goods** |
|---|---|---|---|---|
| 2012 | 364835 | 123694 | 71804 | 207167 |
| 2013 | 436528 | 144056 | 86013 | 234380 |
| 2014 | 502005 | 161629 | 95036 | 262394 |
| 2015 | 551590 | 178933 | 95979 | 300931 |
| 2016 | 596501 | 213096 | 102581 | 332316 |
| | | | | |
| 2017.01 | | | | |
| 2017.02 | 41378 | 14662 | 9854 | |
| 2017.03 | 93777 | 33087 | 19292 | 27864 |
| 2017.04 | 144327 | 51476 | 27732 | 27279 |
| 2017.05 | 203718 | 72912 | 37595 | 29459 |
| 2017.06 | 280605 | 102022 | 50610 | 29808 |
| 2017.07 | 337409 | 123013 | 59761 | 29610 |
| 2017.08 | 394150 | 143827 | 69494 | 30330 |
| 2017.09 | 458478 | 168164 | 80644 | 30870 |
| 2017.10 | 517818 | 189881 | 90544 | 34241 |
| 2017.11 | 575057 | 211295 | 100387 | 34108 |
| 2017.12 | 631684 | 232887 | 109799 | 34734 |
| | | | | |
| 2018.01 | | | | |
| 2018.02 | 44626 | | 10831 | |
| 2018.03 | 100763 | | 21291 | 29194 |
| 2018.04 | 154358 | | 30592 | 28542 |
| 2018.05 | 216043 | | 41420 | 30359 |
| 2018.06 | 297316 | | 55531 | 30842 |
| 2018.07 | 355798 | | 65886 | 30734 |
| 2018.08 | 415158 | | 76519 | 31542 |
| 2018.09 | 483442 | | 88665 | 32005 |
| 2018.10 | 547567 | | 99325 | 35534 |
| 2018.11 | 609267 | | 110083 | 35260 |
| 2018.12 | 635636 | | 120264 | 35893 |
| | | | | |
| 2019.01 | | | | |
| 2019.02 | 44849 | | 12090 | |
| 2019.03 | 101871 | | 23803 | 31726 |
| 2019.04 | 155747 | | 34217 | 30586 |
| 2019.05 | 217555 | | 46075 | 32956 |
| 2019.06 | 299100 | | 61609 | 33878 |
| 2019.07 | 348892 | | 72843 | 33073 |
| 2019.08 | 400628 | | 84589 | 33896 |
| 2019.09 | 461204 | | 98008 | 34495 |
| 2019.10 | 510880 | | 109603 | 38104 |
| 2019.11 | 533718 | | 121265 | 38094 |
| 2019.12 | 551478 | | 132194 | 38777 |

* 自 2011 年起，投资项目统计起点标准由原来的 50 万元调整为 500 万元，"固定资产投资（不含农户）"等于原口径的"城镇固定资产投资"加上"农村企事业组织项目投资"。

* Since 2011, investment indicators have been calculated using new threshold criteria of 5 million yuan instead of 500 thousand yuan in the past. "Fixed Assets Investment(Excluding Rural Households)" equals to "Fixed Assets Investment in Urban Area" under the old creteria plus "Investment of Rural Enterprises and Institutions".

** 自 2010 年 1 月起，"消费品零售额"采用新的分组替代原来的分组。

** Since January 2010, "Total Retail Sales of Consumer Goods" has adopted new categories.

## 1 4 主要经济指标
## Major Economic Indicators

单位：亿美元（除另注明外）
Unit:100 Million USD (unless noted otherwise)

| 时间<br>Time | 人均收入<br>（单位：元人民币）<br>Income Per Capita<br>(Unit:RMB Yuan) | | 进出口总值<br>Trade<br>Volume | | | 贸易差额<br>Trade<br>Balance | 外商直接投资 *<br>Foreign<br>Direct<br>Investment* | 外汇储备 *<br>Foreign<br>Exchange<br>Reserves* |
|---|---|---|---|---|---|---|---|---|
| | 城镇居民可支配收入<br>Disposable Income<br>of Urban Households | 农村居民可支配收入 **<br>Disposable Income of<br>Rural Households** | | 出口<br>Export | 进口<br>Import | | | |
| 2012 | 24565 | 7917 | 38671 | 20487 | 18184 | 2303 | 1117 | 33116 |
| 2013 | 26467 | 9430 | 41590 | 22090 | 19500 | 2590 | 1176 | 38213 |
| 2014 | 28844 | 10489 | 43015 | 23423 | 19592 | 3831 | 1196 | 38430 |
| 2015 | 31195 | 11422 | 39530 | 22735 | 16796 | 5939 | 1263 | 33304 |
| 2016 | 33616 | 12363 | 36856 | 20976 | 15879 | 5097 | 1260 | 30105 |
| 2017.01 | | | 3119 | 1803 | 1316 | 487 | 120 | 29982 |
| 2017.02 | | | 2486 | 1188 | 1298 | -109 | 207 | 30051 |
| 2017.03 | 9986 | 3880 | 3358 | 1792 | 1565 | 227 | 338 | 30091 |
| 2017.04 | | | 3190 | 1778 | 1413 | 365 | 427 | 30295 |
| 2017.05 | | | 3383 | 1891 | 1492 | 399 | 509 | 30536 |
| 2017.06 | 18322 | 6562 | 3483 | 1948 | 1535 | 412 | 657 | 30568 |
| 2017.07 | | | 3394 | 1921 | 1473 | 449 | 721 | 30807 |
| 2017.08 | | | 3560 | 1980 | 1580 | 400 | 815 | 30915 |
| 2017.09 | 27430 | 9778 | 3685 | 1979 | 1706 | 274 | 921 | 31085 |
| 2017.10 | | | 3389 | 1879 | 1510 | 369 | 1011 | 31092 |
| 2017.11 | | | 3932 | 2158 | 1774 | 384 | 1199 | 31193 |
| 2017.12 | 36396 | 13432 | 4092 | 2315 | 1777 | 539 | 1310 | 31399 |
| 2018.01 | | | 3806 | 1995 | 1812 | 183 | 121 | 31615 |
| 2018.02 | | | 3089 | 1705 | 1383 | 322 | 211 | 31345 |
| 2018.03 | 10781 | 4226 | 3536 | 1739 | 1797 | -58 | 345 | 31428 |
| 2018.04 | | | 3717 | 1989 | 1727 | 262 | 436 | 31249 |
| 2018.05 | | | 3998 | 2116 | 1882 | 234 | 527 | 31106 |
| 2018.06 | 19770 | 7142 | 3903 | 2156 | 1747 | 409 | 683 | 31121 |
| 2018.07 | | | 4013 | 2144 | 1869 | 275 | 761 | 31179 |
| 2018.08 | | | 4076 | 2169 | 1907 | 263 | 865 | 31097 |
| 2018.09 | 29599 | 10645 | 4205 | 2254 | 1951 | 303 | 980 | 30870 |
| 2018.10 | | | 3965 | 2148 | 1818 | 330 | 1077 | 30531 |
| 2018.11 | | | 4067 | 2243 | 1824 | 419 | 1213 | 30617 |
| 2018.12 | 39251 | 14617 | 3849 | 2209 | 1641 | 568 | 1350 | 30727 |
| 2019.01 | | | 3976 | 2180 | 1796 | 384 | 124 | 30879 |
| 2019.02 | | | 2676 | 1353 | 1323 | 30 | 217 | 30902 |
| 2019.03 | 11633 | 4600 | 3650 | 1982 | 1668 | 315 | 358 | 30988 |
| 2019.04 | | | 3740 | 1936 | 1805 | 131 | 451 | 30950 |
| 2019.05 | | | 3866 | 2139 | 1727 | 413 | 546 | 31010 |
| 2019.06 | 21342 | 7778 | 3752 | 2124 | 1628 | 496 | 707 | 31192 |
| 2019.07 | | | 3995 | 2218 | 1777 | 441 | 788 | 31037 |
| 2019.08 | | | 3951 | 2149 | 1802 | 346 | 893 | 31072 |
| 2019.09 | 31939 | 11622 | 3966 | 2181 | 1785 | 397 | 1008 | 30924 |
| 2019.10 | | | 3835 | 2130 | 1701 | 428 | 1108 | 31052 |
| 2019.11 | | | 4048 | 2215 | 1830 | 387 | 1244 | 30956 |
| 2019.12 | 42359 | 16021 | 4285 | 2377 | 1909 | 468 | 1381 | 31079 |

\*　月度外商直接投资为累计数，外汇储备为余额数。

\*　Monthly data for foreign direct investment are grand totals. Data for foreign exchange reserves sure outstanding amounts.

\*\*　自 2015 年起，本表中"农村居民现金收入"更名为"农村居民可支配收入"；对 2015 年以前该项数据未作调整。

\*\*　Since 2015, in this table, as "Cash Income of Rural Households", "Disposable Income of Rural Households" has been used, the data before 2015 are unchanged.

1 5 主要经济指标
## Major Economic Indicators

单位：亿特别提款权
Unit:100 Million SDR

| 时间<br>Time | 进出口总值<br>Trade<br>Volume | | | 贸易差额<br>Trade<br>Balance | 外商直接投资<br>Foreign<br>Direct<br>Investment |
|---|---|---|---|---|---|
| | | 出口<br>Export | 进口<br>Import | | |
| 2016 | 26539.1 | 15103.5 | 11435.6 | 3667.9 | 906.9 |
| 2017.01 | 2307.6 | 1333.9 | 973.7 | 360.2 | 88.8 |
| 2017.02 | 1834.5 | 876.9 | 957.6 | -80.7 | 153.0 |
| 2017.03 | 2478.6 | 1323.1 | 1155.5 | 167.6 | 249.8 |
| 2017.04 | 2343.8 | 1306.0 | 1037.8 | 268.2 | 315.3 |
| 2017.05 | 2460.7 | 1375.5 | 1085.1 | 290.4 | 374.4 |
| 2017.06 | 2517.4 | 1407.6 | 1109.7 | 297.9 | 481.3 |
| 2017.07 | 2432.0 | 1376.7 | 1055.3 | 321.4 | 527.8 |
| 2017.08 | 2523.0 | 1403.4 | 1119.6 | 283.8 | 594.2 |
| 2017.09 | 2594.6 | 1393.7 | 1200.9 | 192.7 | 668.7 |
| 2017.10 | 2404.1 | 1332.9 | 1071.2 | 261.8 | 732.8 |
| 2017.11 | 2792.4 | 1532.7 | 1259.7 | 272.9 | 866.2 |
| 2017.12 | 2891.5 | 1636.0 | 1255.5 | 380.5 | 944.9 |
| 2018.01 | 2646.3 | 1386.8 | 1259.5 | 127.4 | 83.9 |
| 2018.02 | 2128.4 | 1175.1 | 953.2 | 221.9 | 145.9 |
| 2018.03 | 2433.9 | 1197.0 | 1236.9 | -39.9 | 238.4 |
| 2018.04 | 2562.3 | 1371.5 | 1190.8 | 180.7 | 301.1 |
| 2018.05 | 2806.9 | 1485.7 | 1321.3 | 164.4 | 364.7 |
| 2018.06 | 2760.2 | 1524.7 | 1235.4 | 289.3 | 475.5 |
| 2018.07 | 2855.9 | 1525.8 | 1330.2 | 195.6 | 530.6 |
| 2018.08 | 2921.2 | 1554.8 | 1366.4 | 188.5 | 605.4 |
| 2018.09 | 3003.3 | 1609.7 | 1393.6 | 216.1 | 687.2 |
| 2018.10 | 2851.1 | 1544.1 | 1307.0 | 237.1 | 757.0 |
| 2018.11 | 2937.7 | 1620.0 | 1317.7 | 302.3 | 855.2 |
| 2018.12 | 2778.6 | 1594.3 | 1184.3 | 410.0 | 954.2 |
| 2019.01 | 2852.1 | 1563.8 | 1288.3 | 275.5 | 89.0 |
| 2019.02 | 1922.5 | 972.1 | 950.3 | 21.8 | 155.7 |
| 2019.03 | 2623.3 | 1424.7 | 1198.6 | 226.1 | 257.1 |
| 2019.04 | 2696.1 | 1395.2 | 1300.9 | 94.3 | 324.4 |
| 2019.05 | 2797.9 | 1548.3 | 1249.6 | 298.6 | 393.0 |
| 2019.06 | 2708.3 | 1533.2 | 1175.2 | 357.9 | 509.4 |
| 2019.07 | 2892.1 | 1605.6 | 1286.5 | 319.1 | 567.7 |
| 2019.08 | 2877.9 | 1565.0 | 1312.9 | 252.1 | 643.9 |
| 2019.09 | 2898.4 | 1594.1 | 1304.3 | 289.8 | 728.1 |
| 2019.10 | 2795.3 | 1552.7 | 1240.0 | 312.0 | 801.0 |
| 2019.11 | 2943.3 | 1610.5 | 1330.8 | 281.6 | 900.0 |
| 2019.12 | 3107.6 | 1723.5 | 1384.1 | 339.3 | 999.7 |

注 1：外商直接投资为累计值。

Note 1: Monthly data for foreign direct investment are grand totals.

注 2：进出口、贸易差额和外商直接投资数据以 SDR 为计值单位。具体方法为：以商务部和中国海关总署发布的美元计值的月度外商直接
　　　投资和进出口、贸易差额发生额数据为基础，根据国际货币基金组织每个工作日公布的 SDR 对美元汇率计算月均汇率，折算以 SDR
　　　计值的月度数据。季度和年度数据均由 SDR 计值月度数据累计相加获得。

Note 2: Data for import, export, trade balance and foreign direct qnvestment are measured in SDR. The method is to convert the monthly data for
　　　foreign direct investment, imports, exports and trade balance measured by US dollar, which are published by the Ministry of Commerce
　　　and the General Administration of Customs of China, to monthly data measured in SDR. The monthly SDR value is averaged by the daily
　　　SDR value against US dollar published by IMF. Quarterly and annual data are aggregated from the converted monthly data.

## 2.1 ■ 主要金融指标
## Major Financial Indicators

単位：亿元
Unit:100 Million Yuan

| 时间<br>Time | 社会融资规模增量<br>Aggregate Financing to<br>the Real Economy(AFRE, Flow) | M2 | M1 | M0 | 金融机构人民币各项存款<br>Total Deposits by All<br>Financial Institutions | 储蓄存款 *<br>Savings Deposits* | 金融机构人民币各项贷款<br>Total Loans by All<br>Financial Institutions |
|---|---|---|---|---|---|---|---|
| 2012 | 157631 | 974148.8 | 308664.2 | 54659.8 | 917554.8 | 399551.0 | 629909.6 |
| 2013 | 173169 | 1106525 | 337291 | 58574 | 1043847 | 447602 | 718961 |
| 2014 | 158761 | 1228375 | 348056 | 60260 | 1138645 | 485261 | 816770 |
| 2015 | 154063 | 1392278 | 400953 | 63217 | 1357022 | 546078 | 939540 |
| 2016 | 177999 | 1550067 | 486557 | 68304 | 1505864 | 597751 | 1066040 |
| 2017.01 | 37720 | 1575946 | 472526 | 86599 | 1520724 | 629064 | 1086367 |
| 2017.02 | 48775 | 1582913 | 476528 | 71728 | 1543814 | 630077 | 1098024 |
| 2017.03 | 74247 | 1599610 | 488770 | 68605 | 1556487 | 637409 | 1108256 |
| 2017.04 | 93806 | 1596332 | 490180 | 68393 | 1559118 | 625236 | 1119234 |
| 2017.05 | 111618 | 1601360 | 496390 | 67333 | 1570194 | 626485 | 1130353 |
| 2017.06 | 137504 | 1631283 | 510228 | 66978 | 1596636 | 637138 | 1145721 |
| 2017.07 | 158692 | 1628997 | 510485 | 67129 | 1604795 | 629623 | 1153976 |
| 2017.08 | 179177 | 1645157 | 518114 | 67551 | 1618426 | 632213 | 1164896 |
| 2017.09 | 204616 | 1655662 | 517863 | 69749 | 1622758 | 642591 | 1177617 |
| 2017.10 | 220477 | 1653434 | 525977 | 68231 | 1633319 | 634539 | 1184249 |
| 2017.11 | 243433 | 1670013 | 535565 | 68623 | 1648974 | 635994 | 1195477 |
| 2017.12 | 261536 | 1676769 | 543790 | 70646 | 1641044 | 643768 | 1201321 |
| 2018.01 | 31417 | 1720814 | 543247 | 74636 | 1679728 | 652744 | 1230255 |
| 2018.02 | 43482 | 1729070 | 517036 | 81424 | 1676717 | 681474 | 1238649 |
| 2018.03 | 60573 | 1739859 | 523540 | 72693 | 1691816 | 686804 | 1249814 |
| 2018.04 | 82816 | 1737684 | 525448 | 71476 | 1697168 | 673585 | 1261589 |
| 2018.05 | 94050 | 1743064 | 526277 | 69775 | 1710216 | 675751 | 1273112 |
| 2018.06 | 114423 | 1770178 | 543945 | 69589 | 1731176 | 686695 | 1291534 |
| 2018.07 | 132805 | 1776196 | 536624 | 69531 | 1741463 | 683763 | 1306067 |
| 2018.08 | 156883 | 1788670 | 538325 | 69775 | 1752365 | 687226 | 1318822 |
| 2018.09 | 179944 | 1801666 | 538574 | 71254 | 1761267 | 700518 | 1332663 |
| 2018.10 | 189482 | 1795560 | 540128 | 70107 | 1764802 | 697171 | 1339633 |
| 2018.11 | 205609 | 1813175 | 543499 | 70563 | 1774310 | 704576 | 1352127 |
| 2018.12 | 224920 | 1826744 | 551686 | 73208 | 1775226 | 716038 | 1362967 |
| 2019.01 | 46791 | 1865935 | 545638 | 87471 | 1807904 | 754594 | 1395256 |
| 2019.02 | 56456 | 1867427 | 527190 | 79485 | 1820995 | 767902 | 1404114 |
| 2019.03 | 86059 | 1889412 | 547576 | 74942 | 1838227 | 776654 | 1421057 |
| 2019.04 | 102768 | 1884670 | 540615 | 73966 | 1840833 | 770406 | 1431218 |
| 2019.05 | 119892 | 1891154 | 544356 | 72798 | 1853010 | 772823 | 1443055 |
| 2019.06 | 146135 | 1921360 | 567696 | 72581 | 1875680 | 784172 | 1459691 |
| 2019.07 | 159007 | 1919411 | 553043 | 72689 | 1882100 | 783140 | 1470249 |
| 2019.08 | 180963 | 1935492 | 556798 | 73153 | 1900148 | 785854 | 1482338 |
| 2019.09 | 206105 | 1952250 | 557138 | 74130 | 1907341 | 801298 | 1499247 |
| 2019.10 | 214785 | 1945601 | 558144 | 73395 | 1909713 | 795286 | 1505861 |
| 2019.11 | 234722 | 1961430 | 562487 | 73974 | 1922791 | 797752 | 1519741 |
| 2019.12 | 255753 | 1986489 | 576009 | 77189 | 1928785 | 813017 | 1531123 |

注 1：　自 2011 年起增加社会融资规模增量指标。社会融资规模增量是指在一定时期内（每月、每季度或每年）实体经济从金融体系获得的资金总额。统计数据为年累计数，当期数据为初步数据。
Note 1: Aggregate Financing to the Real Economy(AFRE, flow) has been included as a new indicator since 2011. It includes all the funding from the financial system to the real economy during a certain period, such as a month, a quarter or a year. In this sheet, data of "AFRE, flow" are yearly accumulated amounts. Statistics for the current period are preliminary.

注 2：　自 2011 年 10 月起，货币供应量已包括住房公积金中心存款和非存款类金融机构在存款类金融机构的存款。
Note 2: Since October 2011, money supply has already included deposits in housing provident fund management centers, as well as deposit of un-depository financial institutions with depository financial institutions.

*　　　"居民储蓄存款" 更名为 "储蓄存款"。
*　　　"Household Savings Deposits" is renamed as "Savings Deposits".

注 3：　自 2019 年 12 月起，中国人民银行进一步完善社会融资规模统计，将 "国债" 和 "地方政府一般债券" 纳入社会融资规模统计，与原有 "地方政府专项债券" 合并为 "政府债券" 指标。指标数值为托管机构的托管面值。自 2019 年 9 月起，中国人民银行完善 "社会融资规模" 中的 "企业债券" 统计，将 "自交易所企业资产支持证券" 纳入 "企业债券" 指标。自 2018 年 9 月起，中国人民银行将 "地方政府专项债券" 纳入社会融资规模统计。自 2018 年 7 月起，中国人民银行完善社会融资规模统计方法，将 "存款类金融机构资产支持证券" 和 "贷款核销" 纳入社会融资规模统计，在 "其他融资" 项下单独列示。当期数据为初步统计数。2017 年 1 月以来数据进行了可比口径调整，详见中国人民银行官网社会融资规模数据表附注。
Note 3: Since December 2019, the People's Bank of China has made further efforts to improve the statistical method of AFRE. "Treasury Bonds" and "Local Government General Bonds" have been newly introduced into AFRE and have merged with "Local Government Special Bonds" into "Government Bonds" ,which is recorded at face value at depositories. Since September 2019, the People's Bank of China has improved the statistics of "Net Financing of Corporate Bonds" in AFRE, and has incorporated "Asset-backed Securities of Non-Financial Enterprises" into "Net Financing of Corporate Bonds". Since September 2018, the People's Bank of China has incorporated "Local Government Special Bonds" into AFRE. Since July 2018, the People's Bank of China has improved the statistical method of AFRE, and has incorporated "Asset-backed Securities of Depository Financial Institutions" and "Loans Written off" into AFRE, which is reflected as a sub-item of "Other Financing". Data for the current period are preliminary. Data are comparably adjusted as of January, 2017. Please refer to the notes of the AFRE release on the website of the PBC for details.

2.2 ■ 主要金融指标（消除季节因素）
Major Financial Indicators (Seasonally Adjusted)

单位：亿元
Unit:100 Million Yuan

| 时间<br>Time | M2 | M1 | M0 | 金融机构各项存款<br>Total Deposits by All<br>Financial Institutions | 储蓄存款 *<br>Savings Deposits* | 金融机构各项贷款 **<br>Total Loans by All<br>Financial Institutions** |
|---|---|---|---|---|---|---|
| 2012 | 974547.8 | 297717.4 | 53596.6 | 924390.6 | 404985.3 | 654075.0 |
| 2013 | 1108443 | 326484 | 57585 | 1055003 | 451765 | 742747 |
| 2014 | 1231646 | 335230 | 60101 | 1149996 | 492945 | 841866 |
| 2015 | 1401059 | 387380 | 63096 | 1372276 | 532681 | 946431 |
| 2016 | 1557929 | 472141 | 67769 | 1520677 | 573783 | 1072919 |
| 2017.01 | 1575406 | 468863 | 75874 | 1543169 | 591026 | 1085834 |
| 2017.02 | 1585054 | 487322 | 66873 | 1547418 | 583391 | 1096415 |
| 2017.03 | 1589598 | 486160 | 65365 | 1554097 | 585514 | 1103454 |
| 2017.04 | 1596623 | 498381 | 69022 | 1562537 | 586912 | 1118073 |
| 2017.05 | 1595916 | 500831 | 69874 | 1560956 | 591885 | 1129165 |
| 2017.06 | 1610591 | 503330 | 69975 | 1577324 | 592610 | 1139714 |
| 2017.07 | 1623660 | 512494 | 70090 | 1590990 | 593339 | 1151903 |
| 2017.08 | 1639242 | 517719 | 70311 | 1606603 | 596006 | 1165315 |
| 2017.09 | 1656244 | 522936 | 70873 | 1620670 | 598387 | 1176067 |
| 2017.10 | 1671263 | 525359 | 70963 | 1638294 | 600119 | 1188856 |
| 2017.11 | 1687374 | 530198 | 70997 | 1653000 | 601688 | 1203718 |
| 2017.12 | 1688864 | 530623 | 70759 | 1661762 | 602648 | 1210909 |
| 2018.01 | 1699713 | 536030 | 66273 | 1681486 | 599186 | 1225160 |
| 2018.02 | 1714853 | 528504 | 74532 | 1688945 | 610160 | 1236312 |
| 2018.03 | 1718695 | 528494 | 71641 | 1691797 | 602890 | 1247066 |
| 2018.04 | 1726605 | 533156 | 72038 | 1698949 | 605869 | 1259271 |
| 2018.05 | 1729086 | 533544 | 72037 | 1703208 | 608118 | 1273143 |
| 2018.06 | 1738695 | 536614 | 72285 | 1711411 | 610246 | 1285112 |
| 2018.07 | 1754858 | 538923 | 72946 | 1727847 | 613122 | 1303308 |
| 2018.08 | 1762573 | 537450 | 72998 | 1738360 | 615170 | 1316614 |
| 2018.09 | 1779392 | 542714 | 72883 | 1760205 | 620534 | 1330351 |
| 2018.10 | 1806646 | 537054 | 73380 | 1765267 | 629446 | 1346136 |
| 2018.11 | 1825597 | 536017 | 72939 | 1777230 | 633886 | 1360952 |
| 2018.12 | 1836845 | 535700 | 73304 | 1790188 | 636585 | 1386643 |
| 2019.01 | 1853092 | 540543 | 73737 | 1589929 | 654146 | 1399499 |
| 2019.02 | 1862957 | 546024 | 75257 | 1604967 | 650695 | 1412462 |
| 2019.03 | 1877569 | 552623 | 74601 | 1611709 | 653032 | 1428367 |
| 2019.04 | 1888386 | 548590 | 74969 | 1609531 | 662608 | 1440739 |
| 2019.05 | 1898785 | 552535 | 75042 | 1609372 | 665047 | 1452979 |
| 2019.06 | 1911095 | 559310 | 75756 | 1612626 | 669340 | 1466513 |
| 2019.07 | 1923244 | 553335 | 76106 | 1605868 | 679141 | 1478618 |
| 2019.08 | 1937860 | 555435 | 75825 | 1603932 | 682052 | 1493363 |
| 2019.09 | 1952932 | 559374 | 75472 | 1605202 | 685198 | 1508754 |
| 2019.10 | 1959169 | 557558 | 76239 | 1595650 | 691370 | 1521876 |
| 2019.11 | 1976101 | 557144 | 76357 | 1592264 | 694686 | 1536995 |
| 2019.12 | 1995729 | 562439 | 77045 | 1632903 | 700878 | 1549227 |

\* "居民储蓄存款"更名为"储蓄存款"。

\* "Household Savings Deposits" is renamed as "Savings Deposits".

\*\* 各项贷款按可比口径数据计算，包含2001—2008年剥离出去的不良贷款数据。

\*\* Total loans are calculated on the basis of comparable basis, which include the non-performing loans separated from financial institutions from 2001 to 2008.

## 2.3 社会融资规模增量统计表
## Aggregate Financing to the Real Economy (Flow)

单位：亿元
Unit: 100 Million Yuan

| 时间<br>Time | 社会融资<br>规模增量<br>AFRE<br>(Flow) | 其中 Of Which | | 委托贷款<br>Entrusted<br>Loans | 信托贷款<br>Trust<br>Loans | 未贴现的银行<br>承兑汇票<br>Undiscounted<br>Bankers'<br>Acceptances | 企业债券<br>Net<br>Financing<br>of Corporate<br>Bonds | 政府债券<br>Government<br>Bonds | 非金融企业<br>境内股票融资<br>Equity Financing on<br>the Domestic Stock<br>Market by Non-<br>financial Enterprises | 存款类金融机构资产<br>支持证券<br>Asset-backed<br>Securities of<br>Depository Financial<br>Institutions | 贷款核销<br>Loans Written off |
|---|---|---|---|---|---|---|---|---|---|---|---|
| | | 人民币<br>贷款<br>RMB<br>Loans | 外币贷款<br>(折合人民币)<br>Foreign Currency-<br>denominated<br>Loans<br>(RMB Equivalent) | | | | | | | | |
| 2009.01 | 13990 | 16177 | -582 | 262 | -346 | -2232 | 507 | — | 14 | — | — |
| 2009.02 | 11131 | 10715 | -288 | 347 | 38 | -305 | 447 | — | 48 | — | — |
| 2009.03 | 22011 | 18920 | 291 | 407 | -137 | 972 | 1240 | — | 119 | — | — |
| 2009.04 | 5452 | 5918 | 478 | 339 | 75 | -3247 | 1557 | — | 137 | — | — |
| 2009.05 | 14959 | 6669 | 1054 | 619 | 292 | 5035 | 876 | — | 238 | — | — |
| 2009.06 | 21067 | 15304 | 2542 | 678 | 297 | 613 | 1238 | — | 190 | — | — |
| 2009.07 | 7388 | 3691 | 752 | 502 | 572 | 295 | 587 | — | 788 | — | — |
| 2009.08 | 7650 | 4104 | 1315 | 776 | 482 | -103 | 634 | — | 234 | — | — |
| 2009.09 | 11871 | 5167 | 1208 | 1125 | 869 | 1310 | 1678 | — | 299 | — | — |
| 2009.10 | 5985 | 2530 | 1112 | 708 | 218 | 217 | 723 | — | 302 | — | — |
| 2009.11 | 9501 | 2948 | 1131 | 670 | 1294 | 1178 | 1909 | — | 168 | — | — |
| 2009.12 | 8100 | 3800 | 252 | 347 | 710 | 874 | 973 | — | 815 | — | — |
| 2010.01 | 20550 | 13934 | 641 | 857 | 265 | 3449 | 664 | — | 519 | — | — |
| 2010.02 | 10877 | 6999 | 663 | 96 | 496 | 1425 | 688 | — | 366 | — | — |
| 2010.03 | 13830 | 5107 | 662 | 567 | 1377 | 4208 | 1324 | — | 365 | — | — |
| 2010.04 | 14919 | 7740 | 349 | 635 | 2039 | 2309 | 1192 | — | 432 | — | — |
| 2010.05 | 10805 | 6493 | -112 | 623 | 762 | 1213 | 1356 | — | 253 | — | — |
| 2010.06 | 10196 | 6027 | -18 | 421 | 1077 | 1105 | 872 | — | 468 | — | — |
| 2010.07 | 7202 | 5327 | -378 | 706 | 231 | 900 | -69 | — | 262 | — | — |
| 2010.08 | 10646 | 5446 | 166 | 521 | -761 | 3381 | 1208 | — | 419 | — | — |
| 2010.09 | 11224 | 6004 | 918 | 626 | -713 | 1679 | 1883 | — | 543 | — | — |
| 2010.10 | 8608 | 5877 | 346 | 1027 | -297 | 306 | 629 | — | 483 | — | — |
| 2010.11 | 10554 | 5689 | 526 | 1121 | -324 | 1796 | 719 | — | 722 | — | — |
| 2010.12 | 10780 | 4807 | 1090 | 1549 | -288 | 1576 | 594 | — | 954 | — | — |
| 2011.01 | 17560 | 10263 | 862 | 1272 | -98 | 3157 | 1012 | — | 731 | — | — |
| 2011.02 | 6468 | 5377 | 347 | 419 | 141 | -1176 | 877 | — | 270 | — | — |
| 2011.03 | 18212 | 6794 | 572 | 1513 | 47 | 5631 | 2682 | — | 557 | — | — |
| 2011.04 | 13673 | 7430 | 492 | 1407 | 501 | 2332 | 761 | — | 448 | — | — |
| 2011.05 | 10854 | 5516 | 842 | 1216 | 180 | 1695 | 721 | — | 351 | — | — |
| 2011.06 | 10873 | 6339 | 245 | 1202 | 141 | 1630 | 536 | — | 320 | — | — |
| 2011.07 | 5393 | 4916 | 9 | 1232 | -28 | -1726 | 422 | — | 252 | — | — |
| 2011.08 | 10741 | 5484 | 376 | 1409 | 176 | 1652 | 898 | — | 350 | — | — |
| 2011.09 | 4279 | 4693 | 1025 | 1008 | -223 | -3361 | 520 | — | 236 | — | — |
| 2011.10 | 7908 | 5868 | 415 | 518 | 90 | -1186 | 1639 | — | 244 | — | — |
| 2011.11 | 9581 | 5629 | 49 | 595 | 716 | -227 | 2077 | — | 268 | — | — |
| 2011.12 | 12744 | 6406 | 478 | 1173 | 389 | 1851 | 1514 | — | 350 | — | — |
| 2012.01 | 9754 | 7381 | -148 | 1646 | 247 | -214 | 442 | — | 81 | — | — |
| 2012.02 | 10431 | 7107 | 526 | 394 | 522 | -284 | 1544 | — | 229 | — | — |
| 2012.03 | 18703 | 10114 | 950 | 770 | 1018 | 2821 | 1974 | — | 565 | — | — |
| 2012.04 | 9637 | 6818 | 96 | 1015 | 37 | 279 | 887 | — | 190 | — | — |
| 2012.05 | 11432 | 7932 | 302 | 215 | 557 | 380 | 1441 | — | 184 | — | — |
| 2012.06 | 17802 | 9198 | 1040 | 789 | 988 | 3113 | 1982 | — | 246 | — | — |
| 2012.07 | 10522 | 5401 | 70 | 1279 | 384 | 218 | 2486 | — | 316 | — | — |
| 2012.08 | 12475 | 7039 | 743 | 1046 | 1238 | -846 | 2579 | — | 208 | — | — |
| 2012.09 | 16462 | 6226 | 1764 | 1449 | 2012 | 2155 | 2278 | — | 158 | — | — |
| 2012.10 | 12906 | 5054 | 1290 | 941 | 1444 | 729 | 2992 | — | 88 | — | — |
| 2012.11 | 11225 | 5220 | 1045 | 1218 | 1802 | -489 | 1820 | — | 107 | — | — |
| 2012.12 | 16282 | 4546 | 1486 | 2079 | 2598 | 2637 | 2126 | — | 135 | — | — |

## 2.3 ■ 社会融资规模增量统计表
## Aggregate Financing to the Real Economy (Flow)

单位：亿元
Unit: 100 Million Yuan

| 时间<br>Time | 社会融资<br>规模增量<br>AFRE<br>(Flow) | 其中　Of Which | | | | | | | | | |
|---|---|---|---|---|---|---|---|---|---|---|---|
| | | 人民币<br>贷款<br>RMB<br>Loans | 外币贷款<br>（折合人民币）<br>Foreign Currency-<br>denominated<br>Loans<br>(RMB Equivalent) | 委托贷款<br>Entrusted<br>Loans | 信托贷款<br>Trust<br>Loans | 未贴现的银行<br>承兑汇票<br>Undiscounted<br>Bankers'<br>Acceptances | 企业债券<br>Net<br>Financing<br>of Corporate<br>Bonds | 政府债券<br>Government<br>Bonds | 非金融企业<br>境内股票融资<br>Equity Financing on<br>the Domestic Stock<br>Market by Non-<br>financial Enterprises | 存款类金融机构资产<br>支持证券<br>Asset-backed<br>Securities of<br>Depository Financial<br>Institutions | 贷款核销<br>Loans Written off |
| 2013.01 | 25446 | 10721 | 1795 | 2061 | 2108 | 5798 | 2249 | — | 244 | — | — |
| 2013.02 | 10705 | 6200 | 1149 | 1426 | 1825 | -1823 | 1454 | — | 165 | — | — |
| 2013.03 | 25503 | 10625 | 1509 | 1748 | 4312 | 2731 | 3870 | — | 208 | — | — |
| 2013.04 | 17629 | 7923 | 847 | 1926 | 1942 | 2218 | 2039 | — | 274 | — | — |
| 2013.05 | 11871 | 6694 | 357 | 1967 | 971 | -1141 | 2230 | — | 231 | — | — |
| 2013.06 | 10375 | 8628 | 133 | 1990 | 1208 | -2615 | 323 | — | 126 | — | — |
| 2013.07 | 8191 | 6997 | -1157 | 1927 | 1151 | -1777 | 476 | — | 128 | — | — |
| 2013.08 | 15841 | 7128 | -360 | 2938 | 1209 | 3049 | 1240 | — | 136 | — | — |
| 2013.09 | 14120 | 7870 | 891 | 2218 | 1130 | -79 | 1443 | — | 113 | — | — |
| 2013.10 | 8645 | 5060 | 53 | 1834 | 431 | -345 | 1078 | — | 78 | — | — |
| 2013.11 | 12310 | 6246 | 122 | 2704 | 1006 | 60 | 1424 | — | 147 | — | — |
| 2013.12 | 12532 | 4824 | 509 | 2727 | 1111 | 1679 | 287 | — | 369 | — | — |
| | | | | | | | | | | | |
| 2014.01 | 25902 | 13176 | 1500 | 3971 | 1059 | 4902 | 375 | — | 454 | — | — |
| 2014.02 | 8924 | 6434 | 1128 | 540 | 747 | -1419 | 1026 | — | 169 | — | — |
| 2014.03 | 20194 | 10202 | 1201 | 2130 | 1071 | 2252 | 2464 | — | 352 | — | — |
| 2014.04 | 14992 | 7734 | 69 | 1365 | 398 | 789 | 3664 | — | 582 | — | — |
| 2014.05 | 13583 | 8791 | -342 | 1655 | 125 | -94 | 2797 | — | 162 | — | — |
| 2014.06 | 18957 | 10780 | 131 | 2139 | 1200 | 1445 | 2626 | — | 154 | — | — |
| 2014.07 | 1861 | 3754 | -511 | 783 | -158 | -4157 | 1435 | — | 332 | — | — |
| 2014.08 | 9547 | 7003 | -109 | 1651 | -515 | -1116 | 1934 | — | 217 | — | — |
| 2014.09 | 10883 | 8573 | -684 | 1314 | -326 | -1410 | 2338 | — | 612 | — | — |
| 2014.10 | 6537 | 5521 | -689 | 1043 | -215 | -2411 | 2590 | — | 279 | — | — |
| 2014.11 | 11270 | 8543 | -281 | 1319 | -314 | -668 | 1807 | — | 379 | — | — |
| 2014.12 | 15674 | 6940 | -179 | 3831 | 2102 | 688 | 836 | — | 658 | — | — |
| | | | | | | | | | | | |
| 2015.01 | 20516 | 14708 | 212 | 832 | 52 | 1946 | 1868 | — | 526 | — | — |
| 2015.02 | 13609 | 11437 | -146 | 1299 | 38 | -592 | 716 | — | 542 | — | — |
| 2015.03 | 12433 | 9920 | -4 | 1111 | -77 | -910 | 1344 | — | 639 | — | — |
| 2015.04 | 10582 | 8045 | -265 | 344 | -46 | -74 | 1616 | — | 597 | — | — |
| 2015.05 | 12397 | 8510 | 81 | 324 | -195 | 961 | 1710 | — | 584 | — | — |
| 2015.06 | 18384 | 13240 | 560 | 1414 | 536 | -1028 | 2132 | — | 1051 | — | — |
| 2015.07 | 7511 | 5890 | -133 | 1137 | 99 | -3317 | 2832 | — | 615 | — | — |
| 2015.08 | 11097 | 7756 | -620 | 1198 | 317 | -1577 | 3121 | — | 479 | — | — |
| 2015.09 | 13571 | 10417 | -2344 | 2422 | -159 | -1279 | 3805 | — | 349 | — | — |
| 2015.10 | 5593 | 5574 | -1317 | 1390 | -201 | -3697 | 3331 | — | 121 | — | — |
| 2015.11 | 10255 | 8873 | -1142 | 910 | -301 | -2545 | 3378 | — | 568 | — | — |
| 2015.12 | 18114 | 8323 | -1308 | 3530 | 370 | 1546 | 3535 | — | 1518 | — | — |
| | | | | | | | | | | | |
| 2016.01 | 34758 | 25370 | -1727 | 2175 | 552 | 1327 | 5083 | — | 1469 | — | — |
| 2016.02 | 8312 | 8105 | -569 | 1650 | 308 | -3705 | 1386 | — | 810 | — | — |
| 2016.03 | 23931 | 13176 | 6 | 1660 | 732 | 173 | 7081 | — | 562 | — | — |
| 2016.04 | 7809 | 5642 | -706 | 1694 | 269 | -2776 | 2366 | — | 951 | — | — |
| 2016.05 | 6720 | 9374 | -524 | 1566 | 121 | -5067 | -300 | — | 1073 | — | — |
| 2016.06 | 16464 | 13141 | -267 | 1721 | 809 | -2720 | 1993 | — | 1158 | — | — |
| 2016.07 | 4791 | 4550 | -401 | 1775 | 210 | -5118 | 2208 | — | 1135 | — | — |
| 2016.08 | 14605 | 7969 | 70 | 1432 | 736 | -376 | 3236 | — | 1075 | — | — |
| 2016.09 | 17085 | 12628 | -487 | 1451 | 1057 | -2230 | 2842 | — | 1368 | — | — |
| 2016.10 | 8825 | 6010 | -335 | 725 | 530 | -1801 | 2152 | — | 1125 | — | — |
| 2016.11 | 18303 | 8463 | -310 | 1994 | 1625 | 1171 | 3834 | — | 861 | — | — |
| 2016.12 | 16397 | 9943 | -389 | 4011 | 1643 | 1606 | -2016 | — | 828 | — | — |

## 2.3 ■ 社会融资规模增量统计表
## Aggregate Financing to the Real Economy (Flow)

单位：亿元
Unit: 100 Million Yuan

| 时间<br>Time | 社会融资<br>规模增量<br>AFRE<br>(Flow) | 其中 Of Which | | | | | | | | | |
| --- | --- | --- | --- | --- | --- | --- | --- | --- | --- | --- | --- |
| | | 人民币<br>贷款<br>RMB<br>Loans | 外币贷款<br>(折合人民币)<br>Foreign Currency-<br>denominated<br>Loans<br>(RMB Equivalent) | 委托贷款<br>Entrusted<br>Loans | 信托贷款<br>Trust<br>Loans | 未贴现的银行<br>承兑汇票<br>Undiscounted<br>Bankers'<br>Acceptances | 企业债券<br>Net<br>Financing<br>of Corporate<br>Bonds | 政府债券<br>Government<br>Bonds | 非金融企业<br>境内股票融资<br>Equity Financing on<br>the Domestic Stock<br>Market by Non-<br>financial Enterprises | 存款类金融机构资产<br>支持证券<br>Asset-backed<br>Securities of<br>Depository Financial<br>Institutions | 贷款核销<br>Loans Written off |
| 2017.01 | 37720 | 23133 | 126 | 3142 | 3128 | 6130 | -510 | 665 | 1225 | -129 | 253 |
| 2017.02 | 11055 | 10317 | 368 | 1181 | 1026 | -1719 | -899 | -191 | 570 | -10 | 149 |
| 2017.03 | 25472 | 11586 | 288 | 2043 | 3020 | 2390 | 264 | 3230 | 800 | 164 | 846 |
| 2017.04 | 19559 | 10806 | -283 | -48 | 1381 | 345 | 628 | 5939 | 769 | -505 | 210 |
| 2017.05 | 17812 | 11780 | -99 | -274 | 1791 | -1245 | -2365 | 6505 | 458 | 294 | 277 |
| 2017.06 | 25886 | 14474 | 73 | -26 | 2485 | -230 | -5 | 6571 | 487 | 113 | 1309 |
| 2017.07 | 21188 | 9152 | -213 | 187 | 1245 | -2037 | 2642 | 9472 | 536 | -505 | 205 |
| 2017.08 | 20486 | 11466 | -332 | -70 | 1218 | 242 | 1525 | 4420 | 653 | 446 | 250 |
| 2017.09 | 25439 | 11885 | -232 | 783 | 2362 | 784 | 1669 | 5486 | 519 | 324 | 1276 |
| 2017.10 | 15861 | 6635 | -44 | 108 | 1013 | 12 | 1628 | 4968 | 601 | 61 | 271 |
| 2017.11 | 22956 | 11428 | 198 | 306 | 1400 | 15 | 979 | 5979 | 1324 | 248 | 481 |
| 2017.12 | 18103 | 5769 | 169 | 661 | 2163 | 676 | 688 | 2759 | 817 | 1476 | 2059 |
| 2018.01 | 31417 | 26850 | 266 | -709 | 397 | 1437 | 1894 | 5 | 500 | -137 | 320 |
| 2018.02 | 12064 | 10199 | 86 | -750 | 674 | 106 | 734 | 175 | 379 | -146 | 261 |
| 2018.03 | 17091 | 11425 | 139 | -1850 | -343 | -323 | 3611 | 1816 | 404 | 387 | 1234 |
| 2018.04 | 22243 | 10987 | -26 | -1481 | -101 | 1454 | 4042 | 5303 | 533 | 821 | 259 |
| 2018.05 | 11234 | 11396 | -228 | -1570 | -936 | -1741 | -351 | 2728 | 438 | 377 | 479 |
| 2018.06 | 20373 | 16787 | -364 | -1642 | -1576 | -3649 | 1308 | 6509 | 258 | 272 | 1737 |
| 2018.07 | 18382 | 12861 | -773 | -950 | -1205 | -2744 | 2189 | 7998 | 175 | 123 | 176 |
| 2018.08 | 24078 | 13140 | -344 | -1207 | -685 | -779 | 3541 | 8651 | 141 | 501 | 377 |
| 2018.09 | 23061 | 14341 | -670 | -1432 | -890 | -548 | 15 | 9108 | 272 | 895 | 1615 |
| 2018.10 | 9538 | 7141 | -800 | -949 | -1366 | -453 | 1523 | 3032 | 176 | 188 | 446 |
| 2018.11 | 16127 | 12302 | -787 | -1310 | -455 | -127 | 3918 | -247 | 200 | 1157 | 729 |
| 2018.12 | 19311 | 9281 | -702 | -2210 | -488 | 1023 | 3895 | 3452 | 130 | 1503 | 2522 |
| 2019.01 | 46791 | 35668 | 343 | -699 | 345 | 3787 | 4829 | 1700 | 289 | -466 | 249 |
| 2019.02 | 9665 | 7641 | -105 | -508 | -37 | -3103 | 875 | 4347 | 119 | -14 | 201 |
| 2019.03 | 29602 | 19584 | 3 | -1070 | 528 | 1365 | 3546 | 3412 | 122 | 261 | 1227 |
| 2019.04 | 16710 | 8733 | -330 | -1197 | 129 | -357 | 3949 | 4433 | 262 | 243 | 316 |
| 2019.05 | 17124 | 11855 | 191 | -631 | -52 | -768 | 1033 | 3857 | 259 | 383 | 392 |
| 2019.06 | 26243 | 16737 | -4 | -827 | 15 | -1311 | 1439 | 6867 | 153 | 607 | 1806 |
| 2019.07 | 12872 | 8086 | -221 | -987 | -676 | -4562 | 2944 | 6427 | 593 | 286 | 244 |
| 2019.08 | 21956 | 13045 | -247 | -513 | -658 | 157 | 3384 | 5059 | 256 | 269 | 351 |
| 2019.09 | 25142 | 17612 | -440 | -22 | -672 | -431 | 2431 | 3777 | 289 | 284 | 1692 |
| 2019.10 | 8680 | 5470 | -10 | -667 | -624 | -1053 | 2032 | 1871 | 180 | 623 | 416 |
| 2019.11 | 19937 | 13633 | -249 | -959 | -673 | 570 | 3330 | 1716 | 524 | 693 | 639 |
| 2019.12 | 21030 | 10770 | -205 | -1316 | -1092 | 951 | 2625 | 3738 | 432 | 865 | 3018 |

注1：社会融资规模增量是指一定时期内实体经济从金融体系获得的资金额。
Note 1: AFRE(flow) refers to the total volume of financing provided by the financial system to the real economy during a certain period of time.
注2：社会融资规模中的本外币贷款是指一定时期内实体经济从金融体系获得的人民币和外币贷款，不包含银行业金融机构拆放给非银行业金融机构的款项和境外贷款。
Note 2: RMB loans and foreign currency loans in AFRE refer to those issued to the real economy by the financial system during a certain period of time,barring the funds lend to non-bank financial institutions by the banking financial institutions and external loans.
注3：数据来源于中国人民银行、中国银行保险监督管理委员会、中国证券监督管理委员会、中央国债登记结算有限责任公司和中国银行间市场交易商协会等。
Note 3: Source of data: the PBC, CBIRC, CSRC, CCDC and NAFMII.
注4：自2019年12月起，中国人民银行进一步完善社会融资规模统计，将"国债"和"地方政府一般债券"纳入社会融资规模统计，与原有"地方政府专项债券"合并为"政府债券"指标。指标数值为托管机构的托管面值。自2019年9月起，中国人民银行完善"社会融资规模"中的"企业债券"统计，将"交易所企业资产支持证券"纳入"企业债券"指标。自2018年9月起，中国人民银行将"地方政府专项债券"纳入社会融资规模统计。自2018年7月起，中国人民银行完善社会融资规模统计方法，将"存款类金融机构资产支持证券"和"贷款核销"纳入社会融资规模统计，在"其他融资"项下单独列示。
Note 4: Since December 2019,the People's Bank of China has made further efforts to improve the statistical method of AFRE. "Treasury Bonds" and "Local Government General Bonds" have been newly introduced into AFRE and have merged with "Local Government Special Bonds" into "Government Bonds" ,which is recorded at face value at depositories. Since September 2019, the People's Bank of China has improved the statistics of "Net Financing of Corporate Bonds" in AFRE, and has incorporated "Asset-backed Securities of Non-Financial Enterprises" into "Net Financing of Corporate Bonds". Since September 2018, the People's Bank of China has incorporated "Local Government Special Bonds" into AFRE. Since July 2018, the People's Bank of China has improved the statistical method of AFRE, and has incorporated "Asset-backed Securities of Depository Financial Institutions" and "Loans Written off" into AFRE, which is reflected as a sub-item of "Other Financing".
注5：当期数据为初步统计数。2017年1月以来数据进行了可比口径调整，详见中国人民银行官网最新社会融资规模数据表附注。
Note 5: Data for the current period are preliminary. Data are comparably adjusted as of January, 2017. Please refer to the notes of the latest AFRE release on the website of the PBC for details.

## 2.3 ■ 2019 年地区社会融资规模增量统计表
### Aggregate Financing to the Real Economy (flow) by Province(2019)

单位：亿元
Unit:100 Million Yuan

| 地区<br>Province | 地区社会融资规模增量<br>Aggregate Financing to the Real Economy(flow) by Province | 人民币贷款<br>RMB Loans | 外币贷款(折合人民币)<br>Foreign Currency-denominated Loans (RMB Equivalent) | 委托贷款<br>Entrusted Loans | 信托贷款<br>Trust Loans | 未贴现银行承兑汇票<br>Undiscounted Bank'ers' Acceptances | 企业债券<br>Net Financing of Corporate Bonds | 政府债券<br>Government Bonds | 非金融企业境内股票融资<br>Equity Financing on the Domestic Stock Market by Non-financial Enterprises | 存款类金融机构资产支持证券<br>Asset-backed Securities of Depository Financial Institutions | 贷款核销<br>Loans Written off |
|---|---|---|---|---|---|---|---|---|---|---|---|
| 北京 Beijing | 14630 | 6489 | 120 | -1730 | -1290 | -1295 | 6975 | 1009 | 486 | 3310 | 177 |
| 天津 Tianjin | 2866 | 2317 | -269 | -638 | -352 | -764 | 875 | 920 | 109 | 61 | 516 |
| 河北 Hebei | 8339 | 5367 | -63 | 169 | 173 | -375 | 623 | 1577 | 41 | -2 | 474 |
| 山西 Shanxi | 4222 | 2569 | 170 | -20 | -33 | -37 | 575 | 661 | 33 | -40 | 171 |
| 内蒙古 Inner Mongolia | 1492 | 900 | -14 | 18 | 37 | -729 | 17 | 904 | 44 | 0 | 188 |
| 辽宁 Liaoning | 2942 | 4624 | -146 | -819 | -186 | -1347 | -296 | 447 | 29 | 4 | 397 |
| 吉林 Jilin | 2965 | 1773 | -12 | 23 | -98 | -37 | 227 | 693 | 18 | 0 | 209 |
| 黑龙江 Heilongjiang | 3097 | 1107 | -1 | -21 | 963 | -46 | 40 | 733 | 10 | 0 | 96 |
| 上海 Shanghai | 8642 | 5204 | 169 | -658 | -885 | 564 | 2746 | 763 | 403 | -196 | 119 |
| 江苏 Jiangsu | 24104 | 17345 | -291 | -836 | 368 | 975 | 3139 | 1874 | 289 | 49 | 552 |
| 浙江 Zhejiang | 22162 | 16003 | -174 | -409 | 72 | 1017 | 2679 | 1530 | 333 | 7 | 461 |
| 安徽 Anhui | 7255 | 5302 | 31 | -584 | 446 | -487 | 532 | 1394 | 90 | 70 | 155 |
| 福建 Fujian | 8974 | 5697 | -78 | -152 | -493 | 1049 | 860 | 1032 | 145 | 262 | 365 |
| 江西 Jiangxi | 6726 | 5033 | -20 | -173 | -200 | -357 | 1008 | 947 | 29 | -3 | 259 |
| 山东 Shandong | 13831 | 8483 | -145 | -438 | -276 | 186 | 1829 | 1811 | 162 | -12 | 1664 |
| 河南 Henan | 11323 | 7554 | 142 | -298 | 395 | 295 | 681 | 1448 | 94 | 0 | 540 |
| 湖北 Hubei | 8734 | 6096 | 142 | -97 | -495 | -165 | 1058 | 1435 | 131 | 33 | 277 |
| 湖南 Hunan | 8850 | 5828 | 16 | 57 | 114 | -147 | 936 | 1521 | 42 | -22 | 195 |
| 广东 Guangdong | 29190 | 22125 | -464 | -689 | -1378 | 78 | 4787 | 2076 | 549 | 555 | 562 |
| 广西 Guangxi | 5484 | 3714 | -29 | -99 | 0 | 403 | 217 | 890 | 51 | 11 | 149 |
| 海南 Hainan | 954 | 641 | -38 | -62 | 0 | 16 | -35 | 330 | 5 | 0 | 105 |
| 重庆 Chongqing | 5970 | 4710 | -2 | -98 | 91 | -147 | 149 | 951 | 19 | -11 | 156 |
| 四川 Sichuan | 9653 | 6464 | 43 | -482 | -373 | 52 | 1659 | 1356 | 52 | -3 | 534 |
| 贵州 Guizhou | 5367 | 3485 | 4 | -134 | 336 | 51 | 369 | 870 | 14 | 6 | 209 |
| 云南 Yunnan | 4926 | 3003 | -39 | -198 | 25 | -82 | 607 | 1133 | 45 | -25 | 259 |
| 西藏 Tibet | 23 | 139 | 0 | 32 | -275 | -83 | 68 | 122 | 7 | 0 | 0 |
| 陕西 Shaanxi | 4522 | 3519 | -7 | 15 | -1030 | -7 | 857 | 795 | 76 | -20 | 137 |
| 甘肃 Gansu | 2445 | 1246 | -40 | -56 | 320 | -256 | 183 | 722 | 29 | 0 | 157 |
| 青海 Qinghai | 1278 | 27 | 2 | 16 | 687 | 1 | 14 | 382 | 0 | 0 | 124 |
| 宁夏 Ningxia | 801 | 370 | -5 | -19 | 0 | -10 | -26 | 266 | 86 | 0 | 106 |
| 新疆 Xinjiang | 2948 | 1646 | -14 | -167 | -168 | 40 | 196 | 1084 | 59 | 0 | 92 |

注 1：地区社会融资规模增量是指一定时期内、一定区域内实体经济从金融体系获得的资金总额。

Note 1: Aggregate Financing to the Real Economy(AFRE, flow) by province refers to the total volume of financing provided by the financial system to the real economy during a certain period of time in each province.

注 2：表中数据为初步统计数。

Note 2: The statistics are preliminary.

注 3：数据来源于中国人民银行、中国银行保险监督管理委员会、中国证券监督管理委员会、中央国债登记结算有限责任公司和中国银行间市场交易商协会等。

Note 3: Source of data: the PBC, CBIRC, CSRC, CCDC and NAFMII.

注 4：由金融机构总行（或总部）提供的社会融资规模为 2.25 万亿元。

Note 4: AFRE provided by headquarters of financial institutions is 2.25 trillion yuan.

注 5：自 2019 年 12 月起，中国人民银行进一步完善社会融资规模统计，将"国债"和"地方政府一般债券"纳入社会融资规模统计，与原有"地方政府专项债券"合并为"政府债券"指标，指标数值为托管机构的托管面值。自 2019 年 9 月起，中国人民银行进一步完善"社会融资规模"中的"企业债券"统计，将"交易所企业资产支持证券"纳入"企业债券"指标。自 2018 年 9 月起，中国人民银行将"地方政府专项债券"纳入社会融资规模统计，地方政府专项债券按照债权债务在托管机构登记日统计。自 2018 年 7 月起，中国人民银行完善社会融资规模统计方法，将"存款类金融机构资产支持证券"和"贷款核销"纳入社会融资规模统计，在"其他融资"项下单独列示。

Note 5: Since December 2019,the People's Bank of China has made further efforts to improve the statistical method of AFRE. "Treasury Bonds" and "Local Government General Bonds" have been newly introduced into AFRE and has merged with "Local Government Special Bonds" into "Government Bonds ",which is recorded at face value at depositories. Since September 2019, the People's Bank of China has improved the statistics of Net Financing of Corporate Bonds in AFRE, and has incorporated "Asset-backed Securities of Non-Financial Enterprises" into "Net Financing of Corporate Bonds". Since September 2018, the People's Bank of China has incorporated "Local government special bonds" into AFRE, which is recorded when claims and obligations are registered at depositories. Since July 2018, the People's Bank of China has improved the statistical method of AFRE, and has incorporated "Asset-backed Securities of Depository Financial Institutions" and "Loans Written off " into AFRE, which is reflected as a sub-item of "Other Financing".

## 2.4 ■ 社会融资规模存量统计表
## Aggregate Financing to the Real Economy (Stock)

单位：亿元，%
Unit:100 Million Yuan，%

| 时间<br>Time | 社会融资<br>规模增量<br>AFRE<br>(Flow) | 社会融资<br>规模存量<br>同比增速<br>(Stock,<br>Growth Rate) | 其中 Of Which | | | | | | | | | |
|---|---|---|---|---|---|---|---|---|---|---|---|---|
| | | | 人民币<br>贷款<br>RMB<br>Loans | 外币贷款<br>(折合人民币)<br>Foreign Currency-<br>denominated<br>Loans<br>(RMB Equivalent) | 委托贷款<br>Entrusted<br>Loans | 信托贷款<br>Trust<br>Loans | 未贴现的银行<br>承兑汇票<br>Undiscounted<br>Bankers'<br>Acceptances | 企业债券<br>Net<br>Financing<br>of Corporate<br>Bonds | 政府债券<br>Government<br>Bonds | 非金融企业<br>境内股票融资<br>Equity Financing on<br>the Domestic Stock<br>Market by Non-<br>financial Enterprises | 存款类金融机构<br>资产支持证券<br>Asset-backed<br>Securities of<br>Depository Financial<br>Institutions | 贷款核销<br>Loans<br>Written off |
| 2003 | 181655 | 22.3 | 21.4 | 26.6 | 13.3 | — | 126.0 | 132.9 | — | 8.0 | — | — |
| 2004 | 204143 | 14.9 | 14.3 | 16.8 | 61.6 | — | -8.0 | 4.0 | — | 8.5 | — | — |
| 2005 | 224265 | 13.5 | 13.3 | 11.0 | 11.8 | — | 0.7 | 129.1 | — | 4.2 | — | — |
| 2006 | 264500 | 18.1 | 16.3 | 9.0 | 20.0 | — | 44.9 | 68.7 | — | 12.5 | — | — |
| 2007 | 321326 | 21.5 | 16.4 | 21.9 | 29.9 | 84.0 | 138.4 | 41.0 | — | 45.8 | — | — |
| 2008 | 379765 | 20.5 | 18.7 | 5.1 | 29.1 | 84.3 | 9.2 | 78.7 | — | 17.7 | — | — |
| 2009 | 511835 | 34.8 | 31.3 | 55.5 | 35.8 | 63.4 | 36.5 | 86.2 | — | 18.3 | — | — |
| 2010 | 649869 | 27.0 | 19.9 | 15.9 | 44.2 | 34.4 | 135.5 | 42.3 | — | 30.9 | — | — |
| 2011 | 767791 | 18.3 | 16.1 | 13.1 | 21.2 | 13.5 | 25.6 | 36.2 | — | 17.7 | — | — |
| 2012 | 914675 | 19.1 | 15.0 | 27.2 | 17.1 | 75.0 | 21.0 | 44.4 | — | 8.6 | — | — |
| 2013 | 1075217 | 17.6 | 14.2 | 7.2 | 39.7 | 61.1 | 12.7 | 24.2 | — | 6.7 | — | — |
| 2014 | 1229386 | 14.3 | 13.6 | 4.1 | 29.2 | 10.8 | -1.1 | 25.8 | — | 11.8 | — | — |
| 2015 | 1382824 | 12.5 | 13.9 | -13.0 | 18.0 | 2.0 | -14.8 | 25.1 | — | 20.2 | — | — |
| 2016 | 1559884 | 12.8 | 13.4 | -12.9 | 19.8 | 15.8 | -33.3 | 22.4 | — | 27.6 | — | — |
| 2017 | 2059098 | 14.1 | 13.2 | -5.8 | 5.9 | 35.9 | 13.7 | 3.9 | 24.7 | 15.2 | 40.5 | 61.4 |
| 2018 | 2270356 | 10.3 | 13.2 | -10.7 | -11.5 | -8.0 | -14.3 | 9.8 | 17.2 | 5.4 | 86.7 | 50.9 |
| 2019.01 | 2315476 | 10.9 | 13.6 | -11.1 | -11.6 | -8.2 | -8.7 | 11.5 | 17.8 | 5.1 | 83.5 | 49.8 |
| 2019.02 | 2324102 | 10.6 | 13.3 | -12.0 | -11.4 | -8.9 | -15.7 | 11.2 | 19.3 | 4.7 | 87.4 | 48.8 |
| 2019.03 | 2352400 | 11.2 | 13.8 | -11.3 | -11.0 | -7.9 | -12.1 | 10.9 | 19.7 | 4.2 | 80.7 | 46.0 |
| 2019.04 | 2368118 | 10.8 | 13.5 | -13.3 | -10.9 | -7.7 | -15.6 | 11.0 | 19.1 | 3.8 | 64.8 | 45.7 |
| 2019.05 | 2384958 | 11.0 | 13.4 | -10.6 | -10.4 | -6.7 | -14.0 | 11.6 | 19.3 | 3.5 | 61.9 | 44.4 |
| 2019.06 | 2410483 | 11.2 | 13.2 | -12.4 | -9.9 | -4.9 | -9.6 | 12.1 | 19.0 | 3.3 | 63.8 | 41.5 |
| 2019.07 | 2421940 | 10.8 | 12.7 | -13.0 | -10.0 | -4.3 | -15.0 | 12.8 | 18.0 | 3.9 | 64.8 | 41.5 |
| 2019.08 | 2443064 | 10.7 | 12.6 | -10.3 | -9.5 | -4.3 | -12.8 | 12.6 | 16.3 | 4.1 | 58.7 | 40.7 |
| 2019.09 | 2466786 | 10.7 | 12.7 | -10.6 | -8.5 | -4.1 | -12.7 | 14.1 | 14.2 | 4.1 | 47.2 | 38.5 |
| 2019.10 | 2474237 | 10.6 | 12.5 | -9.0 | -8.4 | -3.4 | -14.5 | 14.5 | 13.8 | 4.1 | 50.7 | 37.8 |
| 2019.11 | 2492701 | 10.7 | 12.5 | -6.9 | -8.2 | -3.7 | -12.7 | 13.8 | 14.4 | 4.5 | 41.4 | 36.5 |
| 2019.12 | 2513120 | 10.7 | 12.5 | -4.6 | -7.6 | -4.4 | -12.5 | 13.4 | 14.3 | 5.0 | 31.5 | 35.1 |

注 1：社会融资规模存量是指一定时期末实体经济从金融体系获得的资金余额。
Note 1: AFRE (Stock) refers to the outstanding of financing provided by the financial system to the real economy at the end of a period.

注 2：存量数据基于账面值或面值计算。
Note 2: Stock figures are based on book-value or face-value.

注 3：数据来源于中国人民银行、中国银行保险监督管理委员会、中国证券监督管理委员会、中央国债登记结算有限责任公司和中国银行间市场交易商协会等。
Note 3: Source of data: the PBC, CBIRC,CSRC,CCDC and NAFMII.

注 4：自 2019 年 12 月起，中国人民银行进一步完善社会融资规模统计，将"国债"和"地方政府一般债券"纳入社会融资规模统计，与原有"地方政府专项债券"合并为"政府债券"指标。指标数值为托管机构的托管面值。自 2019 年 9 月起，中国人民银行完善"社会融资规模"中的"企业债券"统计，将"交易所企业资产支持证券"纳入"企业债券"指标。自 2018 年 9 月起，中国人民银行将"地方政府专项债券"纳入社会融资规模统计。自 2018 年 7 月起，中国人民银行完善社会融资规模统计方法，将"存款类金融机构资产支持证券"和"贷款核销"纳入社会融资规模统计，在"其他融资"项下单独列示。
Note 4: Since December 2019,the People's Bank of China has made further efforts to improve the statistical method of AFRE. "Treasury Bonds" and "Local Government General Bonds" have been newly introduced into AFRE and have merged with "Local Government Special Bonds" into "Government Bonds ",which is recorded at face value at depositories. Since September 2019, the People's Bank of China has improved the statistics of "Net Financing of Corporate Bonds" in AFRE, and has incorporated "Asset-backed Securities of Non-Financial Enterprises" into "Net Financing of Corporate Bonds". Since September 2018, the People's Bank of China has incorporated "Local Government Special Bonds" into AFRE. Since July 2018, the People's Bank of China has improved the statistical method of AFRE, and has incorporated "Asset-backed Securities of Depository Financial Institutions" and "Loans Written off" into AFRE, which is reflected as a sub-item of "Other Financing".

注 5：当期数据为初步统计数。2017 年 1 月以来数据进行了可比口径调整，详见中国人民银行官网最新社会融资规模数据表附注。
Note 5: Data for the current period are preliminary. Data are comparably adjusted as of January 2017. Please refer to the notes of the latest AFRE release on the website of the PBC for details.

## 2.5　金融机构信贷收支表（人民币）
## Sources and Uses of Credit Funds of Financial Institutions (RMB)

单位：亿元
Unit:100 Million Yuan

| 时间<br>Time | 资金来源总计<br>Total Funds Sources | 各项存款<br>Total Deposits | 非金融企业存款<br>Deposits of Non-financial Enterprises | 财政存款<br>Fiscal Deposits | 住户存款<br>Deposits of Households | 活期及临时性存款<br>Demand & Temporary Deposits | 定期及其他存款 *<br>Time & Other Deposits* | 其他类存款 **<br>Other Deposits** | 金融债券<br>Financial Bonds | 流通中现金<br>Currency in Circulation | 对国际金融机构负债<br>Liabilities to International Financial Institutions | 其他<br>Other Items |
|---|---|---|---|---|---|---|---|---|---|---|---|---|
| 2008 | 538405.6 | 466203.3 | 157632.2 | 18040.0 | 217885.4 | 78585.2 | 139300.2 | 72645.7 | 20852.5 | 34219.0 | 732.6 | 16398.2 |
| 2009 | 681874.8 | 597741.1 | 217110.0 | 22411.5 | 260771.7 | 100541.3 | 160230.4 | 97447.8 | 16203.4 | 38246.0 | 761.7 | 28922.6 |
| 2010 | 805879.1 | 718237.9 | 244495.6 | 25455.0 | 303302.5 | 124888.6 | 178413.9 | 144984.8 | 13526.9 | 44628.2 | 720.1 | 28766.0 |
| 2011.03 | 828977.4 | 752838.4 | 281727.1 | 29981.6 | 327629.2 | 130028.6 | 197600.5 | 113500.5 | 6042.6 | 44845.2 | 774.2 | 24477.0 |
| 2011.06 | 851311.8 | 786432.6 | 294263.3 | 36271.4 | 333678.6 | 132640.3 | 201038.2 | 122219.3 | 7597.4 | 44477.8 | 795.1 | 12008.9 |
| 2011.09 | 878645.1 | 794100.4 | 290918.5 | 38160.1 | 337212.3 | 130681.8 | 206530.5 | 127809.5 | 7393.6 | 47145.3 | 797.3 | 29208.5 |
| 2011.12 | 900401.6 | 809368.3 | 303504.3 | 26223.1 | 348045.6 | 137576.2 | 210469.4 | 131595.4 | 10638.8 | 50748.5 | 776.5 | 29469.5 |
| 2012.03 | 931667.6 | 846931.7 | 299252.9 | 26886.6 | 380498.1 | 145083.5 | 235414.6 | 140294.1 | 9016.7 | 49595.7 | 765.5 | 25358.0 |
| 2012.06 | 958431.0 | 883068.7 | 311166.7 | 31522.0 | 391186.0 | 148865.3 | 242320.7 | 149194.0 | 7220.7 | 49284.6 | 780.4 | 18076.6 |
| 2012.09 | 983508.1 | 899647.1 | 313959.7 | 32503.8 | 398069.7 | 150832.9 | 247236.8 | 155113.9 | 7695.3 | 53433.5 | 793.6 | 21938.6 |
| 2012.12 | 1002434.4 | 917554.8 | 327393.7 | 24426.4 | 406191.6 | 158271.8 | 247919.8 | 159543.1 | 8487.6 | 54659.8 | 827.7 | 20904.5 |
| 2013.03 | 1046828 | 979301 | 342606 | 25316 | 443408 | 173557 | 269851 | 167971 | 5508 | 55461 | 794 | 5764 |
| 2013.06 | 1076338 | 1009122 | 349741 | 33953 | 447772 | 169140 | 278632 | 177656 | 4375 | 54064 | 806 | 7971 |
| 2013.09 | 1105735 | 1030892 | 350387 | 38965 | 456348 | 171759 | 284589 | 185192 | 5728 | 56493 | 846 | 11772 |
| 2013.12 | 1132914 | 1043847 | 361555 | 30133 | 461370 | 178050 | 283320 | 190789 | 6681 | 58574 | 854 | 22958 |
| 2014.03 | 1221581 | 1091022 | 531168 | 31063 | 494023 | 189049 | 304974 | 204142 | 9349 | 58329 | 880 | 12465 |
| 2014.06 | 1204845 | 1136075 | 383718 | 36674 | 501628 | 187221 | 314407 | 214055 | 10049 | 56951 | 894 | 876 |
| 2014.09 | 1229317 | 1126570 | 369510 | 41305 | 497860 | 179302 | 318558 | 217895 | 10570 | 58845 | 880 | 32452 |
| 2014.12 | 1258000 | 1138645 | 378334 | 35665 | 502504 | 182705 | 319799 | 222142 | 9843 | 60260 | 867 | 48385 |

注1：对金融机构信贷收支表的说明详见第 96 页。
Note 1: Notes to the sheet of the Sources and Uses of Credit Funds of Financial Institutions can be read on page 96.

注2：自 2011 年一季度起，部分指标名称和统计口径变动。以前年度数据未作调整。（1）"企业定活期存款"更名为"非金融企业存款"。（2）"储蓄存款"更名为"住户存款"。（3）"活期储蓄"更名为"活期及临时性存款"。（4）"定期储蓄"更名为"定期及其他存款"。

Note 2: As of 2011 Q1, changes have taken place in the name and statistical coverage for certain indicators. Historical data for previous periods are not adjusted accordingly.(1) "Demand & Time Deposits of Enterprises" is renamed as "Deposits of Non-financial Enterprises". (2) "Savings Deposits" is renamed as "Deposits of Households". (3) "Demand Deposits" under the category of saving deposits is renamed as "Demand & Temporary Deposits". (4) "Time Deposits" under the category of savings deposits is renamed as "Time & Other Deposits".

* 定期及其他存款包括定期存款、通知存款、定活两便存款、协议存款、协定存款、保证金存款、结构性存款。
* Time & other deposits cover the components of time deposits, notice deposits, savings & time optional deposits, agreed-term deposits, corporate agreement savings deposits, margin deposits and structure deposits.

** 其他类存款包括各项存款中除非金融企业存款、财政存款、住户存款之外的所有存款。
** Other deposits cover all the other deposits under total deposits excluding deposits of non-financial enterprises, fiscal deposits and deposits of households.

## 2.5 ■ 金融机构信贷收支表（人民币）
## Sources and Uses of Credit Funds of Financial Institutions (RMB)

单位：亿元<br>Unit:100 Million Yuan

| 时间<br>Time | 资金运用总计<br>Total Funds Uses | 各项贷款<br>Total Loans | 境内短期贷款<br>Domestic Short-term Loans | 境内中长期贷款<br>Domestic Medium- and Long-term Loans | 其他类贷款*<br>Other Loans* | 有价证券及投资<br>Portfolio Investment | 黄金占款**<br>Position for Gold Purchase** | 外汇占款**<br>Position for Foreign Exchange Purchase** | 财政借款<br>Fiscal Debts | 国际金融机构资产<br>Assets with International Financial Institutions |
|---|---|---|---|---|---|---|---|---|---|---|
| 2008 | 538405.6 | 303394.6 | 125181.7 | 154999.8 | 23213.2 | 65301.9 | 337.2 | 168431.1 | | 940.7 |
| 2009 | 681874.8 | 399684.8 | 146611.3 | 222418.8 | 30654.7 | 86643.2 | 669.8 | 193112.5 | | 1764.5 |
| 2010 | 805879.1 | 479195.6 | 166233.4 | 288930.4 | 24031.8 | 98526.1 | 669.8 | 225795.1 | | 1692.5 |
| 2011.03 | 828977.4 | 494740.7 | 174954.9 | 302720.9 | 17064.9 | 94682.7 | 669.8 | 237036.0 | | 1848.2 |
| 2011.06 | 851311.8 | 514025.4 | 184264.6 | 311026.9 | 18733.9 | 88091.4 | 669.8 | 246680.6 | | 1844.6 |
| 2011.09 | 878645.1 | 529118.3 | 191783.3 | 316972.4 | 20362.6 | 91968.6 | 669.8 | 255118.2 | | 1770.2 |
| 2011.12 | 900401.6 | 547946.7 | 203132.6 | 323806.5 | 21007.6 | 96479.4 | 669.8 | 253587.0 | | 1718.7 |
| 2012.03 | 931667.6 | 572474.8 | 215703.9 | 332492.4 | 24278.5 | 100323.2 | 669.8 | 256493.9 | | 1705.9 |
| 2012.06 | 958431.0 | 596422.6 | 226373.8 | 339859.8 | 30189.0 | 103046.9 | 669.8 | 256613.4 | | 1678.4 |
| 2012.09 | 983508.1 | 615089.5 | 235942.5 | 347726.9 | 31420.1 | 108368.1 | 669.8 | 257707.6 | | 1673.1 |
| 2012.12 | 1002434.4 | 629909.6 | 248272.8 | 352907.4 | 28729.4 | 111680.9 | 669.8 | 258533.5 | | 1640.6 |
| 2013.03 | 1046828 | 657592 | 259872 | 367239 | 30481 | 116271 | 670 | 270687 | | 1608 |
| 2013.06 | 1076338 | 680837 | 269169 | 378833 | 32835 | 119373 | 670 | 273887 | | 1571 |
| 2013.09 | 1105753 | 702832 | 280495 | 391820 | 30517 | 125480 | 670 | 275179 | | 1592 |
| 2013.12 | 1132914 | 718961 | 290238 | 398862 | 29861 | 125399 | 670 | 286304 | | 1580 |
| 2014.03 | 1172045 | 749090 | 302593 | 416371 | 30126 | 126834 | 670 | 293852 | | 1599 |
| 2014.06 | 1204845 | 776337 | 310624 | 431646 | 34067 | 131723 | 670 | 294513 | | 1602 |
| 2014.09 | 1229317 | 795786 | 311674 | 444289 | 39823 | 136712 | 670 | 294592 | | 1557 |
| 2014.12 | 1258000 | 816770 | 314796 | 459482 | 42492 | 144954 | 670 | 294090 | | 1516 |

\* 其他类贷款包括各项贷款中除境内短期贷款和境内中长期贷款之外的所有贷款。

\* Other loans include all the loans except domestic short-term loans, domestic medium- and long-term loans.

\*\* 中国人民银行 2001 年 12 月、2002 年 12 月对"金银占款"进行了两次调整，自 2002 年一季度起对"外汇占款"进行了调整。自 2009 年 6 月起，本表"金银占款"更名为"黄金占款"。

\*\* Adjustments were made on "Position for Gold and Silver Purchase" by the PBC in December 2001 and December 2002. Adjustments have also been made on "Position for Foreign Exchange Purchased" since 2002 Q1. "Position for Gold and Silver Purchase" has been renamed as "Position for Gold Purchase" since June 2009.

## 2.5 金融机构信贷收支表（人民币）
## Sources and Uses of Credit Funds of Financial Institutions (RMB)

单位：亿元
Unit:100 Million Yuan

| 时间<br>Time | 资金来源合计<br>Total Funds Sources | 各项存款<br>Total Deposits | 境内存款<br>Domestic Deposits | 住户存款<br>Deposits of Households | 活期存款<br>Demand Deposits | 定期及其他存款<br>Time & Other Deposits | 非金融企业存款<br>Deposits of Non-financial Enterprises | 活期存款<br>Demand Deposits | 定期及其他存款<br>Time & Other Deposits | 政府存款<br>Deposits of Government | 非银行业金融机构<br>Deposits of Non-banking Financial Institutions | 境外存款<br>Overseas Deposits | 金融债券<br>Financial Bonds | 流通中货币<br>Currency in Circulation | 其他<br>Other Items |
|---|---|---|---|---|---|---|---|---|---|---|---|---|---|---|---|
| 2014.03 | 1277171 | 1134571 | 1118049 | 494023 | 189049 | 304974 | 361793 | 134251 | 227542 | 200459 | 61774 | 16522 | 9349 | 58329 | 74922 |
| 2014.06 | 1328807 | 1191306 | 1174482 | 501628 | 187221 | 314407 | 383717 | 141436 | 242281 | 214796 | 74341 | 16824 | 10049 | 56951 | 70501 |
| 2014.09 | 1346639 | 1187288 | 1169198 | 497860 | 179302 | 318558 | 369509 | 129490 | 240019 | 224609 | 77220 | 18090 | 10570 | 58845 | 89936 |
| 2014.12 | 1378334 | 1206922 | 1188257 | 502504 | 182705 | 319799 | 378333 | 143310 | 235023 | 221794 | 85626 | 18665 | 9843 | 60260 | 101309 |
| | | | | | | | | | | | | | | | |
| 2015.03 | 1434519 | 1248866 | 1232919 | 538399 | 189934 | 348465 | 373435 | 132701 | 240734 | 224339 | 96746 | 15947 | 11612 | 61950 | 112091 |
| 2015.06 | 1499209 | 1318292 | 1301334 | 532829 | 187645 | 345184 | 398245 | 144245 | 254000 | 241883 | 128377 | 16958 | 8836 | 58604 | 113477 |
| 2015.09 | 1534889 | 1337338 | 1323229 | 541749 | 194150 | 347599 | 404797 | 147153 | 257643 | 250356 | 126327 | 14109 | 9768 | 61023 | 126760 |
| 2015.12 | 1586049 | 1357022 | 1345783 | 546078 | 202869 | 343209 | 430247 | 174586 | 255661 | 241832 | 127625 | 11239 | 10062 | 63217 | 155749 |
| | | | | | | | | | | | | | | | |
| 2016.03 | 1604474 | 1411183 | 1400021 | 580800 | 217001 | 363799 | 445248 | 175269 | 269980 | 249960 | 124012 | 11162 | 17762 | 64651 | 110878 |
| 2016.06 | 1673236 | 1462397 | 1450753 | 581521 | 216945 | 364576 | 465346 | 191138 | 274208 | 271954 | 131932 | 11644 | 25335 | 62819 | 122685 |
| 2016.09 | 1722228 | 1485214 | 1474865 | 592909 | 225331 | 367578 | 480303 | 192839 | 287464 | 277665 | 123988 | 10350 | 28660 | 65069 | 143285 |
| 2016.12 | 1759952 | 1505864 | 1497169 | 597751 | 231630 | 366121 | 502178 | 215107 | 287072 | 270379 | 126860 | 8695 | 31579 | 68304 | 154206 |
| | | | | | | | | | | | | | | | |
| 2017.03 | 1810979 | 1556487 | 1547169 | 637409 | 241907 | 395502 | 503768 | 212132 | 291636 | 277556 | 128436 | 9318 | 38147 | 68605 | 147741 |
| 2017.06 | 1852410 | 1596636 | 1585978 | 637138 | 242055 | 395083 | 515971 | 222012 | 293960 | 295245 | 137624 | 10657 | 40007 | 66978 | 148790 |
| 2017.09 | 1898731 | 1622758 | 1612133 | 642591 | 246818 | 395772 | 521823 | 219597 | 302226 | 308039 | 139681 | 10624 | 43235 | 69749 | 162990 |
| 2017.12 | 1931934 | 1641044 | 1630577 | 643768 | 248239 | 395529 | 542405 | 237888 | 304517 | 304853 | 139552 | 10467 | 48000 | 70646 | 172245 |
| | | | | | | | | | | | | | | | |
| 2018.03 | 1982829 | 1691816 | 1681636 | 686804 | 258521 | 428283 | 529321 | 219818 | 309503 | 310348 | 155163 | 10180 | 53003 | 72693 | 165317 |
| 2018.06 | 2024395 | 1731176 | 1720273 | 686695 | 255578 | 431117 | 544362 | 230035 | 314327 | 326867 | 162348 | 10903 | 55887 | 69589 | 167743 |
| 2018.09 | 2075626 | 1761267 | 1749826 | 700518 | 258601 | 441917 | 547417 | 220860 | 326557 | 342685 | 159206 | 11441 | 60255 | 71254 | 182850 |
| 2018.12 | 2109164 | 1775226 | 1764398 | 716038 | 267215 | 448824 | 562976 | 236190 | 326786 | 325585 | 159798 | 10828 | 65433 | 73208 | 195297 |
| | | | | | | | | | | | | | | | |
| 2019.03 | 2188083 | 1838227 | 1826924 | 776654 | 275339 | 501315 | 565751 | 226505 | 339246 | 334297 | 150222 | 11303 | 68790 | 74942 | 206124 |
| 2019.06 | 2232785 | 1875680 | 1864210 | 784172 | 277699 | 506473 | 580837 | 236266 | 344571 | 350642 | 148559 | 11470 | 72815 | 72581 | 211709 |
| 2019.09 | 2278779 | 1907341 | 1895803 | 801298 | 286136 | 515162 | 577652 | 226300 | 351353 | 355732 | 161121 | 11538 | 76972 | 74130 | 220336 |
| 2019.12 | 2317003 | 1928785 | 1917482 | 813017 | 294712 | 518305 | 595365 | 242504 | 352861 | 337671 | 171429 | 11304 | 82924 | 77189 | 228104 |

注1：本表机构包括中国人民银行、银行业存款类金融机构、银行业非存款类金融机构。
Note 1: Financial institutions in this table include the PBC, banking depository financial institutions and banking non-depository financial institutions.

注2：银行业存款类金融机构包括银行、信用社和财务公司。银行业非存款类金融机构包括信托投资公司、金融租赁公司、汽车金融公司和贷款公司等。
Note 2: Banking depository financial institutions include banks, credit cooperatives and finance companies. Banking non-depository financial institutions include financial trust and investment corporations, financial leasing companies, auto-financing companies, as well as loan companies.

注3：自2015年起，各项存款含非银行业金融机构存放款项，各项贷款含拆放给非银行业金融机构款项。
Note 3: Since 2015, deposits of non-banking financial institutions have been covered in total deposits and loans to non-banking financial institutions are covered in total loans.

注4：本表2014年数据，按2015年统计口径调整。
Note 4: Historical data for 2014 are adjusted, according to the changes of the statistical coverage as of 2015.

## 2.5 金融机构信贷收支表（人民币）
## Sources and Uses of Credit Funds of Financial Institutions (RMB)

单位：亿元
Unit:100 Million Yuan

| 时间<br>Time | 资金运用总计<br>Total Funds Uses | 各项贷款<br>Total Loans | 境内贷款<br>Domestic Loans | 住户贷款<br>Loans to Households | 非金融企业及机关团体贷款<br>Loans to Non-financial Enterprises and Government Departments & Organizations | 非银行业金融机构贷款<br>Loans to Non-banking Financial Institutions | 境外贷款<br>Overseas Loans | 债券投资<br>Portfolio Investments | 股权及其他投资<br>Shares and Other Investments | 黄金占款<br>Position for Bullion Purchase | 外汇买卖<br>Position for Forex Purchase | 其他资产<br>Other Assets |
|---|---|---|---|---|---|---|---|---|---|---|---|---|
| 2014.03 | 1277171 | 753655 | 751688 | 207795 | 539337 | 4556 | 1967 | 126834 | 51802 | 670 | 293852 | 50358 |
| 2014.06 | 1328807 | 783181 | 781198 | 217290 | 557095 | 6813 | 1983 | 131723 | 56855 | 670 | 294513 | 61865 |
| 2014.09 | 1346639 | 798506 | 796478 | 225062 | 568717 | 2699 | 2028 | 136716 | 58324 | 670 | 294592 | 57831 |
| 2014.12 | 1378334 | 822031 | 819850 | 231410 | 583322 | 5118 | 2181 | 144954 | 67503 | 670 | 294090 | 49086 |
| 2015.03 | 1434519 | 859069 | 856785 | 240385 | 610996 | 5404 | 2284 | 150172 | 83278 | 670 | 291865 | 49465 |
| 2015.06 | 1499209 | 887947 | 885445 | 251030 | 630088 | 4327 | 2502 | 163373 | 107246 | 2059 | 291574 | 47011 |
| 2015.09 | 1534889 | 921337 | 917947 | 261515 | 643631 | 12801 | 3391 | 179326 | 112720 | 2172 | 274232 | 45102 |
| 2015.12 | 1586049 | 939540 | 936387 | 270214 | 657633 | 8539 | 3153 | 197636 | 134326 | 2293 | 265859 | 46395 |
| 2016.03 | 1604474 | 985613 | 982366 | 282755 | 691731 | 7880 | 3247 | 200143 | 174485 | 2417 | 238366 | 3451 |
| 2016.06 | 1673236 | 1014859 | 1011385 | 299767 | 702833 | 8785 | 3474 | 224182 | 191888 | 2488 | 236308 | 3510 |
| 2016.09 | 1722228 | 1041138 | 1037376 | 317526 | 710199 | 9652 | 3761 | 238372 | 207563 | 2530 | 229109 | 3515 |
| 2016.12 | 1759952 | 1066040 | 1061667 | 333615 | 718521 | 9532 | 4373 | 247604 | 220820 | 2542 | 219425 | 3521 |
| 2017.03 | 1810979 | 1108256 | 1103898 | 352174 | 744996 | 6729 | 4358 | 251996 | 230536 | 2542 | 216210 | 1441 |
| 2017.06 | 1852410 | 1145721 | 1141256 | 371453 | 762748 | 7055 | 4465 | 265485 | 222083 | 2542 | 215153 | 1427 |
| 2017.09 | 1898731 | 1177617 | 1173283 | 391026 | 775678 | 6579 | 4335 | 281209 | 220870 | 2541 | 215107 | 1386 |
| 2017.12 | 1931934 | 1201321 | 1196900 | 405045 | 785496 | 6359 | 4421 | 294382 | 217589 | 2541 | 214788 | 1313 |
| 2018.03 | 1982829 | 1249814 | 1245104 | 422733 | 816154 | 6217 | 4710 | 290080 | 224151 | 2541 | 214952 | 1290 |
| 2018.06 | 2024395 | 1291534 | 1286781 | 441217 | 836871 | 8692 | 4753 | 303205 | 210536 | 2541 | 215194 | 1386 |
| 2018.09 | 2075626 | 1332663 | 1327637 | 462053 | 856352 | 9232 | 5025 | 325869 | 199035 | 2541 | 214084 | 1433 |
| 2018.12 | 2109164 | 1362967 | 1357891 | 478843 | 868289 | 10760 | 5075 | 333467 | 196190 | 2570 | 212557 | 1414 |
| 2019.03 | 2188083 | 1421057 | 1415914 | 496985 | 913048 | 5881 | 5143 | 348157 | 202286 | 2664 | 212537 | 1382 |
| 2019.06 | 2232785 | 1459691 | 1454547 | 516449 | 930903 | 7195 | 5145 | 360177 | 196276 | 2782 | 212455 | 1403 |
| 2019.09 | 2278779 | 1499247 | 1494009 | 535666 | 950424 | 7919 | 5238 | 375447 | 187411 | 2856 | 212354 | 1464 |
| 2019.12 | 2317003 | 1531123 | 1525755 | 553191 | 962737 | 9827 | 5368 | 385520 | 183730 | 2856 | 212317 | 1457 |

## 2.6 1 存款性公司概览（资产）
## Depository Corporations Survey (Assets)

单位：亿元
Unit: 100 Million Yuan

| 时间<br>Time | 国外净资产<br>Net Foreign Assets | 国内信贷<br>Domestic Credit | 对政府债权（净）<br>Claims on Government (Net) |
|---|---|---|---|
| 2012 | 258850.9 | 805593.8 | 50683.7 |
| 2013 | 280986 | 927007 | 49044 |
| 2014.03 | 284032 | 972329 | 48407 |
| 2014.06 | 289009 | 1016864 | 46666 |
| 2014.09 | 288866 | 1032886 | 47087 |
| 2014.12 | 288390 | 1076962 | 55047 |
| 2015.03 | 294637 | 1136552 | 56176 |
| 2015.06 | 294660 | 1199812 | 61493 |
| 2015.09 | 287168 | 1255732 | 74882 |
| 2015.12 | 280639 | 1332693 | 98297 |
| 2016.03 | 271903 | 1425207 | 105297 |
| 2016.06 | 270808 | 1496112 | 128868 |
| 2016.09 | 268411 | 1544356 | 146868 |
| 2016.12 | 263948 | 1600067 | 162352 |
| 2017.03 | 260793 | 1650629 | 166269 |
| 2017.06 | 255508 | 1701411 | 176481 |
| 2017.09 | 254785 | 1740947 | 190194 |
| 2017.12 | 253287 | 1780278 | 204892 |
| 2018.03 | 255448 | 1841753 | 214981 |
| 2018.06 | 257147 | 1873240 | 220423 |
| 2018.09 | 256694 | 1927674 | 238970 |
| 2018.12 | 255736 | 1965451 | 251378 |
| 2019.03 | 260083 | 2039204 | 260601 |
| 2019.06 | 261731 | 2074943 | 266279 |
| 2019.09 | 262994 | 2124548 | 276851 |
| 2019.12 | 264599 | 2172833 | 290116 |

注：自 2005 年起，将货币当局资产负债表和其他存款性公司资产负债表合并，编制存款性公司概览。2005 年之前，原银行概览可以替代存款性公司概览。

Note: Since 2005, the balance sheet of monetary authority and that of other depository corporations have been consolidated to compile the depository corporations survey. To keep comparability, the original banking survey could be used as the substitution for depository corporation survey before 2005.

2.6 **1** 存款性公司概览（资产）
Depository Corporations Survey (Assets)

单位：亿元
Unit: 100 Million Yuan

| 时间<br>Time | 对非金融部门债权<br>Claims on Non-financial Corporations | 对其他金融部门债权<br>Claims on Other Financial Corporations |
| --- | --- | --- |
| 2012 | 694351.5 | 60558.5 |
| 2013 | 796464 | 81500 |
| 2014.03 | 831078 | 92845 |
| 2014.06 | 858228 | 111971 |
| 2014.09 | 878407 | 107392 |
| 2014.12 | 902513 | 119402 |
| 2015.03 | 943331 | 137045 |
| 2015.06 | 978254 | 160065 |
| 2015.09 | 1011362 | 169488 |
| 2015.12 | 1051160 | 183236 |
| 2016.03 | 1089233 | 230676 |
| 2016.06 | 1118050 | 249194 |
| 2016.09 | 1139688 | 257801 |
| 2016.12 | 1166093 | 271623 |
| 2017.03 | 1200190 | 284170 |
| 2017.06 | 1234070 | 290859 |
| 2017.09 | 1265935 | 284818 |
| 2017.12 | 1288783 | 286603 |
| 2018.03 | 1338831 | 287941 |
| 2018.06 | 1373058 | 279760 |
| 2018.09 | 1423655 | 265050 |
| 2018.12 | 1450737 | 263336 |
| 2019.03 | 1514311 | 264292 |
| 2019.06 | 1550378 | 258286 |
| 2019.09 | 1601534 | 246163 |
| 2019.12 | 1631601 | 251116 |

2.6 2 存款性公司概览（负债）
## Depository Corporations Survey (Liabilities)

单位：亿元
Unit: 100 Million Yuan

| 时间<br>Time | 货币和<br>准货币<br>Money and<br>Quasi-money | 货币<br>Money | 流通中<br>现金<br>Currency<br>in<br>Circulation | 活期存款<br>Demand<br>Deposits | 准货币<br>Quasi-<br>money | 定期存款<br>Time<br>Deposits | 储蓄存款<br>Savings<br>Deposits | 其他存款<br>Other<br>Deposits |
|---|---|---|---|---|---|---|---|---|
| 2012 | 974148.8 | 308664.2 | 54659.8 | 254004.5 | 665484.6 | 195940.1 | 411362.6 | 58181.9 |
| 2013 | 1106525 | 337291 | 58574 | 278717 | 769234 | 232697 | 467031 | 69506 |
| 2014.03 | 1160687 | 327684 | 58329 | 269354 | 833004 | 250779 | 500399 | 81825 |
| 2014.06 | 1209587 | 341487 | 56951 | 284536 | 868100 | 265644 | 508025 | 94431 |
| 2014.09 | 1202051 | 327220 | 58845 | 268375 | 874831 | 272197 | 504262 | 98372 |
| 2014.12 | 1228375 | 348056 | 60260 | 287797 | 880318 | 264056 | 508878 | 107385 |
| 2015.03 | 1275333 | 337211 | 61950 | 275261 | 938122 | 275189 | 544694 | 118239 |
| 2015.06 | 1333375 | 356083 | 58604 | 297479 | 977293 | 289329 | 539127 | 148836 |
| 2015.09 | 1359824 | 364417 | 61023 | 303394 | 995407 | 298571 | 547874 | 148962 |
| 2015.12 | 1392278 | 400953 | 63217 | 337737 | 991325 | 288241 | 552073 | 151011 |
| 2016.03 | 1446198 | 411581 | 64651 | 346930 | 1034617 | 300623 | 586856 | 147138 |
| 2016.06 | 1490492 | 443644 | 62819 | 380825 | 1046848 | 301674 | 587549 | 157625 |
| 2016.09 | 1516361 | 454340 | 65069 | 389272 | 1062020 | 315077 | 598881 | 148063 |
| 2016.12 | 1550067 | 486557 | 68304 | 418253 | 1063509 | 307990 | 603504 | 152016 |
| 2017.03 | 1599610 | 488770 | 68605 | 420165 | 1110839 | 317183 | 643278 | 150378 |
| 2017.06 | 1631283 | 510228 | 66978 | 443250 | 1121054 | 317003 | 642932 | 161119 |
| 2017.09 | 1655662 | 517863 | 69749 | 448114 | 1137799 | 326614 | 648350 | 162835 |
| 2017.12 | 1676769 | 543790 | 70646 | 473145 | 1132978 | 320196 | 649341 | 163441 |
| 2018.03 | 1739859 | 523540 | 72693 | 450847 | 1216319 | 332606 | 692564 | 191150 |
| 2018.06 | 1770178 | 543945 | 69589 | 474355 | 1226234 | 334425 | 692441 | 199368 |
| 2018.09 | 1801666 | 538574 | 71254 | 467320 | 1263091 | 349827 | 706256 | 207008 |
| 2018.12 | 1826744 | 551686 | 73208 | 478478 | 1275058 | 340179 | 721689 | 213191 |
| 2019.03 | 1889412 | 547576 | 74942 | 472634 | 1341837 | 359015 | 782606 | 200215 |
| 2019.06 | 1921360 | 567696 | 72581 | 495115 | 1353664 | 362163 | 790201 | 201300 |
| 2019.09 | 1952250 | 557138 | 74130 | 483008 | 1395113 | 374318 | 807437 | 213357 |
| 2019.12 | 1986489 | 576009 | 77189 | 498820 | 1410480 | 363486 | 819162 | 227832 |

注：自 2001 年 6 月起，将证券公司存放在金融机构的客户保证金计入货币和准货币，包含在其他存款（净）项内。

Note: Since June 2001, the margin account of securities companies maintained with financial institutions, as part of other items (net), has been included in money and quasi-money.

## 2.6 2 存款性公司概览（负债）
## Depository Corporations Survey (Liabilities)

单位：亿元
Unit: 100 Million Yuan

| 时间<br>Time | 不纳入广义<br>货币的存款<br>Deposits Excluded<br>from Broad Money | 债券<br>Bonds | 实收资本<br>Paid-in Capital | 其他<br>（净）<br>Other Items<br>(Net) |
|---|---|---|---|---|
| 2012 | 24454.1 | 92318.3 | 30945.0 | -57421.5 |
| 2013 | 25940 | 103672 | 32766 | -60910 |
| 2014.03 | 28640 | 108254 | 33107 | -74327 |
| 2014.06 | 32792 | 113378 | 33666 | -83550 |
| 2014.09 | 33008 | 118474 | 34121 | -65903 |
| 2014.12 | 31136 | 123119 | 36630 | -53908 |
| 2015.03 | 36495 | 129897 | 37931 | -48466 |
| 2015.06 | 34231 | 139065 | 39132 | -51331 |
| 2015.09 | 36665 | 147649 | 40956 | -42192 |
| 2015.12 | 36440 | 160004 | 43214 | -18604 |
| 2016.03 | 38640 | 172911 | 44208 | -4848 |
| 2016.06 | 39130 | 181275 | 44560 | 11464 |
| 2016.09 | 40162 | 191977 | 45563 | 18705 |
| 2016.12 | 44874 | 201111 | 47167 | 20796 |
| 2017.03 | 48588 | 213157 | 47799 | 2269 |
| 2017.06 | 49139 | 218172 | 48377 | 9948 |
| 2017.09 | 46694 | 223472 | 49563 | 20341 |
| 2017.12 | 47043 | 225877 | 52048 | 31828 |
| 2018.03 | 48088 | 230069 | 52128 | 27057 |
| 2018.06 | 47685 | 236917 | 53052 | 22554 |
| 2018.09 | 46714 | 242696 | 53578 | 39715 |
| 2018.12 | 45211 | 255388 | 54432 | 39412 |
| 2019.03 | 46939 | 263847 | 55041 | 44047 |
| 2019.06 | 47448 | 268946 | 57368 | 41552 |
| 2019.09 | 46835 | 272586 | 61934 | 53935 |
| 2019.12 | 48195 | 280399 | 64796 | 57555 |

## 2.7 1 货币当局资产负债表（资产）
## Balance Sheet of Monetary Authority (Assets)

单位：亿元
Unit: 100 Million Yuan

| 时间<br>Time | 国外资产 *<br>Foreign Assets* | 外汇 **<br>Foreign Exchange** | 货币黄金 **<br>Monetary Gold** | 其他国外资产<br>Other Foreign Assets | 对政府债权 ***<br>Claims on Government*** |
|---|---|---|---|---|---|
| 2012 | 241416.9 | 236669.9 | 669.8 | 4077.1 | 15313.7 |
| 2013 | 272234 | 264270 | 670 | 7294 | 15313 |
| 2014.03 | 280178 | 272149 | 670 | 7359 | 15313 |
| 2014.06 | 280169 | 272131 | 670 | 7369 | 15313 |
| 2014.09 | 280121 | 272018 | 670 | 7433 | 15313 |
| 2014.12 | 278623 | 270681 | 670 | 7272 | 15313 |
| 2015.03 | 276073 | 268161 | 670 | 7242 | 15313 |
| 2015.06 | 276555 | 267149 | 2095 | 7311 | 15313 |
| 2015.09 | 262214 | 258244 | 2208 | 1762 | 15313 |
| 2015.12 | 253831 | 248538 | 2330 | 2964 | 15313 |
| 2016.03 | 246545 | 238366 | 2417 | 5763 | 15313 |
| 2016.06 | 245224 | 236308 | 2488 | 6428 | 15274 |
| 2016.09 | 238943 | 229109 | 2530 | 7304 | 15274 |
| 2016.12 | 229796 | 219425 | 2541 | 7829 | 15274 |
| 2017.03 | 224290 | 216210 | 2541 | 5539 | 15274 |
| 2017.06 | 223008 | 215153 | 2541 | 5313 | 15274 |
| 2017.09 | 222589 | 215107 | 2541 | 4941 | 15274 |
| 2017.12 | 221164 | 214788 | 2541 | 3834 | 15274 |
| 2018.03 | 220278 | 214952 | 2541 | 2784 | 15274 |
| 2018.06 | 220183 | 215194 | 2541 | 2448 | 15274 |
| 2018.09 | 218811 | 214084 | 2541 | 2185 | 15274 |
| 2018.12 | 217648 | 212557 | 2570 | 2522 | 15250 |
| 2019.03 | 218110 | 212537 | 2664 | 2909 | 15250 |
| 2019.06 | 218522 | 212455 | 2782 | 3285 | 15250 |
| 2019.09 | 218768 | 212354 | 2856 | 3558 | 15250 |
| 2019.12 | 218639 | 212317 | 2856 | 3466 | 15250 |

注：自 2008 年起，本表增设"不计入储备货币的金融性公司存款"项目，删除原表中"非金融性公司存款"项目及其子项"活期存款"。
Note: Since 2008, the item of "Deposits of Financial Corporations not Included in Reserve Money" has been added to the balance sheet and the items of "Deposits of Non-financial Corporations" and "Demand Deposits" have been excluded from the balance sheet.

\* 国外资产：自 2005 年起，本表国外资产不再以净值反映。
\* Foreign Assets: Since 2005, foreign assets have been no longer presented on a net basis for this sheet.

\*\* 中国人民银行 2001 年 12 月、2002 年 12 月对"金银占款"进行了两次调整，自 2002 年一季度起对"外汇占款"进行了调整。
\*\* Adjustments were made on "Position for Gold and Silver Purchase" by the PBC in December 2001 and December 2002. Adjustments have also been made on "Position for Foreign Exchange Purchased" since 2002 Q1.

\*\*\* 自 2001 年起，包括中国人民银行所持有的国家债券。
\*\*\* Since 2001, the government bonds held by the PBC have been included in this item.

## 2.7 ① 货币当局资产负债表（资产）
## Balance Sheet of Monetary Authority (Assets)

单位：亿元
Unit: 100 Million Yuan

| 时间<br>Time | 对其他<br>存款性公司债权 *<br>Claims on<br>Other Depository<br>Corporations* | 对其他<br>金融性公司债权 *<br>Claims on<br>Other Financial<br>Corporations* | 对非金融性公司<br>债权<br>Claims on<br>Non-financial<br>Corporations | 其他资产<br>Other Assets | 总资产<br>Total Assets |
|---|---|---|---|---|---|
| 2012 | 16701.1 | 10038.6 | 25.0 | 11041.9 | 294537.2 |
| 2013 | 13148 | 8907 | 25 | 7652 | 317279 |
| 2014.03 | 12384 | 8818 | 25 | 9930 | 326647 |
| 2014.06 | 14557 | 8809 | 25 | 10826 | 329699 |
| 2014.09 | 21015 | 8732 | 25 | 11055 | 336262 |
| 2014.12 | 24985 | 7849 | 12 | 11467 | 338249 |
| 2015.03 | 31479 | 7847 | 41 | 11473 | 342226 |
| 2015.06 | 23264 | 7696 | 55 | 14193 | 337076 |
| 2015.09 | 25235 | 9697 | 57 | 13523 | 326039 |
| 2015.12 | 26626 | 6657 | 72 | 15339 | 317837 |
| 2016.03 | 44158 | 6655 | 72 | 13474 | 326216 |
| 2016.06 | 57566 | 6658 | 75 | 13346 | 338142 |
| 2016.09 | 61905 | 6658 | 72 | 12098 | 334950 |
| 2016.12 | 84739 | 6324 | 81 | 7497 | 343712 |
| 2017.03 | 80711 | 6316 | 117 | 10644 | 337354 |
| 2017.06 | 85907 | 6318 | 97 | 14422 | 345026 |
| 2017.09 | 89149 | 6318 | 95 | 16571 | 349997 |
| 2017.12 | 102230 | 5987 | 102 | 18174 | 362932 |
| 2018.03 | 99902 | 5950 | 36 | 18169 | 359608 |
| 2018.06 | 103424 | 5948 | 54 | 17819 | 362702 |
| 2018.09 | 109333 | 5957 | 45 | 16810 | 366230 |
| 2018.12 | 111517 | 4643 | 28 | 23406 | 372492 |
| 2019.03 | 93668 | 4709 | 27 | 16790 | 348553 |
| 2019.06 | 101860 | 4842 | 0 | 23121 | 363595 |
| 2019.09 | 106775 | 5168 | 0 | 16007 | 361967 |
| 2019.12 | 117749 | 4623 | 0 | 14869 | 371130 |

\* 自 2005 年起，本表采用其他存款性公司和其他金融性公司分类，其机构范围详见第 94 页 [注 1]。2005 年之前，存款货币银行和特定存款机构加总的数据可以替代其他存款性公司数据，其他金融机构的数据可以替代其他金融性公司数据。

\* For this sheet, new classification has been adopted since 2005. Please refer to the monete 1 on page 94 for the particular institution coverage of other depository corporations and other financial corporations. To keep comparability, the data of other depository corporations before 2005 could be approximately substituted by the aggregation of deposit money banks and specific monetary institutions. Similarly, data of other financial corporations could be substituted by data of other financial institutions before 2005.

2.7 2 货币当局资产负债表（负债）

## Balance Sheet of Monetary Authority (Liabilities)

单位：亿元

Unit: 100 Million Yuan

| 时间<br>Time | 储备货币<br>Reserve<br>Money | 货币发行<br>Currency<br>Issue | 金融性<br>公司存款<br>Deposits of<br>Financial<br>Corporations | 其他存款性<br>公司存款 *<br>Deposits of<br>Other Depository<br>Corporations* | 其他金融性<br>公司存款 *<br>Deposits of<br>Other Financial<br>Corporations* | 非金融性<br>公司存款<br>Deposits of<br>Non-financial<br>Corporations | 不计入储备货币的<br>金融性公司存款<br>Deposits of Financial<br>Corporations not<br>Included in<br>Reserve Money |
|---|---|---|---|---|---|---|---|
| 2012 | 252345.2 | 60646.0 | 191699.2 | 191699.2 | — | 0.0 | 1348.9 |
| 2013 | 271023 | 64981 | 206042 | 206042 | — | 0.0 | 1330 |
| 2014.03 | 274741 | 64816 | 209925 | 209925 | — | 0.0 | 1366 |
| 2014.06 | 279899 | 63260 | 216638 | 216638 | — | 0.0 | 1571 |
| 2014.09 | 285299 | 65545 | 219754 | 219754 | — | 0.0 | 1662 |
| 2014.12 | 294093 | 67151 | 226942 | 226942 | — | 0.0 | 1558 |
| 2015.03 | 295753 | 69078 | 226675 | 226675 | — | 0.0 | 1729 |
| 2015.06 | 288780 | 65112 | 223668 | 223668 | — | 0.0 | 1692 |
| 2015.09 | 279677 | 68455 | 211222 | 211222 | — | 0.0 | 1843 |
| 2015.12 | 276377 | 69886 | 206492 | 206492 | — | 0.0 | 2826 |
| 2016.03 | 283377 | 71353 | 212024 | 212024 | — | 0.0 | 3910 |
| 2016.06 | 289071 | 69031 | 220040 | 220040 | — | 0.0 | 4760 |
| 2016.09 | 290707 | 71920 | 218786 | 218786 | — | 0.0 | 5713 |
| 2016.12 | 308980 | 74884 | 234095 | 234095 | — | 0.0 | 6485 |
| 2017.03 | 302387 | 75247 | 227141 | 227141 | — | 0.0 | 7744 |
| 2017.06 | 303772 | 73269 | 229662 | 229662 | — | 841 | 7597 |
| 2017.09 | 306044 | 76626 | 228516 | 228516 | — | 901 | 6047 |
| 2017.12 | 321871 | 77074 | 243802 | 243802 | — | 995 | 5019 |
| 2018.03 | 321350 | 79453 | 238740 | 238740 | — | 3158 | 4168 |
| 2018.06 | 318471 | 75658 | 237805 | 237805 | — | 5008 | 3746 |
| 2018.09 | 317918 | 78117 | 231051 | 231051 | — | 8750 | 3549 |
| 2018.12 | 330957 | 79146 | 235511 | 235511 | — | 16300 | 4016 |
| 2019.03 | 303711 | 81311 | 209648 | 209648 | — | 12752 | 4693 |
| 2019.06 | 313086 | 78237 | 221817 | 221817 | — | 13032 | 4237 |
| 2019.09 | 305882 | 80218 | 212230 | 212230 | — | 13435 | 4775 |
| 2019.12 | 324175 | 82859 | 226024 | 226024 | — | 15292 | 4574 |

注：自 2011 年起，采用国际货币基金组织关于储备货币的定义，不再将其他金融性公司在货币当局的存款计入储备货币。

Note : Since 2011, new definition of reserve money defined by IMF has been adopted. Deposits of other financial corporations with the monetary authority have no longer been included in reserve money.

\* 见第 25 页脚注。

\* See footnote on page 25.

2.7 2 货币当局资产负债表（负债）

# Balance Sheet of Monetary Authority (Liabilities)

单位：亿元
Unit: 100 Million Yuan

| 时间<br>Time | 债券发行<br>Bonds Issue | 国外负债<br>Foreign<br>Liabilities | 政府存款<br>Government<br>Deposits | 自有资金<br>Self-owned<br>Capital | 其他负债<br>Other Liabilities | 总负债<br>Total Liabilities |
|---|---|---|---|---|---|---|
| 2012 | 13880.0 | 1464.2 | 20753.3 | 219.8 | 4525.9 | 294537.2 |
| 2013 | 7762 | 2088 | 28611 | 220 | 6245 | 317279 |
| 2014.03 | 7762 | 1999 | 28963 | 220 | 11594 | 326647 |
| 2014.06 | 7132 | 1477 | 33283 | 220 | 6171 | 329699 |
| 2014.09 | 6922 | 1964 | 36787 | 220 | 3407 | 336262 |
| 2014.12 | 6522 | 1834 | 31275 | 220 | 2747 | 338249 |
| 2015.03 | 6522 | 1405 | 29829 | 220 | 6768 | 342226 |
| 2015.06 | 6522 | 1466 | 32481 | 220 | 5915 | 337076 |
| 2015.09 | 6522 | 1650 | 31542 | 220 | 4585 | 326039 |
| 2015.12 | 6572 | 1807 | 27179 | 220 | 2855 | 317837 |
| 2016.03 | 6572 | 3828 | 27339 | 220 | 972 | 326216 |
| 2016.06 | 6572 | 3882 | 31797 | 220 | 1841 | 338142 |
| 2016.09 | 764 | 3787 | 29920 | 220 | 3840 | 334950 |
| 2016.12 | 500 | 3195 | 25063 | 220 | -731 | 343712 |
| 2017.03 | 500 | 1099 | 24026 | 220 | 1378 | 337354 |
| 2017.06 | 0 | 1599 | 28113 | 220 | 3725 | 345026 |
| 2017.09 | 0 | 1025 | 31095 | 220 | 5565 | 349997 |
| 2017.12 | 0 | 880 | 28626 | 220 | 6316 | 362932 |
| 2018.03 | 0 | 929 | 26374 | 220 | 6567 | 359608 |
| 2018.06 | 0 | 1118 | 32041 | 220 | 7106 | 362702 |
| 2018.09 | 0 | 2050 | 34795 | 220 | 7698 | 366230 |
| 2018.12 | 200 | 1165 | 28225 | 220 | 7710 | 372492 |
| 2019.03 | 315 | 819 | 31407 | 220 | 7387 | 348553 |
| 2019.06 | 740 | 904 | 35683 | 220 | 8727 | 363595 |
| 2019.09 | 940 | 1106 | 38527 | 220 | 10517 | 361967 |
| 2019.12 | 1020 | 842 | 32415 | 220 | 7884 | 371130 |

## 2.8 1 其他存款性公司资产负债表（资产）
## Balance Sheet of Other Depository Corporations (Assets)

单位：亿元
Unit: 100 Million Yuan

| 时间<br>Time | 国外资产<br>Foreign Assets | 储备资产<br>Reserve Assets | | | 对政府债权<br>Claims on<br>Government | 对中央银行债权<br>Claims on<br>Central Bank |
|---|---|---|---|---|---|---|
| | | | 准备金存款<br>Deposits with<br>Central Bank | 库存现金<br>Cash in Vault | | |
| 2012 | 28798.5 | 197132.5 | 191146.3 | 5986.2 | 56123.3 | 12709.0 |
| 2013 | 28814 | 211776 | 205369 | 6406 | 62341 | 10301 |
| 2014.03 | 29879 | 216345 | 209859 | 6486 | 62057 | 15966 |
| 2014.06 | 35152 | 223025 | 216716 | 6309 | 64636 | 10314 |
| 2014.09 | 35940 | 226343 | 219644 | 6700 | 68562 | 7579 |
| 2014.12 | 36689 | 233489 | 226597 | 6892 | 71010 | 6564 |
| 2015.03 | 40916 | 233401 | 226272 | 7128 | 70692 | 6569 |
| 2015.06 | 40915 | 233977 | 227469 | 6508 | 78662 | 6429 |
| 2015.09 | 43383 | 224110 | 216678 | 7432 | 91111 | 6403 |
| 2015.12 | 41595 | 219330 | 212661 | 6669 | 110163 | 6229 |
| 2016.03 | 41063 | 221687 | 214986 | 6701 | 117323 | 6161 |
| 2016.06 | 42585 | 230117 | 223905 | 6212 | 145391 | 5696 |
| 2016.09 | 46034 | 230546 | 223694 | 6852 | 161514 | 677 |
| 2016.12 | 50020 | 246447 | 239867 | 6581 | 172140 | 525 |
| 2017.03 | 52879 | 239252 | 232611 | 6642 | 175020 | 522 |
| 2017.06 | 52266 | 243285 | 236994 | 6291 | 189320 | 3 |
| 2017.09 | 53361 | 242297 | 235419 | 6878 | 206015 | 3 |
| 2017.12 | 53482 | 256108 | 249680 | 6428 | 218244 | 0 |
| 2018.03 | 55833 | 244963 | 238203 | 6760 | 226081 | 0 |
| 2018.06 | 57795 | 244261 | 238193 | 6068 | 237190 | 0 |
| 2018.09 | 59782 | 238907 | 232044 | 6863 | 258491 | 0 |
| 2018.12 | 60146 | 243161 | 237224 | 5937 | 264353 | 0 |
| 2019.03 | 61768 | 223796 | 217427 | 6369 | 276758 | 0 |
| 2019.06 | 62600 | 236259 | 230603 | 5656 | 286711 | 0 |
| 2019.09 | 64271 | 225915 | 219827 | 6088 | 300128 | 0 |
| 2019.12 | 63618 | 236958 | 231289 | 5670 | 307281 | 0 |

注：自 2008 年起，本表项目中原"央行债券"更名为"对中央银行债权"。
Note: Since 2008, the item of "Central Bank Bonds" has been renamed as "Claims on Central Bank".

## 2.8 1 其他存款性公司资产负债表（资产）
## Balance Sheet of Other Depository Corporations (Assets)

单位：亿元
Unit: 100 Million Yuan

| 时间<br>Time | 对其他存款性<br>公司债权 *<br>Claims on Other<br>Depository<br>Corporations* | 对其他金融性<br>公司债权 *<br>Claims on Other<br>Financial<br>Corporations* | 对非金融性<br>公司债权<br>Claims on<br>Non-financial<br>Corporations | 对其他居民部门<br>债权<br>Claims on<br>Other Resident<br>Sectors | 其他资产<br>Other Assets | 总资产<br>Total Assets |
|---|---|---|---|---|---|---|
| 2012 | 237024.6 | 50519.9 | 534132.7 | 160193.8 | 60228.6 | 1336862.8 |
| 2013 | 260442 | 72592 | 599575 | 196864 | 82046 | 1524752 |
| 2014.03 | 279595 | 84027 | 625037 | 206016 | 84970 | 1603891 |
| 2014.06 | 293407 | 103162 | 642770 | 215432 | 85778 | 1673677 |
| 2014.09 | 278523 | 98661 | 655324 | 223057 | 88931 | 1682922 |
| 2014.12 | 280389 | 111553 | 673286 | 229216 | 79835 | 1722030 |
| 2015.03 | 279794 | 129198 | 705301 | 237989 | 86130 | 1789988 |
| 2015.06 | 302876 | 152369 | 729637 | 248562 | 86872 | 1880298 |
| 2015.09 | 301714 | 159792 | 752395 | 258910 | 95716 | 1933533 |
| 2015.12 | 314186 | 176579 | 783762 | 267326 | 72385 | 1991556 |
| 2016.03 | 300636 | 224021 | 809470 | 279691 | 75906 | 2075960 |
| 2016.06 | 304320 | 242537 | 821461 | 296514 | 81626 | 2170247 |
| 2016.09 | 304522 | 251143 | 825632 | 313984 | 82686 | 2216738 |
| 2016.12 | 315878 | 265299 | 836468 | 329544 | 87435 | 2303756 |
| 2017.03 | 311845 | 277853 | 852222 | 347851 | 103578 | 2361022 |
| 2017.06 | 296902 | 284541 | 866964 | 367009 | 103915 | 2404204 |
| 2017.09 | 292933 | 278500 | 879635 | 386205 | 102809 | 2441757 |
| 2017.12 | 296043 | 280617 | 889011 | 399669 | 104049 | 2497224 |
| 2018.03 | 283167 | 281991 | 921705 | 417091 | 101406 | 2532235 |
| 2018.06 | 282345 | 273812 | 937323 | 435680 | 101298 | 2569704 |
| 2018.09 | 280218 | 259093 | 967287 | 456323 | 100214 | 2620314 |
| 2018.12 | 287239 | 258694 | 977946 | 472762 | 103033 | 2667335 |
| 2019.03 | 294876 | 259583 | 1023575 | 490709 | 109325 | 2740389 |
| 2019.06 | 295166 | 253445 | 1040312 | 510066 | 109708 | 2794267 |
| 2019.09 | 290077 | 240995 | 1072307 | 529227 | 110959 | 2833878 |
| 2019.12 | 296766 | 246493 | 1085250 | 546351 | 110002 | 2892720 |

* 自 2005 年起，本表采用其他存款性公司和其他金融性公司分类，其机构范围详见第 94 页 [ 注 1]。2005 年之前，存款货币银行和特定存款机构加总的数据可以替代其他存款性公司数据，其他金融机构的数据可以替代其他金融性公司数据。

* For this sheet, new classification has been adopted since 2005. Please refer to the note 1 on page 94 for the particular institution coverage of other depository corporations and other financial corporations. To keep comparability, the data of other depository corporations before 2005 could be approximately substituted by the aggregation of deposit money banks and specific monetary institutions. Similarly, data of other financial corporations could be substituted by data of other financial institutions before 2005.

## 2.8 2 其他存款性公司资产负债表（负债）
## Balance Sheet of Other Depository Corporations (Liabilities)

单位：亿元
Unit: 100 Million Yuan

| 时间<br>Time | 对非金融机构及住户负债<br>Liabilities to Non-financial Institutions & Households | 纳入广义货币的存款<br>Deposits Included in Broad Money | 企业活期存款<br>Demand Deposits of Enterprises | 企业定期存款<br>Time Deposits of Enterprises | 居民储蓄存款<br>Household Savings Deposits | 不纳入广义货币的存款<br>Deposits Excluded from Broad Money | 可转让存款<br>Transferable Deposits | 其他存款<br>Other Deposits | 其他负债<br>Other Liabilities | 对中央银行负债<br>Liabilities to Central Bank |
|---|---|---|---|---|---|---|---|---|---|---|
| 2012 | 891427.9 | 861307.2 | 254004.5 | 195940.1 | 411362.6 | 24454.1 | 8036.1 | 16418.0 | 5666.6 | 13903.1 |
| 2013 | 1012779 | 978444 | 278717 | 232697 | 467031 | 25940 | 7454 | 18486 | 8394 | 11663 |
| 2014.03 | 1056771 | 1020533 | 269354 | 250779 | 500399 | 28640 | 7253 | 21387 | 7598 | 11691 |
| 2014.06 | 1097646 | 1058206 | 284536 | 265644 | 508025 | 32792 | 7928 | 24864 | 6648 | 15285 |
| 2014.09 | 1086316 | 1044834 | 268375 | 272197 | 504262 | 33008 | 7815 | 25194 | 8473 | 21890 |
| 2014.12 | 1102203 | 1060731 | 287797 | 264056 | 508878 | 31136 | 8157 | 22979 | 10336 | 26617 |
| 2015.03 | 1143386 | 1095144 | 275261 | 275189 | 544694 | 36495 | 8966 | 27529 | 11748 | 34527 |
| 2015.06 | 1173336 | 1125935 | 297479 | 289329 | 539127 | 34231 | 8509 | 25723 | 13170 | 32126 |
| 2015.09 | 1203732 | 1149839 | 303394 | 298571 | 547874 | 36665 | 9381 | 27283 | 17228 | 31296 |
| 2015.12 | 1249743 | 1178051 | 337737 | 288241 | 552073 | 36440 | 10806 | 25634 | 35252 | 33638 |
| 2016.03 | 1314172 | 1234409 | 346930 | 300623 | 586856 | 38640 | 11354 | 27286 | 41123 | 46855 |
| 2016.06 | 1356213 | 1270047 | 380825 | 301674 | 587549 | 39130 | 11065 | 28066 | 47035 | 60247 |
| 2016.09 | 1387791 | 1303229 | 389272 | 315077 | 598881 | 40162 | 12078 | 28084 | 44400 | 64388 |
| 2016.12 | 1420679 | 1329747 | 418253 | 307990 | 603504 | 44874 | 14028 | 30846 | 46057 | 87880 |
| 2017.03 | 1469485 | 1380627 | 420165 | 317183 | 643278 | 48588 | 13977 | 34611 | 40271 | 83858 |
| 2017.06 | 1491234 | 1403185 | 443250 | 317003 | 642932 | 49139 | 14683 | 34456 | 38910 | 90884 |
| 2017.09 | 1511037 | 1423079 | 448114 | 326614 | 648350 | 46694 | 13811 | 32883 | 41265 | 93245 |
| 2017.12 | 1531979 | 1442682 | 473145 | 320196 | 649341 | 47043 | 15267 | 31777 | 42253 | 105470 |
| 2018.03 | 1573169 | 1476017 | 450847 | 332606 | 692564 | 48088 | 15643 | 32445 | 49064 | 95168 |
| 2018.06 | 1591690 | 1501221 | 474355 | 334425 | 692441 | 47685 | 15029 | 32656 | 42784 | 94315 |
| 2018.09 | 1624130 | 1523403 | 467320 | 349827 | 706256 | 46714 | 14652 | 32062 | 54013 | 99762 |
| 2018.12 | 1641201 | 1540345 | 478478 | 340179 | 721689 | 45211 | 15356 | 29856 | 55644 | 104475 |
| 2019.03 | 1716456 | 1614256 | 472634 | 359015 | 782606 | 46939 | 15018 | 31921 | 55262 | 99705 |
| 2019.06 | 1749287 | 1647479 | 495115 | 362163 | 790201 | 47448 | 14927 | 32521 | 54360 | 108057 |
| 2019.09 | 1778065 | 1664764 | 483008 | 374318 | 807437 | 46835 | 14019 | 32816 | 66466 | 90790 |
| 2019.12 | 1798147 | 1681468 | 498820 | 363486 | 819162 | 48195 | 15660 | 32534 | 68485 | 98826 |

2.8 2 其他存款性公司资产负债表（负债）
## Balance Sheet of Other Depository Corporations (Liabilities)

单位：亿元
Unit: 100 Million Yuan

| 时间<br>Time | 对其他存款性<br>公司负债 *<br>Liabilities to<br>Other Depository<br>Corporations* | 对其他金融性<br>公司负债 *<br>Liabilities to<br>Other Financial<br>Corporations* | 计入广义<br>货币的存款<br>Deposits Included<br>in Broad Money | 国外<br>负债<br>Foreign<br>Liabilities | 债券发行<br>Bonds<br>Issue | 实收资本<br>Paid-in<br>Capital | 其他负债<br>Other<br>Liabilities | 总负债<br>Total<br>Liabilities |
|---|---|---|---|---|---|---|---|---|
| 2012 | 108636.3 | 62999.2 | 58181.9 | 9900.3 | 92318.3 | 30725.3 | 126952.6 | 1336862.8 |
| 2013 | 110398 | 74805 | 69506 | 17973 | 103672 | 32546 | 160916 | 1524752 |
| 2014.03 | 112140 | 86323 | 81825 | 24025 | 108254 | 32888 | 171800 | 1603891 |
| 2014.06 | 114186 | 98502 | 94431 | 24835 | 113378 | 33446 | 176399 | 1673677 |
| 2014.09 | 107682 | 103207 | 98372 | 25232 | 118474 | 33901 | 186219 | 1682922 |
| 2014.12 | 111118 | 112401 | 107385 | 25088 | 123119 | 36410 | 185075 | 1722030 |
| 2015.03 | 107779 | 122365 | 118239 | 20946 | 129897 | 37711 | 193378 | 1789988 |
| 2015.06 | 118407 | 154897 | 148836 | 21344 | 139065 | 38912 | 202210 | 1880298 |
| 2015.09 | 117975 | 152605 | 148962 | 16779 | 147649 | 40736 | 222763 | 1933533 |
| 2015.12 | 131306 | 155915 | 151011 | 12978 | 160004 | 42995 | 204978 | 1991556 |
| 2016.03 | 123721 | 150576 | 147138 | 11879 | 172911 | 43988 | 211858 | 2075960 |
| 2016.06 | 131786 | 160884 | 157625 | 13119 | 181275 | 44340 | 222383 | 2170247 |
| 2016.09 | 135593 | 151794 | 148063 | 12780 | 191977 | 45343 | 227071 | 2216738 |
| 2016.12 | 144837 | 157275 | 152016 | 12673 | 201111 | 46947 | 232355 | 2303756 |
| 2017.03 | 133600 | 154081 | 150378 | 15277 | 213157 | 47579 | 243985 | 2361022 |
| 2017.06 | 122165 | 163227 | 160279 | 18167 | 218172 | 48158 | 252199 | 2404204 |
| 2017.09 | 119270 | 166742 | 161934 | 20140 | 223472 | 49343 | 258509 | 2441757 |
| 2017.12 | 126116 | 168351 | 162446 | 20479 | 225877 | 51828 | 267124 | 2497224 |
| 2018.03 | 112176 | 179403 | 175839 | 19734 | 230069 | 51908 | 270608 | 2532235 |
| 2018.06 | 110739 | 184890 | 181610 | 19714 | 236917 | 52832 | 278607 | 2569704 |
| 2018.09 | 107848 | 182569 | 177897 | 19849 | 242696 | 53358 | 290103 | 2620314 |
| 2018.12 | 108916 | 184311 | 179375 | 20894 | 255388 | 54213 | 297939 | 2667335 |
| 2019.03 | 108129 | 172181 | 168963 | 18975 | 263847 | 54821 | 306274 | 2740389 |
| 2019.06 | 107772 | 171809 | 168314 | 18487 | 268946 | 57149 | 312761 | 2794267 |
| 2019.09 | 106142 | 186008 | 181042 | 18940 | 272586 | 61714 | 319633 | 2833878 |
| 2019.12 | 114185 | 198935 | 193524 | 16816 | 280399 | 64576 | 320835 | 2892720 |

* 见第 29 页脚注。
* See footnote on page 29.

## 2.9 1 中资大型银行资产负债表（资产）
## Balance Sheet of Large-sized Domestic Banks (Assets)

单位：亿元
Unit: 100 Million Yuan

| 时间<br>Time | 国外资产<br>Foreign Assets | 储备资产<br>Reserve Assets | 准备金存款<br>Deposits with<br>Central Bank | 库存现金<br>Cash in Vault | 对政府债权<br>Claims on<br>Government | 对中央银行债权<br>Claims on<br>Central Bank |
|---|---|---|---|---|---|---|
| 2011.12 | 17393.5 | 102283.7 | 99371.7 | 2912.0 | 33518.2 | 19509.6 |
| 2012.03 | 20822.2 | 108535.4 | 105862.5 | 2672.9 | 33560.0 | 20535.1 |
| 2012.06 | 24421.0 | 107861.8 | 105114.0 | 2747.8 | 34620.9 | 17186.2 |
| 2012.09 | 23873.5 | 108784.6 | 105463.1 | 3321.6 | 37737.1 | 13530.5 |
| 2012.12 | 20196.3 | 111464.9 | 108019.0 | 3445.9 | 38753.5 | 11466.8 |
| 2013.03 | 19957 | 115378 | 112076 | 3302 | 38837 | 13446 |
| 2013.06 | 19929 | 116172 | 113009 | 3163 | 40139 | 8890 |
| 2013.09 | 18978 | 117421 | 113672 | 3749 | 40712 | 5735 |
| 2013.12 | 19356 | 114779 | 111158 | 3621 | 40884 | 9906 |
| 2014.03 | 20058 | 122260 | 118656 | 3605 | 40642 | 13725 |
| 2014.06 | 23244 | 123488 | 120044 | 3444 | 41468 | 9585 |
| 2014.09 | 22990 | 125882 | 122057 | 3825 | 42802 | 7073 |
| 2014.12 | 23268 | 122515 | 118638 | 3877 | 43799 | 6230 |
| 2015.03 | 26644 | 132277 | 128436 | 3841 | 43798 | 6190 |
| 2015.06 | 26415 | 129927 | 126453 | 3474 | 48492 | 5998 |
| 2015.09 | 26227 | 122904 | 118657 | 4247 | 55820 | 5968 |
| 2015.12 | 24885 | 111191 | 107457 | 3734 | 70540 | 5908 |
| 2016.03 | 24543 | 119904 | 116271 | 3632 | 75560 | 5910 |
| 2016.06 | 24980 | 120200 | 116829 | 3371 | 93250 | 5400 |
| 2016.09 | 26959 | 122195 | 118346 | 3850 | 103001 | 656 |
| 2016.12 | 28224 | 126354 | 122710 | 3643 | 110144 | 500 |
| 2017.03 | 30284 | 127992 | 124346 | 3646 | 112832 | 500 |
| 2017.06 | 29270 | 128580 | 125140 | 3439 | 122519 | 0 |
| 2017.09 | 29761 | 128481 | 124607 | 3873 | 132967 | 0 |
| 2017.12 | 29052 | 130449 | 126967 | 3482 | 140119 | 0 |
| 2018.03 | 30976 | 127903 | 124291 | 3613 | 145469 | 0 |
| 2018.06 | 31919 | 126423 | 123221 | 3202 | 153150 | 0 |
| 2018.09 | 32888 | 124009 | 120343 | 3666 | 165963 | 0 |
| 2018.12 | 32428 | 117999 | 114844 | 3155 | 169057 | 0 |
| 2019.03 | 33608 | 114264 | 111007 | 3256 | 176290 | 0 |
| 2019.06 | 34433 | 121144 | 118292 | 2853 | 181812 | 0 |
| 2019.09 | 34651 | 116632 | 113529 | 3103 | 187999 | 0 |
| 2019.12 | 33061 | 115340 | 112447 | 2893 | 190308 | 0 |

2.9 1 中资大型银行资产负债表（资产）
## Balance Sheet of Large-sized Domestic Banks (Assets)

单位：亿元
Unit: 100 Million Yuan

| 时间<br>Time | 对其他存款性<br>公司债权<br>Claims on Other<br>Depository<br>Corporations | 对其他金融性<br>公司债权<br>Claims on Other<br>Financial<br>Corporations | 对非金融性<br>公司债权<br>Claims on<br>Non-financial<br>Corporations | 对其他居民<br>部门债权<br>Claims on<br>Other Resident<br>Sectors | 其他资产<br>Other Assets | 总资产<br>Total Assets |
|---|---|---|---|---|---|---|
| 2011.12 | 79116.9 | 20576.7 | 266750.3 | 73526.7 | 34048.3 | 646723.8 |
| 2012.03 | 95425.3 | 22733.7 | 278972.2 | 76067.5 | 33845.6 | 690497.0 |
| 2012.06 | 102779.8 | 23844.6 | 286210.4 | 79054.1 | 36365.6 | 712344.4 |
| 2012.09 | 97779.0 | 23636.0 | 291755.8 | 83408.8 | 37806.8 | 718312.1 |
| 2012.12 | 102248.2 | 24668.7 | 297056.5 | 86878.8 | 39975.2 | 732708.7 |
| 2013.03 | 115153 | 22626 | 309102 | 91904 | 45244 | 771646 |
| 2013.06 | 116535 | 20811 | 314164 | 97432 | 49267 | 783339 |
| 2013.09 | 114513 | 20966 | 322991 | 102191 | 50038 | 793545 |
| 2013.12 | 112958 | 22269 | 328233 | 105640 | 59570 | 813596 |
| 2014.03 | 117008 | 24782 | 339685 | 110341 | 61508 | 850008 |
| 2014.06 | 124525 | 36375 | 347254 | 114987 | 60473 | 881399 |
| 2014.09 | 118424 | 33304 | 353218 | 118820 | 62409 | 884922 |
| 2014.12 | 119072 | 36984 | 359189 | 121801 | 53023 | 885880 |
| 2015.03 | 116838 | 40069 | 374416 | 126419 | 55683 | 922334 |
| 2015.06 | 135279 | 38927 | 385118 | 131496 | 54604 | 956256 |
| 2015.09 | 126981 | 43583 | 398181 | 137370 | 61483 | 978518 |
| 2015.12 | 131167 | 47455 | 416235 | 142373 | 38640 | 988393 |
| 2016.03 | 126253 | 49824 | 434838 | 149576 | 41926 | 1028334 |
| 2016.06 | 126138 | 53321 | 440333 | 158546 | 45920 | 1068087 |
| 2016.09 | 120418 | 53858 | 440416 | 167364 | 45766 | 1080633 |
| 2016.12 | 116795 | 57489 | 442330 | 174812 | 46962 | 1103610 |
| 2017.03 | 115450 | 61777 | 443513 | 183580 | 54725 | 1130653 |
| 2017.06 | 111009 | 68994 | 447919 | 192271 | 53320 | 1153881 |
| 2017.09 | 106320 | 65083 | 452121 | 201112 | 51925 | 1167769 |
| 2017.12 | 105575 | 64262 | 453332 | 207600 | 51792 | 1182180 |
| 2018.03 | 107667 | 64343 | 465839 | 215652 | 47520 | 1205369 |
| 2018.06 | 105551 | 63250 | 467388 | 223673 | 46551 | 1217907 |
| 2018.09 | 104842 | 62199 | 483710 | 231687 | 45130 | 1250428 |
| 2018.12 | 103994 | 62477 | 486979 | 237933 | 44609 | 1255477 |
| 2019.03 | 110879 | 60248 | 507840 | 246082 | 51284 | 1300495 |
| 2019.06 | 106288 | 58906 | 511601 | 254095 | 51199 | 1319477 |
| 2019.09 | 104356 | 56649 | 530200 | 261743 | 52360 | 1344591 |
| 2019.12 | 108628 | 59675 | 531981 | 269474 | 49340 | 1357807 |

## 2.9 2 中资大型银行资产负债表（负债）
## Balance Sheet of Large-sized Domestic Banks (Liabilities)

单位：亿元
Unit:100 Million Yuan

| 时间<br>Time | 对非金融机构<br>及住户负债<br>Liabilities to<br>Non-financial<br>Institutions<br>& Households | 纳入广义<br>货币的存款<br>Deposits<br>Included in<br>Broad Money | 企业活期<br>存款<br>Demand<br>Deposits of<br>Enterprises | 企业定期<br>存款<br>Time<br>Deposits of<br>Enterprises | 居民储蓄<br>存款<br>Household<br>Savings<br>Deposits | 不纳入<br>广义货币的<br>存款<br>Deposits<br>Excluded from<br>Broad Money | 可转让<br>存款<br>Transferable<br>Deposits | 其他<br>存款<br>Other<br>Deposits | 其他<br>负债<br>Other<br>Liabilities | 对中央银行<br>负债<br>Liabilities to<br>Central Bank |
|---|---|---|---|---|---|---|---|---|---|---|
| 2011.12 | 458964.2 | 445941.3 | 134650.3 | 76395.0 | 234896.1 | 9357.3 | 3636.1 | 5721.2 | 3665.6 | 2076.6 |
| 2012.03 | 484574.0 | 469257.8 | 129832.8 | 82129.6 | 257295.4 | 12142.7 | 3716.8 | 8425.8 | 3173.6 | 2828.0 |
| 2012.06 | 498794.6 | 480646.1 | 134296.5 | 83849.5 | 262500.1 | 14502.0 | 4002.7 | 10499.3 | 3646.4 | 3102.1 |
| 2012.09 | 504604.9 | 486132.9 | 130754.4 | 89723.8 | 265654.7 | 14459.0 | 3862.0 | 10597.0 | 4013.1 | 5872.6 |
| 2012.12 | 508789.6 | 491047.7 | 139933.0 | 84401.2 | 266713.6 | 13487.5 | 4070.8 | 9416.7 | 4254.4 | 4071.3 |
| 2013.03 | 541026 | 522616 | 140834 | 92649 | 289133 | 14443 | 4164 | 10279 | 3967 | 3389 |
| 2013.06 | 545125 | 527835 | 141671 | 98046 | 288118 | 13778 | 4235 | 9543 | 3511 | 6845 |
| 2013.09 | 552735 | 535314 | 139302 | 102987 | 293025 | 13831 | 3948 | 9883 | 3590 | 7274 |
| 2013.12 | 559213 | 540342 | 148850 | 98546 | 292946 | 13077 | 3587 | 9490 | 5793 | 4128 |
| 2014.03 | 584020 | 564109 | 146816 | 105647 | 311646 | 14590 | 3567 | 11024 | 5320 | 3541 |
| 2014.06 | 597192 | 576593 | 152656 | 111297 | 312639 | 16277 | 3601 | 12677 | 4322 | 6309 |
| 2014.09 | 588747 | 567165 | 144757 | 112863 | 309544 | 15609 | 3534 | 12074 | 5973 | 12162 |
| 2014.12 | 588823 | 567167 | 149263 | 107492 | 310412 | 14089 | 3732 | 10357 | 7566 | 12630 |
| 2015.03 | 618824 | 592156 | 148110 | 111368 | 332678 | 17598 | 4116 | 13482 | 9070 | 17731 |
| 2015.06 | 626352 | 599891 | 158510 | 115631 | 325750 | 16340 | 3957 | 12382 | 10121 | 20556 |
| 2015.09 | 640429 | 608856 | 159844 | 118251 | 330761 | 17388 | 4216 | 13172 | 14185 | 18985 |
| 2015.12 | 661772 | 612007 | 169087 | 112676 | 330244 | 17738 | 5022 | 12716 | 32028 | 19560 |
| 2016.03 | 705597 | 647670 | 177795 | 116977 | 352898 | 20066 | 5423 | 14643 | 37861 | 26001 |
| 2016.06 | 720161 | 656318 | 191172 | 115272 | 349874 | 20836 | 5054 | 15782 | 43007 | 34153 |
| 2016.09 | 735167 | 672723 | 195468 | 119486 | 357769 | 21683 | 5846 | 15837 | 40761 | 34938 |
| 2016.12 | 741532 | 676781 | 200971 | 116788 | 359023 | 23883 | 6599 | 17284 | 40868 | 45262 |
| 2017.03 | 775082 | 713050 | 206923 | 123359 | 382768 | 26305 | 6705 | 19600 | 35727 | 47086 |
| 2017.06 | 778931 | 719281 | 216727 | 123863 | 378690 | 25597 | 6752 | 18845 | 34053 | 50588 |
| 2017.09 | 790054 | 731060 | 220267 | 127755 | 383038 | 24160 | 6596 | 17564 | 34834 | 51259 |
| 2017.12 | 784171 | 726114 | 224714 | 121510 | 379890 | 23798 | 7025 | 16773 | 34260 | 56824 |
| 2018.03 | 819739 | 755247 | 222198 | 128336 | 404713 | 24837 | 7393 | 17444 | 39655 | 51008 |
| 2018.06 | 821638 | 762374 | 234997 | 127376 | 400002 | 24569 | 6924 | 17645 | 34695 | 48232 |
| 2018.09 | 838797 | 770529 | 231897 | 130761 | 407871 | 23787 | 7050 | 16737 | 44481 | 50343 |
| 2018.12 | 835134 | 766507 | 229781 | 124589 | 412136 | 22554 | 7125 | 15429 | 46073 | 51163 |
| 2019.03 | 881378 | 810464 | 235333 | 129918 | 445213 | 24741 | 7335 | 17406 | 46173 | 49225 |
| 2019.06 | 886185 | 816431 | 243249 | 128648 | 444534 | 24537 | 7107 | 17431 | 45217 | 52089 |
| 2019.09 | 902169 | 823408 | 237396 | 133663 | 452350 | 23911 | 6689 | 17223 | 54850 | 43931 |
| 2019.12 | 899124 | 817776 | 235743 | 128904 | 453128 | 24106 | 7167 | 16939 | 57242 | 46898 |

注：“中资大型银行资产负债表”机构范围见第 96 页 [ 注 2]。
Note: Please refer to note 2 on page 96 for the information of institutional coverage of the "Balance Sheet of Large-sized Domestic Banks".

2.9 2 中资大型银行资产负债表（负债）
## Balance Sheet of Large-sized Domestic Banks (Liabilities)

单位：亿元
Unit:100 Million Yuan

| 时间<br>Time | 对其他存款性<br>公司负债<br>Liabilities to<br>Other Depository<br>Corporations | 对其他金融性<br>公司负债<br>Liabilities to<br>Other Financial<br>Corporations | 计入广义<br>货币的存款<br>Deposits Included<br>in Broad Money | 国外负债<br>Foreign<br>Liabilities | 债券发行<br>Bonds<br>Issue | 实收资本<br>Paid-in<br>Capital | 其他负债<br>Other<br>Liabilities | 总负债<br>Total<br>Liabilities |
|---|---|---|---|---|---|---|---|---|
| 2011.12 | 27970.8 | 29337.6 | 24374.9 | 2717.5 | 50957.0 | 15904.7 | 58795.4 | 646723.8 |
| 2012.03 | 34446.2 | 34157.2 | 31226.3 | 3027.5 | 53140.6 | 15945.6 | 62377.9 | 690497.0 |
| 2012.06 | 33143.5 | 34718.8 | 31934.8 | 3642.4 | 56091.5 | 15952.3 | 66899.3 | 712344.4 |
| 2012.09 | 28312.1 | 32073.5 | 29800.1 | 3475.6 | 57901.5 | 16079.5 | 69992.4 | 718312.1 |
| 2012.12 | 30249.6 | 33285.6 | 31754.0 | 4203.3 | 60293.3 | 16070.6 | 75745.6 | 732708.7 |
| 2013.03 | 24549 | 34279 | 32881 | 5673 | 61816 | 16067 | 84846 | 771646 |
| 2013.06 | 21912 | 34269 | 32106 | 5762 | 63405 | 16048 | 89974 | 783339 |
| 2013.09 | 20455 | 34295 | 32260 | 6771 | 64903 | 16051 | 91061 | 793545 |
| 2013.12 | 21960 | 35826 | 34118 | 8669 | 65949 | 16070 | 101781 | 813596 |
| 2014.03 | 18428 | 40013 | 38905 | 12609 | 67593 | 16082 | 107724 | 850008 |
| 2014.06 | 20903 | 49912 | 48914 | 12662 | 69945 | 16082 | 108395 | 881399 |
| 2014.09 | 20268 | 50216 | 49331 | 12483 | 70672 | 16085 | 114290 | 884922 |
| 2014.12 | 21852 | 53509 | 52783 | 11930 | 71222 | 17644 | 108270 | 885880 |
| 2015.03 | 14646 | 58397 | 57726 | 9575 | 71503 | 18424 | 113253 | 922334 |
| 2015.06 | 19921 | 72149 | 71527 | 9811 | 73543 | 18518 | 115408 | 956256 |
| 2015.09 | 26278 | 61679 | 60918 | 7633 | 76658 | 19783 | 127073 | 978518 |
| 2015.12 | 30885 | 61407 | 60136 | 5467 | 80907 | 20437 | 107957 | 988393 |
| 2016.03 | 21771 | 55160 | 54071 | 4874 | 83055 | 20632 | 111242 | 1028334 |
| 2016.06 | 28312 | 60110 | 59099 | 4990 | 84580 | 20608 | 115173 | 1068087 |
| 2016.09 | 30442 | 52332 | 51249 | 5323 | 86123 | 20728 | 115580 | 1080633 |
| 2016.12 | 31388 | 54179 | 52952 | 5356 | 86962 | 20849 | 118082 | 1103610 |
| 2017.03 | 24265 | 47594 | 46554 | 6607 | 87826 | 20834 | 121360 | 1130653 |
| 2017.06 | 20786 | 61291 | 60282 | 7787 | 88502 | 20786 | 125208 | 1153881 |
| 2017.09 | 19166 | 60552 | 59616 | 8034 | 91349 | 21247 | 126108 | 1167769 |
| 2017.12 | 24752 | 60932 | 59851 | 8531 | 94777 | 21813 | 130380 | 1182180 |
| 2018.03 | 16624 | 65091 | 64139 | 7874 | 95876 | 21718 | 127440 | 1205369 |
| 2018.06 | 19243 | 70016 | 68846 | 7198 | 98570 | 22097 | 130911 | 1217907 |
| 2018.09 | 21047 | 72630 | 71479 | 7434 | 102213 | 22199 | 135764 | 1250428 |
| 2018.12 | 23530 | 69786 | 68494 | 8440 | 105420 | 22193 | 139810 | 1255477 |
| 2019.03 | 20706 | 65085 | 63673 | 6326 | 108965 | 22530 | 146279 | 1300495 |
| 2019.06 | 23624 | 66870 | 65435 | 6410 | 113085 | 23327 | 147886 | 1319477 |
| 2019.09 | 21879 | 74352 | 72823 | 7219 | 116591 | 26774 | 151675 | 1344591 |
| 2019.12 | 28760 | 76363 | 74667 | 5416 | 121340 | 26490 | 153416 | 1357807 |

2.10 1 中资中型银行资产负债表（资产）
## Balance Sheet of Medium-sized Domestic Banks (Assets)

单位：亿元
Unit:100 Million Yuan

| 时间<br>Time | 国外资产<br>Foreign Assets | 储备资产<br>Reserve Assets | 准备金存款<br>Deposits with<br>Central Bank | 库存现金<br>Cash in Vault | 对政府债权<br>Claims on<br>Government |
|---|---|---|---|---|---|
| 2011.12 | 5108.5 | 28354.0 | 27885.8 | 468.2 | 7540.0 |
| 2012.03 | 5490.1 | 28777.9 | 28356.4 | 421.4 | 7654.3 |
| 2012.06 | 5969.8 | 30085.6 | 29610.6 | 475.1 | 7743.8 |
| 2012.09 | 6140.7 | 31659.0 | 31149.2 | 509.8 | 8316.0 |
| 2012.12 | 6665.8 | 34937.3 | 34343.8 | 593.5 | 8648.8 |
| 2013.03 | 7060 | 34551 | 33988 | 563 | 8802 |
| 2013.06 | 7195 | 37219 | 36598 | 621 | 9352 |
| 2013.09 | 7373 | 37360 | 36748 | 612 | 10287 |
| 2013.12 | 7937 | 38462 | 37790 | 672 | 10912 |
| 2014.03 | 8212 | 38532 | 37887 | 645 | 10973 |
| 2014.06 | 10120 | 41367 | 40710 | 657 | 11934 |
| 2014.09 | 11004 | 41364 | 40745 | 620 | 13641 |
| 2014.12 | 10802 | 44166 | 43480 | 686 | 14513 |
| 2015.03 | 11677 | 40625 | 39923 | 702 | 14545 |
| 2015.06 | 11689 | 43866 | 43199 | 667 | 16757 |
| 2015.09 | 14057 | 42265 | 41613 | 651 | 19647 |
| 2015.12 | 13433 | 41450 | 40821 | 629 | 21841 |
| 2016.03 | 13501 | 42457 | 41858 | 599 | 23357 |
| 2016.06 | 14613 | 45166 | 44604 | 562 | 30845 |
| 2016.09 | 16239 | 42925 | 42336 | 590 | 34957 |
| 2016.12 | 18574 | 45696 | 45057 | 639 | 36915 |
| 2017.03 | 18931 | 42834 | 42274 | 560 | 36821 |
| 2017.06 | 19107 | 43041 | 42501 | 539 | 39499 |
| 2017.09 | 19678 | 41644 | 41104 | 540 | 43161 |
| 2017.12 | 20462 | 43565 | 42955 | 609 | 45819 |
| 2018.03 | 20982 | 40702 | 40136 | 566 | 47654 |
| 2018.06 | 21710 | 41466 | 40945 | 520 | 49752 |
| 2018.09 | 22703 | 39050 | 38529 | 521 | 53968 |
| 2018.12 | 23271 | 40680 | 40142 | 538 | 54925 |
| 2019.03 | 23766 | 36866 | 36318 | 548 | 57824 |
| 2019.06 | 23657 | 39869 | 39363 | 506 | 59972 |
| 2019.09 | 24963 | 37927 | 37417 | 509 | 62971 |
| 2019.12 | 25406 | 40481 | 39958 | 523 | 65121 |

## 2.10 1 中资中型银行资产负债表（资产）
## Balance Sheet of Medium-sized Domestic Banks (Assets)

单位：亿元
Unit:100 Million Yuan

| 时间<br>Time | 对中央银行<br>债权<br>Claims on<br>Central Bank | 对其他存款性<br>公司债权<br>Claims on<br>Other<br>Depository<br>Corporations | 对其他金融性<br>公司债权<br>Claims on<br>Other<br>Financial<br>Corporations | 对非金融性<br>公司债权<br>Claims on<br>Non-<br>financial<br>Corporations | 对其他居民<br>部门债权<br>Claims on<br>Other<br>Resident<br>Sectors | 其他资产<br>Other Assets | 总资产<br>Total Assets |
|---|---|---|---|---|---|---|---|
| 2011.12 | 1956.8 | 44221.4 | 6670.2 | 105725.0 | 24081.7 | 7331.6 | 230989.0 |
| 2012.03 | 1653.8 | 48143.5 | 8638.6 | 110749.2 | 24573.0 | 7757.7 | 243438.1 |
| 2012.06 | 1570.9 | 60444.7 | 9427.7 | 115480.8 | 25752.2 | 8380.4 | 264856.0 |
| 2012.09 | 1336.4 | 59152.1 | 10350.4 | 120369.5 | 28169.7 | 8435.8 | 273929.4 |
| 2012.12 | 790.1 | 63346.6 | 12867.2 | 124944.1 | 30199.3 | 7534.3 | 289933.6 |
| 2013.03 | 749 | 67541 | 15706 | 131634 | 32310 | 8018 | 306370 |
| 2013.06 | 541 | 65149 | 22048 | 134300 | 34906 | 7913 | 318622 |
| 2013.09 | 91 | 60048 | 24923 | 136831 | 37320 | 8042 | 322275 |
| 2013.12 | 90 | 60806 | 26713 | 138873 | 38771 | 8641 | 331205 |
| 2014.03 | 1405 | 66831 | 30946 | 145600 | 40321 | 8846 | 351664 |
| 2014.06 | 260 | 72688 | 36034 | 149668 | 42122 | 10197 | 374390 |
| 2014.09 | 196 | 66941 | 33205 | 152156 | 43800 | 10554 | 372863 |
| 2014.12 | 127 | 64679 | 40458 | 157577 | 46054 | 10964 | 389341 |
| 2015.03 | 126 | 59815 | 50834 | 165398 | 48011 | 13310 | 404342 |
| 2015.06 | 146 | 59643 | 65765 | 170285 | 50763 | 14824 | 433738 |
| 2015.09 | 124 | 62646 | 65469 | 172923 | 53336 | 15819 | 446286 |
| 2015.12 | 122 | 65521 | 71282 | 180137 | 55929 | 14033 | 463749 |
| 2016.03 | 124 | 58283 | 85589 | 187592 | 58653 | 14428 | 483984 |
| 2016.06 | 122 | 61050 | 91619 | 189253 | 63434 | 14606 | 510709 |
| 2016.09 | 0 | 61246 | 94666 | 190045 | 68857 | 15063 | 523997 |
| 2016.12 | 0 | 63915 | 102137 | 193237 | 74314 | 15323 | 550112 |
| 2017.03 | 0 | 56400 | 103391 | 199442 | 79575 | 17201 | 554594 |
| 2017.06 | 0 | 50032 | 100934 | 203264 | 85072 | 17187 | 558136 |
| 2017.09 | 0 | 49179 | 93653 | 206845 | 90316 | 17670 | 562146 |
| 2017.12 | 0 | 45886 | 96630 | 210329 | 94119 | 18620 | 575429 |
| 2018.03 | 0 | 40316 | 99880 | 220714 | 97903 | 18738 | 586890 |
| 2018.06 | 0 | 41327 | 97733 | 227108 | 102998 | 19265 | 601359 |
| 2018.09 | 0 | 40270 | 87852 | 230936 | 109594 | 17806 | 602178 |
| 2018.12 | 0 | 43056 | 89388 | 231885 | 115302 | 20563 | 619068 |
| 2019.03 | 0 | 39878 | 89914 | 242419 | 119419 | 19350 | 629436 |
| 2019.06 | 0 | 42354 | 91389 | 246838 | 124971 | 20373 | 649423 |
| 2019.09 | 0 | 42024 | 84221 | 253745 | 129645 | 18972 | 654470 |
| 2019.12 | 0 | 41453 | 87301 | 259666 | 133930 | 19640 | 672999 |

## 2.10 2 中资中型银行资产负债表（负债）
## Balance Sheet of Medium-sized Domestic Banks (Liabilities)

单位：亿元
Unit: 100 Million Yuan

| 时间<br>Time | 对非金融机构及住户负债<br>Liabilities to Non-financial Institutions & Households | 纳入广义货币的存款<br>Deposits Included in Broad Money | 企业活期存款<br>Demand Deposits of Enterprises | 企业定期存款<br>Time Deposits of Enterprises | 居民储蓄存款<br>Household Savings Deposits | 不纳入广义货币的存款<br>Deposits Excluded from Broad Money | 可转让存款<br>Transferable Deposits | 其他存款<br>Other Deposits | 其他负债<br>Other Liabilities | 对中央银行负债<br>Liabilities to Central Bank |
|---|---|---|---|---|---|---|---|---|---|---|
| 2011.12 | 130272.5 | 125649.3 | 46817.7 | 50945.0 | 27886.6 | 4025.1 | 1699.0 | 2326.1 | 598.1 | 3096.7 |
| 2012.03 | 134432.1 | 128819.3 | 44792.1 | 54309.0 | 29718.3 | 4989.5 | 1584.4 | 3405.1 | 623.3 | 3195.5 |
| 2012.06 | 144211.5 | 136898.4 | 47493.6 | 57693.0 | 31711.9 | 6668.4 | 1867.8 | 4800.6 | 644.7 | 4829.5 |
| 2012.09 | 150405.8 | 142385.5 | 46602.4 | 63315.1 | 32468.1 | 7282.7 | 1906.0 | 5376.7 | 737.5 | 5891.7 |
| 2012.12 | 156491.9 | 148246.6 | 51219.5 | 62392.5 | 34634.6 | 7469.3 | 2174.0 | 5295.3 | 776.1 | 7112.4 |
| 2013.03 | 169829 | 160267 | 53025 | 69409 | 37833 | 8821 | 2155 | 6666 | 742 | 3566 |
| 2013.06 | 177177 | 167265 | 54373 | 72907 | 39984 | 9005 | 2191 | 6815 | 907 | 5095 |
| 2013.09 | 178430 | 168162 | 52534 | 75288 | 40340 | 9247 | 1988 | 7259 | 1021 | 4872 |
| 2013.12 | 180861 | 170690 | 57170 | 72658 | 40861 | 9020 | 2098 | 6921 | 1152 | 4956 |
| 2014.03 | 189559 | 178219 | 54843 | 79308 | 44068 | 10246 | 2044 | 8202 | 1094 | 5900 |
| 2014.06 | 205344 | 191735 | 59832 | 84582 | 47321 | 12465 | 2606 | 9858 | 1144 | 6127 |
| 2014.09 | 198745 | 184336 | 53463 | 86282 | 44590 | 13135 | 2598 | 10537 | 1274 | 6258 |
| 2014.12 | 201772 | 188105 | 60317 | 83300 | 44488 | 12437 | 2497 | 9941 | 1229 | 10249 |
| 2015.03 | 205713 | 190775 | 56588 | 88974 | 45212 | 13780 | 2808 | 10971 | 1159 | 12655 |
| 2015.06 | 215779 | 201671 | 62044 | 94098 | 45530 | 12745 | 2591 | 10153 | 1363 | 7649 |
| 2015.09 | 219594 | 204401 | 63303 | 95722 | 45376 | 13799 | 2956 | 10843 | 1394 | 8278 |
| 2015.12 | 226091 | 211664 | 75061 | 90444 | 46159 | 13046 | 3342 | 9703 | 1381 | 10209 |
| 2016.03 | 232868 | 218409 | 77981 | 94126 | 46301 | 12969 | 3535 | 9434 | 1490 | 15943 |
| 2016.06 | 242548 | 228097 | 88157 | 93008 | 46932 | 12394 | 3575 | 8818 | 2057 | 19910 |
| 2016.09 | 244359 | 230536 | 87844 | 96924 | 45769 | 12101 | 3608 | 8493 | 1721 | 22649 |
| 2016.12 | 252664 | 236600 | 98437 | 92885 | 45278 | 13738 | 4117 | 9621 | 2327 | 31769 |
| 2017.03 | 255611 | 239139 | 98378 | 93762 | 47000 | 14573 | 4193 | 10380 | 1898 | 28606 |
| 2017.06 | 262823 | 245375 | 102938 | 93879 | 48557 | 15417 | 4738 | 10678 | 2032 | 31813 |
| 2017.09 | 259105 | 242065 | 100493 | 95072 | 46500 | 14255 | 4126 | 10129 | 2785 | 33195 |
| 2017.12 | 264587 | 246848 | 106644 | 92988 | 47216 | 14377 | 4634 | 9743 | 3362 | 37760 |
| 2018.03 | 269820 | 250932 | 102441 | 97287 | 51204 | 15067 | 4938 | 10129 | 3821 | 35525 |
| 2018.06 | 276862 | 258780 | 106540 | 97895 | 54345 | 15314 | 4827 | 10487 | 2769 | 36325 |
| 2018.09 | 280013 | 261442 | 101709 | 104345 | 55387 | 15218 | 4457 | 10761 | 3354 | 38790 |
| 2018.12 | 282199 | 264373 | 104898 | 101411 | 58064 | 14631 | 4615 | 10016 | 3195 | 39696 |
| 2019.03 | 295754 | 278223 | 104160 | 109754 | 64309 | 14661 | 4603 | 10058 | 2870 | 40115 |
| 2019.06 | 308802 | 291253 | 111928 | 111702 | 67622 | 14732 | 4584 | 10147 | 2818 | 42104 |
| 2019.09 | 310633 | 292211 | 107294 | 116149 | 68767 | 14371 | 4080 | 10292 | 4050 | 33555 |
| 2019.12 | 314307 | 296613 | 111424 | 113512 | 71677 | 14638 | 4544 | 10095 | 3056 | 36167 |

注：“中资中型银行资产负债表”机构范围见第96页[注2]。
Note: Please refer to note 2 on page 96 for the information of institutional coverage of the "Balance Sheet of Medium-sized Domestic Banks".

2.10 2 中资中型银行资产负债表（负债）

### Balance Sheet of Medium-sized Domestic Banks (Liabilities)

单位：亿元
Unit: 100 Million Yuan

| 时间<br>Time | 对其他存款性<br>公司负债<br>Liabilities to<br>Other Depository<br>Corporations | 对其他金融性<br>公司负债<br>Liabilities to<br>Other Financial<br>Corporations | 计入广义<br>货币的存款<br>Deposits Included<br>in Broad Money | 国外负债<br>Foreign<br>Liabilities | 债券发行<br>Bonds<br>Issue | 实收资本<br>Paid-in<br>Capital | 其他负债<br>Other<br>Liabilities | 总负债<br>Total<br>Liabilities |
|---|---|---|---|---|---|---|---|---|
| 2011.12 | 29889.2 | 19783.9 | 16295.1 | 725.8 | 23411.1 | 2351.6 | 21458.4 | 230989.0 |
| 2012.03 | 30648.4 | 22631.1 | 20853.0 | 1047.4 | 26007.8 | 2362.6 | 23113.2 | 243438.1 |
| 2012.06 | 37103.2 | 22267.3 | 20332.3 | 1156.3 | 27959.4 | 2379.4 | 24949.4 | 264856.0 |
| 2012.09 | 36448.3 | 23197.7 | 21171.3 | 1013.4 | 29132.2 | 2394.4 | 25446.1 | 273929.4 |
| 2012.12 | 40961.3 | 25625.2 | 23798.7 | 1302.9 | 30544.6 | 2413.0 | 25482.3 | 289933.6 |
| 2013.03 | 44055 | 25648 | 23485 | 1987 | 32512 | 2413 | 26359 | 306370 |
| 2013.06 | 45549 | 25684 | 23006 | 2289 | 33762 | 2443 | 26623 | 318622 |
| 2013.09 | 40824 | 29170 | 26609 | 2762 | 34407 | 2576 | 29234 | 322275 |
| 2013.12 | 43044 | 32295 | 29823 | 3403 | 35736 | 2647 | 28263 | 331205 |
| 2014.03 | 40904 | 38408 | 35811 | 4678 | 38523 | 2656 | 31035 | 351664 |
| 2014.06 | 40834 | 39579 | 37185 | 5667 | 41031 | 2738 | 33071 | 374390 |
| 2014.09 | 37927 | 42119 | 39036 | 5992 | 44456 | 2750 | 34617 | 372863 |
| 2014.12 | 38070 | 46271 | 43431 | 6339 | 46615 | 3030 | 36995 | 389341 |
| 2015.03 | 37940 | 49491 | 47162 | 5188 | 51701 | 3183 | 38471 | 404342 |
| 2015.06 | 38632 | 64244 | 60452 | 4928 | 56202 | 3570 | 42735 | 433738 |
| 2015.09 | 35810 | 67289 | 65854 | 3393 | 59762 | 3612 | 48548 | 446286 |
| 2015.12 | 42451 | 68221 | 66507 | 2388 | 64192 | 4002 | 46195 | 463749 |
| 2016.03 | 40639 | 66474 | 65426 | 2233 | 71672 | 4461 | 49694 | 483984 |
| 2016.06 | 40663 | 70037 | 69064 | 3512 | 76485 | 4511 | 53043 | 510709 |
| 2016.09 | 43836 | 66761 | 65694 | 3338 | 84018 | 4777 | 54258 | 523997 |
| 2016.12 | 49315 | 68878 | 67153 | 3414 | 86079 | 5233 | 52759 | 550112 |
| 2017.03 | 44306 | 70001 | 68569 | 4620 | 91597 | 5302 | 54551 | 554594 |
| 2017.06 | 37126 | 65807 | 64903 | 5376 | 94309 | 5336 | 55547 | 558136 |
| 2017.09 | 38081 | 66074 | 63638 | 6353 | 95916 | 5396 | 58027 | 562146 |
| 2017.12 | 39070 | 67781 | 65259 | 6132 | 94733 | 6222 | 59144 | 575429 |
| 2018.03 | 34800 | 74777 | 73468 | 6191 | 96829 | 6221 | 62727 | 586890 |
| 2018.06 | 35432 | 75117 | 73903 | 6453 | 100168 | 6296 | 64706 | 601359 |
| 2018.09 | 31752 | 70477 | 68172 | 6265 | 101502 | 6330 | 67051 | 602178 |
| 2018.12 | 34694 | 72246 | 69944 | 6374 | 107575 | 6396 | 69889 | 619068 |
| 2019.03 | 35156 | 65135 | 64120 | 6613 | 110745 | 6432 | 69487 | 629436 |
| 2019.06 | 33655 | 66012 | 65252 | 6418 | 113788 | 7560 | 71084 | 649423 |
| 2019.09 | 34915 | 72330 | 70797 | 6389 | 116548 | 8229 | 71871 | 654470 |
| 2019.12 | 35854 | 77678 | 76643 | 6419 | 121923 | 9506 | 71145 | 672999 |

2.11 1 中资小型银行资产负债表（资产）
## Balance Sheet of Small-sized Domestic Banks (Assets)

单位：亿元
Unit: 100 Million Yuan

| 时间<br>Time | 国外资产<br>Foreign Assets | 储备资产<br>Reserve Assets | | | 对政府债权<br>Claims on<br>Government | 对中央银行债权<br>Claims on<br>Central Bank |
| --- | --- | --- | --- | --- | --- | --- |
| | | | 准备金存款<br>Deposits with<br>Central Bank | 库存现金<br>Cash in Vault | | |
| 2011.12 | 317.3 | 24966.1 | 24087.1 | 879.0 | 6234.2 | 715.3 |
| 2012.03 | 336.9 | 23705.0 | 22924.9 | 780.1 | 6394.1 | 571.4 |
| 2012.06 | 377.7 | 24977.5 | 24140.7 | 836.8 | 6469.0 | 540.0 |
| 2012.09 | 186.8 | 26092.0 | 25173.0 | 919.0 | 6730.8 | 493.5 |
| 2012.12 | 219.8 | 32034.0 | 30950.8 | 1083.3 | 6785.1 | 392.7 |
| 2013.03 | 205 | 30894 | 29860 | 1034 | 6808 | 428 |
| 2013.06 | 284 | 32853 | 31836 | 1071 | 7253 | 331 |
| 2013.09 | 212 | 34097 | 32930 | 1166 | 7797 | 102 |
| 2013.12 | 274 | 38957 | 37712 | 1245 | 8322 | 88 |
| 2014.03 | 372 | 37824 | 36558 | 1267 | 8353 | 106 |
| 2014.06 | 352 | 39676 | 38418 | 1258 | 8705 | 99 |
| 2014.09 | 401 | 40433 | 39112 | 1321 | 9328 | 100 |
| 2014.12 | 575 | 45603 | 44155 | 1448 | 9805 | 83 |
| 2015.03 | 517 | 42754 | 41193 | 1561 | 10002 | 97 |
| 2015.06 | 610 | 43901 | 42413 | 1488 | 10853 | 121 |
| 2015.09 | 717 | 43032 | 41422 | 1610 | 12643 | 130 |
| 2015.12 | 694 | 47047 | 45474 | 1573 | 14705 | 88 |
| 2016.03 | 782 | 44807 | 43151 | 1657 | 15452 | 41 |
| 2016.06 | 641 | 49064 | 47502 | 1561 | 17979 | 35 |
| 2016.09 | 664 | 49425 | 47738 | 1687 | 20423 | 19 |
| 2016.12 | 882 | 55724 | 54019 | 1705 | 21709 | 25 |
| 2017.03 | 1388 | 53679 | 51900 | 1779 | 22199 | 22 |
| 2017.06 | 1444 | 56004 | 54292 | 1712 | 23899 | 3 |
| 2017.09 | 1499 | 56695 | 54832 | 1862 | 26302 | 3 |
| 2017.12 | 1461 | 63567 | 61738 | 1830 | 28473 | 0 |
| 2018.03 | 1622 | 60714 | 58730 | 1984 | 29351 | 0 |
| 2018.06 | 1615 | 60325 | 58493 | 1832 | 30695 | 0 |
| 2018.09 | 1578 | 59771 | 57665 | 2106 | 34286 | 0 |
| 2018.12 | 1766 | 66329 | 64499 | 1830 | 35998 | 0 |
| 2019.03 | 1695 | 58544 | 56470 | 2074 | 38174 | 0 |
| 2019.06 | 1856 | 60856 | 58972 | 1884 | 40258 | 0 |
| 2019.09 | 1891 | 56778 | 54735 | 2042 | 44117 | 0 |
| 2019.12 | 2005 | 64860 | 62937 | 1923 | 46624 | 0 |

## 2.11 1 中资小型银行资产负债表（资产）
## Balance Sheet of Small-sized Domestic Banks (Assets)

单位：亿元
Unit: 100 Million Yuan

| 时间<br>Time | 对其他存款性<br>公司债权<br>Claims on Other<br>Depository<br>Corporations | 对其他金融性<br>公司债权<br>Claims on Other<br>Financial<br>Corporations | 对非金融性<br>公司债权<br>Claims on<br>Non-financial<br>Corporations | 对其他居民<br>部门债权<br>Claims on<br>Other Resident<br>Sectors | 其他资产<br>Other Assets | 总资产<br>Total Assets |
|---|---|---|---|---|---|---|
| 2011.12 | 34407.2 | 5125.5 | 56894.2 | 16691.7 | 6003.4 | 151354.9 |
| 2012.03 | 39782.9 | 6127.0 | 62315.9 | 17886.9 | 6638.7 | 163758.9 |
| 2012.06 | 43852.5 | 7119.2 | 66998.9 | 19125.4 | 7534.8 | 176995.1 |
| 2012.09 | 39803.9 | 8327.7 | 69058.4 | 19863.2 | 7258.7 | 177815.2 |
| 2012.12 | 45553.8 | 9916.7 | 72244.7 | 21384.1 | 7250.9 | 195781.9 |
| 2013.03 | 48325 | 15182 | 78050 | 22869 | 7850 | 210610 |
| 2013.06 | 48486 | 16077 | 83117 | 24793 | 8529 | 221722 |
| 2013.09 | 48721 | 17408 | 87252 | 27121 | 8568 | 231276 |
| 2013.12 | 55187 | 19855 | 88879 | 29083 | 8734 | 249379 |
| 2014.03 | 59195 | 23840 | 94935 | 31234 | 8962 | 264821 |
| 2014.06 | 60120 | 25745 | 99966 | 33496 | 9588 | 277747 |
| 2014.09 | 56432 | 27084 | 103794 | 35658 | 10188 | 283418 |
| 2014.12 | 59784 | 28641 | 109411 | 37482 | 10458 | 301841 |
| 2015.03 | 63573 | 32223 | 118064 | 39771 | 11387 | 318387 |
| 2015.06 | 66914 | 40187 | 126159 | 42292 | 11781 | 342819 |
| 2015.09 | 70198 | 42931 | 132841 | 44329 | 12446 | 359267 |
| 2015.12 | 75065 | 50200 | 139039 | 46631 | 13155 | 386624 |
| 2016.03 | 70509 | 80542 | 138423 | 49219 | 13664 | 413439 |
| 2016.06 | 72427 | 89455 | 143308 | 52604 | 14714 | 440228 |
| 2016.09 | 77337 | 94026 | 147683 | 56499 | 15794 | 461870 |
| 2016.12 | 87448 | 97709 | 152228 | 60019 | 16890 | 492633 |
| 2017.03 | 94279 | 104157 | 160373 | 65039 | 18237 | 519373 |
| 2017.06 | 91141 | 105641 | 165294 | 69714 | 18841 | 531980 |
| 2017.09 | 91811 | 110022 | 169154 | 75081 | 18120 | 548687 |
| 2017.12 | 94275 | 110144 | 173386 | 78880 | 18173 | 568359 |
| 2018.03 | 89991 | 108502 | 180762 | 84395 | 19017 | 574355 |
| 2018.06 | 90389 | 103220 | 188116 | 89748 | 19438 | 583547 |
| 2018.09 | 89219 | 98641 | 197445 | 95971 | 20616 | 597526 |
| 2018.12 | 92540 | 97963 | 204553 | 101280 | 21378 | 621807 |
| 2019.03 | 99608 | 100037 | 218027 | 106887 | 22301 | 645274 |
| 2019.06 | 99874 | 94683 | 225586 | 112490 | 21855 | 657457 |
| 2019.09 | 98606 | 90945 | 231032 | 119494 | 22982 | 665844 |
| 2019.12 | 97216 | 91184 | 235858 | 125354 | 24518 | 687620 |

2.11 2 中资小型银行资产负债表（负债）

## Balance Sheet of Small-sized Domestic Banks (Liabilities)

单位：亿元

Unit: 100 Million Yuan

| 时间<br>Time | 对非金融<br>机构及<br>住户负债<br>Liabilities to<br>Non-financial<br>Institutions &<br>Households | 纳入广义<br>货币的存款<br>Deposits<br>Included in<br>Broad Money | 企业活期<br>存款<br>Demand<br>Deposits of<br>Enterprises | 企业定期<br>存款<br>Time<br>Deposits of<br>Enterprises | 居民储蓄<br>存款<br>Household<br>Savings<br>Deposits | 不纳入<br>广义货币<br>的存款<br>Deposits<br>Excluded from<br>Broad Money | 可转让<br>存款<br>Transferable<br>Deposits | 其他<br>存款<br>Other<br>Deposits | 其他<br>负债<br>Other<br>Liabilities | 对中央银行<br>负债<br>Liabilities to<br>Central Bank |
|---|---|---|---|---|---|---|---|---|---|---|
| 2011.12 | 109208.9 | 108395.9 | 37003.3 | 26081.7 | 45311.0 | 498.6 | 263.2 | 235.4 | 314.4 | 418.1 |
| 2012.03 | 113155.5 | 112308.2 | 34210.2 | 28003.7 | 50094.3 | 592.8 | 251.1 | 341.7 | 254.5 | 446.6 |
| 2012.06 | 121359.0 | 120422.8 | 36350.8 | 31015.1 | 53056.9 | 645.3 | 246.9 | 398.4 | 291.0 | 918.2 |
| 2012.09 | 125481.3 | 124432.9 | 35938.2 | 32698.0 | 55796.7 | 708.9 | 255.9 | 453.0 | 339.4 | 1565.8 |
| 2012.12 | 137712.6 | 136460.7 | 41319.3 | 33892.3 | 61249.1 | 784.9 | 344.9 | 440.0 | 467.0 | 1401.2 |
| 2013.03 | 147528 | 146370 | 40519 | 37037 | 68814 | 783 | 287 | 495 | 376 | 710 |
| 2013.06 | 155951 | 154404 | 42851 | 39533 | 72020 | 1077 | 345 | 732 | 470 | 1024 |
| 2013.09 | 162050 | 160469 | 43318 | 41988 | 75163 | 1055 | 342 | 713 | 525 | 1353 |
| 2013.12 | 173424 | 171626 | 48776 | 43004 | 79846 | 1100 | 359 | 741 | 699 | 1121 |
| 2014.03 | 181577 | 179867 | 45953 | 46138 | 87777 | 1068 | 292 | 776 | 642 | 999 |
| 2014.06 | 191979 | 190106 | 48976 | 49679 | 91451 | 1159 | 305 | 854 | 713 | 1376 |
| 2014.09 | 195251 | 193139 | 46872 | 51749 | 94518 | 1424 | 314 | 1110 | 687 | 1837 |
| 2014.12 | 205272 | 202803 | 51315 | 52304 | 99183 | 1536 | 357 | 1179 | 934 | 2188 |
| 2015.03 | 214995 | 212133 | 48236 | 54171 | 109726 | 1976 | 347 | 1629 | 887 | 2669 |
| 2015.06 | 226452 | 223417 | 51942 | 59044 | 112430 | 2142 | 339 | 1803 | 894 | 2419 |
| 2015.09 | 237308 | 233999 | 54792 | 62265 | 116942 | 2334 | 455 | 1880 | 976 | 2575 |
| 2015.12 | 251931 | 248664 | 62771 | 62884 | 123009 | 2208 | 389 | 1819 | 1058 | 2668 |
| 2016.03 | 269327 | 266069 | 64669 | 67014 | 134386 | 2155 | 415 | 1740 | 1103 | 3915 |
| 2016.06 | 286479 | 283048 | 72838 | 69885 | 140326 | 2169 | 404 | 1766 | 1262 | 4963 |
| 2016.09 | 301089 | 297390 | 77206 | 72970 | 147213 | 2327 | 451 | 1876 | 1373 | 5556 |
| 2016.12 | 314329 | 309906 | 84609 | 72680 | 152617 | 2646 | 600 | 2045 | 1777 | 9510 |
| 2017.03 | 332478 | 327205 | 86201 | 73835 | 167168 | 3359 | 599 | 2759 | 1915 | 6941 |
| 2017.06 | 342386 | 336579 | 92950 | 73370 | 170259 | 3776 | 678 | 3098 | 2031 | 7032 |
| 2017.09 | 352193 | 345794 | 95938 | 75228 | 174628 | 3936 | 692 | 3244 | 2463 | 7505 |
| 2017.12 | 366366 | 358988 | 103422 | 76011 | 179555 | 4076 | 854 | 3222 | 3302 | 9510 |
| 2018.03 | 373481 | 365654 | 96210 | 76458 | 192986 | 3942 | 999 | 2943 | 3885 | 7594 |
| 2018.06 | 382249 | 374688 | 100244 | 78492 | 195953 | 3514 | 893 | 2621 | 4046 | 8586 |
| 2018.09 | 391974 | 383900 | 100250 | 81284 | 202367 | 3413 | 861 | 2552 | 4661 | 9609 |
| 2018.12 | 408501 | 400135 | 103423 | 83601 | 213111 | 3359 | 980 | 2379 | 5007 | 12398 |
| 2019.03 | 431793 | 423363 | 100492 | 88712 | 234159 | 3314 | 835 | 2479 | 5115 | 9362 |
| 2019.06 | 444499 | 435576 | 104677 | 90939 | 239961 | 3642 | 926 | 2716 | 5281 | 12898 |
| 2019.09 | 454180 | 444455 | 104402 | 91117 | 248935 | 3787 | 990 | 2796 | 5938 | 12459 |
| 2019.12 | 466769 | 455701 | 107988 | 89184 | 258528 | 4162 | 1102 | 3060 | 6906 | 14790 |

注：　"中资小型银行资产负债表" 机构范围见第96页 [注2]。

Note: Please refer to note 2 on page 96 for the information of institutional coverage of the "Balance Sheet of Small-sized Domestic Banks".

## 2.11 2 中资小型银行资产负债表（负债）
### Balance Sheet of Small-sized Domestic Banks (Liabilities)

单位：亿元
Unit: 100 Million Yuan

| 时间<br>Time | 对其他存款性<br>公司负债<br>Liabilities to<br>Other Depository<br>Corporations | 对其他金融性<br>公司负债<br>Liabilities to<br>Other Financial<br>Corporations | 计入广义<br>货币的存款<br>Deposits Included<br>in Broad Money | 国外负债<br>Foreign<br>Liabilities | 债券发行<br>Bonds<br>Issue | 实收资本<br>Paid-in<br>Capital | 其他负债<br>Other<br>Liabilities | 总负债<br>Total<br>Liabilities |
|---|---|---|---|---|---|---|---|---|
| 2011.12 | 22157.4 | 2066.3 | 1563.3 | 174.4 | 703.0 | 4903.4 | 11723.4 | 151354.9 |
| 2012.03 | 29155.9 | 2171.7 | 1844.9 | 206.0 | 873.0 | 5132.2 | 12617.9 | 163758.9 |
| 2012.06 | 32085.6 | 2352.0 | 2006.1 | 230.2 | 948.4 | 5409.1 | 13692.8 | 176995.1 |
| 2012.09 | 27160.3 | 2295.0 | 1998.3 | 255.2 | 1117.7 | 5572.7 | 14367.2 | 177815.2 |
| 2012.12 | 30553.1 | 2743.0 | 2516.8 | 311.6 | 1320.4 | 5980.9 | 15759.2 | 195781.9 |
| 2013.03 | 34459 | 3320 | 3082 | 636 | 1444 | 6187 | 16328 | 210610 |
| 2013.06 | 34309 | 4190 | 3655 | 645 | 1699 | 6479 | 17425 | 221722 |
| 2013.09 | 34920 | 4894 | 4444 | 601 | 1779 | 6758 | 18920 | 231276 |
| 2013.12 | 39675 | 5429 | 4876 | 633 | 1745 | 7226 | 20127 | 249379 |
| 2014.03 | 43771 | 6839 | 6472 | 714 | 1897 | 7459 | 21564 | 264821 |
| 2014.06 | 42525 | 8025 | 7766 | 703 | 2159 | 7786 | 23195 | 277747 |
| 2014.09 | 39526 | 9839 | 9439 | 786 | 3150 | 8128 | 24901 | 283418 |
| 2014.12 | 42096 | 11288 | 10547 | 753 | 4977 | 8559 | 26708 | 301841 |
| 2015.03 | 43663 | 13038 | 12486 | 806 | 6309 | 8946 | 27960 | 318387 |
| 2015.06 | 47572 | 16594 | 15769 | 978 | 8960 | 9494 | 30349 | 342819 |
| 2015.09 | 43710 | 21709 | 20774 | 863 | 10826 | 9812 | 32464 | 359267 |
| 2015.12 | 47395 | 24055 | 22821 | 850 | 14438 | 10641 | 34646 | 386624 |
| 2016.03 | 47312 | 26728 | 25877 | 840 | 17634 | 11039 | 36645 | 413439 |
| 2016.06 | 49314 | 28573 | 27840 | 671 | 19780 | 11418 | 39029 | 440228 |
| 2016.09 | 48425 | 30873 | 29766 | 718 | 21394 | 11955 | 41860 | 461870 |
| 2016.12 | 52388 | 32397 | 30626 | 642 | 27608 | 12659 | 43099 | 492633 |
| 2017.03 | 52542 | 35066 | 34089 | 800 | 33288 | 13185 | 45073 | 519373 |
| 2017.06 | 51463 | 34683 | 34084 | 920 | 34932 | 13610 | 46954 | 531980 |
| 2017.09 | 50030 | 38620 | 37609 | 969 | 35768 | 14153 | 49449 | 548687 |
| 2017.12 | 50952 | 37994 | 36297 | 924 | 36014 | 14972 | 51628 | 568359 |
| 2018.03 | 48390 | 38021 | 37166 | 924 | 37036 | 15141 | 53768 | 574355 |
| 2018.06 | 44366 | 38303 | 37630 | 966 | 37754 | 15474 | 55849 | 583547 |
| 2018.09 | 43577 | 37892 | 36990 | 1116 | 38400 | 15792 | 59165 | 597526 |
| 2018.12 | 40430 | 40729 | 39697 | 1151 | 41757 | 16546 | 60295 | 621807 |
| 2019.03 | 40333 | 40357 | 39865 | 1190 | 43349 | 16719 | 62172 | 645274 |
| 2019.06 | 38498 | 37091 | 36271 | 1202 | 41197 | 16993 | 65080 | 657457 |
| 2019.09 | 37739 | 37610 | 36070 | 1052 | 38600 | 17427 | 66777 | 665844 |
| 2019.12 | 38823 | 42923 | 40698 | 932 | 36267 | 19063 | 68052 | 687620 |

2.12 1 外资银行资产负债表（资产）
## Balance Sheet of Foreign-funded Banks (Assets)

单位：亿元
Unit: 100 Million Yuan

| 时间<br>Time | 国外资产<br>Foreign Assets | 储备资产<br>Reserve Assets | | 对政府债权<br>Claims on<br>Government | 对中央银行<br>债权<br>Claims on<br>Central Bank |
|---|---|---|---|---|---|
| | | | 准备金存款<br>Deposits with<br>Central Bank | 库存现金<br>Cash in Vault | |
| 2012 | 1612.5 | 3228.5 | 3218.4 | 10.1 | 1294.9 | 0 |
| 2013 | 1128 | 3083 | 3073 | 10 | 1535 | 127 |
| 2014.03 | 1110 | 2951 | 2940 | 12 | 1343 | 659 |
| 2014.06 | 1295 | 3019 | 3008 | 11 | 1799 | 302 |
| 2014.09 | 1443 | 2899 | 2887 | 12 | 2055 | 134 |
| 2014.12 | 1889 | 3205 | 3194 | 11 | 2185 | 40 |
| 2015.03 | 1938 | 2650 | 2639 | 11 | 1695 | 39 |
| 2015.06 | 2054 | 2524 | 2514 | 11 | 1838 | 102 |
| 2015.09 | 2190 | 2439 | 2428 | 11 | 1937 | 120 |
| 2015.12 | 2391 | 2899 | 2889 | 10 | 1793 | 105 |
| 2016.03 | 1984 | 2869 | 2859 | 10 | 1687 | 87 |
| 2016.06 | 2066 | 3107 | 3098 | 9 | 1946 | 138 |
| 2016.09 | 1899 | 3584 | 3575 | 9 | 1807 | 3 |
| 2016.12 | 2071 | 4060 | 4051 | 9 | 1958 | 0 |
| 2017.03 | 2008 | 3478 | 3470 | 8 | 1780 | 0 |
| 2017.06 | 2187 | 3469 | 3461 | 8 | 1952 | 0 |
| 2017.09 | 2192 | 3297 | 3289 | 8 | 2027 | 0 |
| 2017.12 | 2222 | 3766 | 3758 | 7 | 2230 | 0 |
| 2018.03 | 2043 | 3045 | 3038 | 7 | 2020 | 0 |
| 2018.06 | 2328 | 2985 | 2979 | 7 | 2028 | 0 |
| 2018.09 | 2380 | 2832 | 2826 | 6 | 2584 | 0 |
| 2018.12 | 2452 | 3287 | 3281 | 6 | 2681 | 0 |
| 2019.03 | 2501 | 2645 | 2639 | 5 | 2740 | 0 |
| 2019.06 | 2443 | 2904 | 2899 | 5 | 2884 | 0 |
| 2019.09 | 2546 | 2880 | 2875 | 5 | 3096 | 0 |
| 2019.12 | 2950 | 3252 | 3247 | 5 | 3388 | 0 |

注：自 2008 年起，本表项目中原"央行债券"更名为"对中央银行债权"。
Note: Since 2008, the item of "Central Bank Bonds" has been renamed as "Claims on Central Bank".

## 2.12 1 外资银行资产负债表（资产）
## Balance Sheet of Foreign-funded Banks (Assets)

单位：亿元
Unit: 100 Million Yuan

| 时间<br>Time | 对其他存款性<br>公司债权 *<br>Claims on Other<br>Depository<br>Corporations* | 对其他金融性<br>公司债权 *<br>Claims on Other<br>Financial<br>Corporations* | 对非金融性<br>公司债权<br>Claims on<br>Non-financial<br>Corporations | 对其他居民<br>部门债权<br>Claims on<br>Other Resident<br>Sectors | 其他资产<br>Other Assets | 总资产<br>Total Assets |
|---|---|---|---|---|---|---|
| 2012 | 5361.3 | 752.2 | 10510.2 | 603.2 | 1219.6 | 24582.4 |
| 2013 | 6313 | 1400 | 10581 | 790 | 849 | 25805 |
| 2014.03 | 6743 | 1491 | 10875 | 843 | 1057 | 27070 |
| 2014.06 | 6471 | 1578 | 10892 | 891 | 934 | 27181 |
| 2014.09 | 5989 | 1684 | 11035 | 933 | 1064 | 27236 |
| 2014.12 | 5775 | 2125 | 11077 | 970 | 877 | 28143 |
| 2015.03 | 5229 | 2257 | 10949 | 869 | 942 | 26566 |
| 2015.06 | 5281 | 2471 | 10782 | 905 | 944 | 26900 |
| 2015.09 | 4791 | 2398 | 10498 | 942 | 1260 | 26574 |
| 2015.12 | 4689 | 2590 | 10267 | 980 | 1969 | 27684 |
| 2016.03 | 4683 | 2545 | 10316 | 1002 | 1019 | 26191 |
| 2016.06 | 4684 | 2454 | 10252 | 1023 | 1638 | 27308 |
| 2016.09 | 5294 | 2469 | 9832 | 1040 | 1587 | 27515 |
| 2016.12 | 5698 | 2738 | 10254 | 1081 | 3809 | 31670 |
| 2017.03 | 5377 | 2987 | 10206 | 1125 | 8875 | 35836 |
| 2017.06 | 5611 | 3149 | 10522 | 1167 | 10104 | 38160 |
| 2017.09 | 6110 | 3415 | 11023 | 1207 | 10958 | 40230 |
| 2017.12 | 6505 | 3694 | 11020 | 1234 | 11812 | 42483 |
| 2018.03 | 5926 | 3826 | 12082 | 1254 | 12604 | 42800 |
| 2018.06 | 5893 | 3849 | 12009 | 1283 | 12596 | 42972 |
| 2018.09 | 5271 | 3847 | 12367 | 1340 | 13218 | 43840 |
| 2018.12 | 5844 | 3745 | 11649 | 1452 | 13066 | 44177 |
| 2019.03 | 5178 | 3812 | 11983 | 1524 | 12962 | 43344 |
| 2019.06 | 5378 | 3664 | 12132 | 1573 | 12813 | 43791 |
| 2019.09 | 4865 | 3646 | 12633 | 1609 | 13114 | 44389 |
| 2019.12 | 5186 | 3662 | 12266 | 1683 | 12684 | 45071 |

* 自 2005 年起，本表采用其他存款性公司和其他金融性公司分类，其机构范围详见第 94 页 [ 注 1]。2005 年之前，存款货币银行和特定存款机构加总的数据可以替代其他存款性公司数据，其他金融机构的数据可以替代其他金融性公司数据。

* For this sheet, new classification has been adopted since 2005. Please refer to the note 1 on page 94 for the particular institution coverage of other depository corporations and other financial corporations. To keep comparability, the data of other depository corporations before 2005 could be approximately substituted by the aggregation of deposit money banks and specific monetary institutions. Similarly, data of other financial corporations could be substituted by data of other financial institutions before 2005.

2.12 2 外资银行资产负债表（负债）

## Balance Sheet of Foreign-funded Banks (Liabilities)

单位：亿元
Unit: 100 Million Yuan

| 时间<br>Time | 对非金融<br>机构及<br>住户负债<br>Liabilities to<br>Non-financial<br>Institutions &<br>Households | 纳入广义<br>货币的存款<br>Deposits<br>Included in<br>Broad Money | 企业活期<br>存款<br>Demand<br>Deposits of<br>Enterprises | 企业定期<br>存款<br>Time<br>Deposits of<br>Enterprises | 居民储蓄<br>存款<br>Household<br>Savings<br>Deposits | 不纳入广义<br>货币的存款<br>Deposits<br>Excluded from<br>Broad Money | 可转让<br>存款<br>Transferable<br>Deposits | 其他<br>存款<br>Other<br>Deposits | 其他<br>负债<br>Other<br>Liabilities | 对中央银行<br>负债<br>Liabilities to<br>Central Bank |
|---|---|---|---|---|---|---|---|---|---|---|
| 2012 | 13072.2 | 10670.7 | 2912.6 | 5823.0 | 1935.2 | 2401.5 | 1209.5 | 1192.0 | 0.0 | 8.6 |
| 2013 | 15108 | 12120 | 2887 | 7193 | 2040 | 2426 | 1158 | 1268 | 561 | 1 |
| 2014.03 | 15016 | 12169 | 2471 | 7635 | 2063 | 2436 | 1122 | 1314 | 411 | 2 |
| 2014.06 | 15124 | 12220 | 2597 | 7574 | 2049 | 2556 | 1189 | 1367 | 348 | 1 |
| 2014.09 | 15007 | 12087 | 2326 | 7761 | 2001 | 2509 | 1171 | 1338 | 410 | 2 |
| 2014.12 | 15731 | 12685 | 3315 | 7440 | 1930 | 2621 | 1249 | 1372 | 424 | 2 |
| 2015.03 | 14266 | 11235 | 2677 | 6765 | 1793 | 2520 | 1218 | 1302 | 511 | 125 |
| 2015.06 | 14079 | 10899 | 2883 | 6345 | 1671 | 2506 | 1291 | 1216 | 674 | 2 |
| 2015.09 | 13844 | 10738 | 2773 | 6375 | 1589 | 2555 | 1389 | 1166 | 552 | 4 |
| 2015.12 | 14593 | 11213 | 3751 | 5958 | 1504 | 2774 | 1563 | 1211 | 605 | 5 |
| 2016.03 | 13684 | 10315 | 2990 | 5922 | 1402 | 2811 | 1529 | 1282 | 558 | 34 |
| 2016.06 | 14452 | 10781 | 3472 | 5955 | 1354 | 3047 | 1592 | 1456 | 624 | 180 |
| 2016.09 | 15131 | 11473 | 3199 | 6947 | 1328 | 3200 | 1645 | 1554 | 458 | 274 |
| 2016.12 | 17153 | 12731 | 4425 | 6996 | 1310 | 3478 | 1845 | 1633 | 945 | 168 |
| 2017.03 | 16241 | 12213 | 3637 | 7304 | 1272 | 3384 | 1796 | 1588 | 644 | 217 |
| 2017.06 | 16384 | 12319 | 3873 | 7185 | 1261 | 3361 | 1800 | 1561 | 704 | 334 |
| 2017.09 | 17066 | 12639 | 3660 | 7730 | 1249 | 3351 | 1717 | 1635 | 1076 | 259 |
| 2017.12 | 18357 | 13802 | 4886 | 7645 | 1270 | 3373 | 1761 | 1612 | 1182 | 284 |
| 2018.03 | 17732 | 12909 | 3876 | 7786 | 1247 | 3211 | 1668 | 1543 | 1612 | 91 |
| 2018.06 | 17378 | 12865 | 4152 | 7499 | 1214 | 3336 | 1777 | 1559 | 1177 | 226 |
| 2018.09 | 17468 | 12701 | 3650 | 7805 | 1247 | 3347 | 1749 | 1598 | 1420 | 82 |
| 2018.12 | 18386 | 13700 | 4837 | 7565 | 1298 | 3461 | 1876 | 1586 | 1225 | 144 |
| 2019.03 | 17054 | 12744 | 3850 | 7607 | 1288 | 3303 | 1701 | 1602 | 1007 | 85 |
| 2019.06 | 17706 | 13126 | 4131 | 7691 | 1304 | 3625 | 1752 | 1872 | 956 | 161 |
| 2019.09 | 18494 | 13102 | 3870 | 7929 | 1303 | 3850 | 1764 | 2086 | 1542 | 133 |
| 2019.12 | 19486 | 14390 | 5347 | 7706 | 1338 | 3953 | 1946 | 2007 | 1143 | 183 |

## 2.12 2 外资银行资产负债表（负债）
## Balance Sheet of Foreign-funded Banks (Liabilities)

单位：亿元
Unit: 100 Million Yuan

| 时间<br>Time | 对其他存款性<br>公司负债*<br>Liabilities to<br>Other Depository<br>Corporations* | 对其他金融性<br>公司负债*<br>Liabilities to<br>Other Financial<br>Corporations* | 计入广义<br>货币的存款<br>Deposits Included<br>in Broad Money | 国外负债<br>Foreign<br>Liabilities | 债券发行<br>Bonds<br>Issue | 实收资本<br>Paid-in<br>Capital | 其他负债<br>Other<br>Liabilities | 总负债<br>Total<br>Liabilities |
|---|---|---|---|---|---|---|---|---|
| 2012 | 2571.0 | 817.4 | — | 4082.5 | 7.2 | 1941.3 | 2082.1 | 24582.4 |
| 2013 | 1227 | 736 | 552 | 5268 | 81 | 1586 | 1799 | 25805 |
| 2014.03 | 1564 | 647 | 520 | 6023 | 80 | 1618 | 2120 | 27070 |
| 2014.06 | 1874 | 597 | 452 | 5803 | 81 | 1635 | 2067 | 27181 |
| 2014.09 | 1624 | 638 | 460 | 5971 | 86 | 1661 | 2248 | 27236 |
| 2014.12 | 1785 | 709 | 512 | 6057 | 115 | 1654 | 2092 | 28143 |
| 2015.03 | 1856 | 923 | 699 | 5361 | 193 | 1637 | 2205 | 26566 |
| 2015.06 | 1973 | 1101 | 877 | 5593 | 154 | 1705 | 2293 | 26900 |
| 2015.09 | 2038 | 1386 | 1155 | 4856 | 156 | 1710 | 2580 | 26574 |
| 2015.12 | 2019 | 1524 | 1315 | 4241 | 257 | 1744 | 3301 | 27684 |
| 2016.03 | 2484 | 1632 | 1484 | 3905 | 318 | 1748 | 2385 | 26191 |
| 2016.06 | 2313 | 1449 | 1293 | 3927 | 202 | 1781 | 3004 | 27308 |
| 2016.09 | 2474 | 1247 | 1037 | 3384 | 197 | 1758 | 3050 | 27515 |
| 2016.12 | 2611 | 1241 | 1027 | 3247 | 184 | 1761 | 5305 | 31670 |
| 2017.03 | 2768 | 1020 | 879 | 3239 | 199 | 1762 | 10390 | 35836 |
| 2017.06 | 2932 | 896 | 718 | 4078 | 200 | 1763 | 11574 | 38160 |
| 2017.09 | 2705 | 912 | 763 | 4779 | 222 | 1766 | 12521 | 40230 |
| 2017.12 | 2612 | 941 | 772 | 4884 | 226 | 1835 | 13344 | 42483 |
| 2018.03 | 3137 | 903 | 772 | 4735 | 208 | 1830 | 14164 | 42800 |
| 2018.06 | 2832 | 1043 | 936 | 5073 | 323 | 1835 | 14263 | 42972 |
| 2018.09 | 2884 | 1100 | 938 | 5011 | 446 | 1873 | 14977 | 43840 |
| 2018.12 | 2342 | 1116 | 1004 | 4904 | 549 | 1878 | 14858 | 44177 |
| 2019.03 | 2823 | 1128 | 1024 | 4827 | 695 | 1954 | 14777 | 43344 |
| 2019.06 | 2893 | 1163 | 1052 | 4444 | 806 | 1975 | 14642 | 43791 |
| 2019.09 | 2497 | 1211 | 1059 | 4273 | 785 | 1977 | 15019 | 44389 |
| 2019.12 | 2663 | 1264 | 1140 | 4041 | 859 | 1979 | 14597 | 45071 |

* 见第 45 页脚注。
* See footnote on page 45.

## 2.13 1 农村信用社资产负债表（资产）
## Balance Sheet of Rural Credit Cooperatives (Assets)

单位：亿元
Unit: 100 Million Yuan

| 时间<br>Time | 国外资产<br>Foreign Assets | 储备资产<br>Reserve Assets | | | 对政府债权<br>Claims on<br>Government | 对中央银行债权<br>Claims on<br>Central Bank |
| --- | --- | --- | --- | --- | --- | --- |
| | | | 准备金存款<br>Deposits with<br>Central Bank | 库存现金<br>Cash in Vault | | |
| 2012 | 5.1 | 13245.1 | 12391.7 | 853.4 | 537.3 | 58.3 |
| 2013 | 3 | 13855 | 12997 | 858 | 632 | 88 |
| 2014.03 | 4 | 12113 | 11154 | 959 | 690 | 72 |
| 2014.06 | 4 | 12664 | 11726 | 939 | 675 | 69 |
| 2014.09 | 4 | 12798 | 11877 | 921 | 684 | 75 |
| 2014.12 | 3 | 14985 | 14116 | 870 | 654 | 84 |
| 2015.03 | 3 | 12182 | 11168 | 1014 | 595 | 117 |
| 2015.06 | 3 | 11644 | 10776 | 868 | 659 | 62 |
| 2015.09 | 4 | 11488 | 10576 | 912 | 988 | 61 |
| 2015.12 | 3 | 14570 | 13846 | 723 | 1217 | 5 |
| 2016.03 | 3 | 9698 | 8894 | 804 | 1207 | 0 |
| 2016.06 | 4 | 10520 | 9810 | 709 | 1294 | 0 |
| 2016.09 | 4 | 10111 | 9394 | 717 | 1255 | 0 |
| 2016.12 | 4 | 11574 | 10989 | 585 | 1350 | 0 |
| 2017.03 | 4 | 8757 | 8109 | 648 | 1321 | 0 |
| 2017.06 | 4 | 9656 | 9064 | 592 | 1396 | 0 |
| 2017.09 | 4 | 9459 | 8865 | 594 | 1502 | 0 |
| 2017.12 | 4 | 11275 | 10776 | 499 | 1545 | 0 |
| 2018.03 | 4 | 9798 | 9208 | 590 | 1528 | 0 |
| 2018.06 | 3 | 10021 | 9514 | 506 | 1505 | 0 |
| 2018.09 | 7 | 9846 | 9282 | 564 | 1621 | 0 |
| 2018.12 | 7 | 11289 | 10881 | 408 | 1627 | 0 |
| 2019.03 | 7 | 8764 | 8279 | 485 | 1658 | 0 |
| 2019.06 | 7 | 8741 | 8333 | 407 | 1692 | 0 |
| 2019.09 | 5 | 8697 | 8270 | 427 | 1857 | 0 |
| 2019.12 | 5 | 9541 | 9216 | 325 | 1698 | 0 |

注：自 2008 年起，本表项目中原"央行债券"更名为"对中央银行债权"。
Note: Since 2008, the item of "Central Bank Bonds" has been renamed as "Claims on Central Bank".

## 2.13 1 农村信用社资产负债表（资产）
## Balance Sheet of Rural Credit Cooperatives (Assets)

单位：亿元
Unit: 100 Million Yuan

| 时间<br>Time | 对其他存款性<br>公司债权 *<br>Claims on Other<br>Depository<br>Corporations* | 对其他金融性<br>公司债权 *<br>Claims on Other<br>Financial<br>Corporations* | 对非金融性<br>公司债权<br>Claims on<br>Non-financial<br>Corporations | 对其他居民<br>部门债权<br>Claims on<br>Other Resident<br>Sectors | 其他资产<br>Other Assets | 总资产<br>Total Assets |
|---|---|---|---|---|---|---|
| 2012 | 13677.0 | 1803.9 | 19629.5 | 20887.8 | 4004.1 | 73848.1 |
| 2013 | 16287 | 1837 | 21754 | 22226 | 4069 | 80752 |
| 2014.03 | 22299 | 2277 | 22354 | 22891 | 4375 | 87074 |
| 2014.06 | 21577 | 2487 | 22912 | 23526 | 4369 | 88285 |
| 2014.09 | 21180 | 2356 | 22878 | 23415 | 4499 | 87889 |
| 2014.12 | 18939 | 2378 | 22918 | 22443 | 4273 | 86677 |
| 2015.03 | 24671 | 2433 | 23309 | 22420 | 4537 | 90267 |
| 2015.06 | 24024 | 3259 | 23467 | 22583 | 4427 | 90128 |
| 2015.09 | 24133 | 3063 | 23748 | 22361 | 4419 | 90266 |
| 2015.12 | 19771 | 2710 | 22692 | 20729 | 4249 | 85946 |
| 2016.03 | 27003 | 2984 | 21914 | 20485 | 4559 | 87853 |
| 2016.06 | 25248 | 3248 | 20787 | 20089 | 4450 | 85640 |
| 2016.09 | 24680 | 3153 | 19761 | 19306 | 4212 | 82481 |
| 2016.12 | 22290 | 2642 | 19471 | 18259 | 4160 | 79750 |
| 2017.03 | 24981 | 2734 | 18795 | 17493 | 4224 | 78308 |
| 2017.06 | 23708 | 2690 | 18668 | 17730 | 4156 | 78008 |
| 2017.09 | 22618 | 2480 | 18428 | 17369 | 3820 | 75680 |
| 2017.12 | 20412 | 2139 | 17749 | 16597 | 3295 | 73017 |
| 2018.03 | 21762 | 2268 | 17876 | 16604 | 3158 | 72997 |
| 2018.06 | 20486 | 1874 | 17553 | 16671 | 3054 | 71168 |
| 2018.09 | 19709 | 1739 | 17022 | 16363 | 3011 | 69317 |
| 2018.12 | 16429 | 1454 | 15547 | 15328 | 2948 | 64629 |
| 2019.03 | 19770 | 1517 | 15643 | 15310 | 2929 | 65598 |
| 2019.06 | 19639 | 1111 | 15150 | 15476 | 2966 | 64781 |
| 2019.09 | 18916 | 1514 | 14821 | 15359 | 3009 | 64177 |
| 2019.12 | 15994 | 895 | 13808 | 14560 | 3256 | 59756 |

* 自 2005 年起，本表采用其他存款性公司和其他金融性公司分类，其机构范围详见第 94 页 [注 1]。2005 年之前，存款货币银行和特定存款机构加总的数据可以替代其他存款性公司数据，其他金融机构的数据可以替代其他金融性公司数据。

* For this sheet, new classification has been adopted since 2005. Please refer to the note 1 on page 94 for the particular institution coverage of other depository corporations and other financial corporations. To keep comparability, the data of other depository corporations before 2005 could be approximately substituted by the aggregation of deposit money banks and specific monetary institutions. Similarly, data of other financial corporations could be substituted by data of other financial corporations before 2005.

2.13 2 农村信用社资产负债表（负债）
## Balance Sheet of Rural Credit Cooperatives (Liabilities)

单位：亿元
Unit: 100 Million Yuan

| 时间<br>Time | 对非金融<br>机构及<br>住户负债<br>Liabilities to<br>Non-financial<br>Institutions &<br>Households | 纳入广义<br>货币的存款<br>Deposits<br>Included in<br>Broad Money | 企业活期<br>存款<br>Demand<br>Deposits of<br>Enterprises | 企业定期<br>存款<br>Time<br>Deposits of<br>Enterprises | 居民储蓄<br>存款<br>Household<br>Savings<br>Deposits | 不纳入广义<br>货币的存款<br>Deposits<br>Excluded from<br>Broad Money | 可转让<br>存款<br>Transferable<br>Deposits | 其他<br>存款<br>Other<br>Deposits | 其他<br>负债<br>Other<br>Liabilities | 对中央银行<br>负债<br>Liabilities to<br>Central Bank |
|---|---|---|---|---|---|---|---|---|---|---|
| 2012 | 59910.6 | 59740.5 | 10894.0 | 2061.7 | 46829.9 | 8.4 | 0.8 | 7.5 | 161.7 | 1212.5 |
| 2013 | 65313 | 65124 | 11515 | 2271 | 51338 | 8 | 1 | 7 | 180 | 1341 |
| 2014.03 | 68768 | 68640 | 11212 | 2589 | 54840 | 5 | 0 | 5 | 122 | 1138 |
| 2014.06 | 68973 | 68854 | 11406 | 2890 | 54558 | 6 | 1 | 5 | 113 | 1360 |
| 2014.09 | 67661 | 67532 | 11044 | 2884 | 53603 | 9 | 1 | 9 | 120 | 1525 |
| 2014.12 | 66662 | 66484 | 10848 | 2776 | 52861 | 6 | 0 | 6 | 171 | 1435 |
| 2015.03 | 68223 | 68104 | 9895 | 2927 | 55282 | 7 | 0 | 7 | 112 | 1242 |
| 2015.06 | 67026 | 66910 | 10130 | 3037 | 53743 | 7 | 0 | 6 | 109 | 1390 |
| 2015.09 | 66647 | 66526 | 10325 | 2998 | 53203 | 7 | 1 | 6 | 114 | 1343 |
| 2015.12 | 63807 | 63630 | 9916 | 2559 | 51155 | 7 | 1 | 7 | 169 | 1072 |
| 2016.03 | 64256 | 64150 | 9619 | 2664 | 51867 | 6 | 1 | 5 | 101 | 844 |
| 2016.06 | 62306 | 62225 | 10336 | 2828 | 49061 | 5 | 0 | 4 | 76 | 916 |
| 2016.09 | 59913 | 59830 | 10549 | 2481 | 46801 | 5 | 1 | 4 | 78 | 829 |
| 2016.12 | 57662 | 57526 | 10124 | 2127 | 45274 | 6 | 1 | 4 | 130 | 984 |
| 2017.03 | 56991 | 56908 | 9716 | 2125 | 45067 | 6 | 2 | 4 | 77 | 851 |
| 2017.06 | 56526 | 56453 | 10190 | 2102 | 44161 | 4 | 1 | 3 | 69 | 935 |
| 2017.09 | 55228 | 55150 | 10153 | 2067 | 42930 | 4 | 1 | 3 | 74 | 850 |
| 2017.12 | 52983 | 52845 | 9570 | 1870 | 41405 | 5 | 1 | 4 | 133 | 886 |
| 2018.03 | 53375 | 53296 | 9020 | 1867 | 42409 | 1 | 1 | 0 | 78 | 778 |
| 2018.06 | 51972 | 51903 | 9162 | 1820 | 40921 | 1 | 1 | 0 | 69 | 770 |
| 2018.09 | 50183 | 50114 | 8948 | 1789 | 39377 | 0 | 0 | 0 | 69 | 743 |
| 2018.12 | 46535 | 46408 | 7839 | 1497 | 37072 | 0 | 0 | 0 | 127 | 771 |
| 2019.03 | 46880 | 46799 | 7664 | 1505 | 37630 | 0 | 0 | 0 | 80 | 654 |
| 2019.06 | 45976 | 45904 | 7653 | 1479 | 36772 | 0 | 0 | 0 | 71 | 558 |
| 2019.09 | 44995 | 44925 | 7397 | 1454 | 36074 | 0 | 0 | 0 | 70 | 502 |
| 2019.12 | 42228 | 42107 | 6354 | 1271 | 34482 | 1 | 1 | 0 | 121 | 553 |

## 2.13 2 农村信用社资产负债表（负债）
## Balance Sheet of Rural Credit Cooperatives (Liabilities)

单位：亿元
Unit: 100 Million Yuan

| 时间<br>Time | 对其他存款性<br>公司负债*<br>Liabilities to<br>Other Depository<br>Corporations* | 对其他金融性<br>公司负债*<br>Liabilities to<br>Other Financial<br>Corporations* | 计入广义<br>货币的存款<br>Deposits Included<br>in Broad Money | 国外负债<br>Foreign<br>Liabilities | 债券发行<br>Bonds<br>Issue | 实收资本<br>Paid-in<br>Capital | 其他负债<br>Other<br>Liabilities | 总负债<br>Total<br>Liabilities |
|---|---|---|---|---|---|---|---|---|
| 2012 | 3492.2 | 462.8 | 56.9 | 0.0 | 0.0 | 2428.4 | 6341.7 | 73848.1 |
| 2013 | 3936 | 459 | 90 | 0 | 0 | 2570 | 7133 | 80752 |
| 2014.03 | 6915 | 345 | 60 | 0 | 0 | 2524 | 7385 | 87074 |
| 2014.06 | 7415 | 334 | 62 | 0 | 0 | 2550 | 7654 | 88285 |
| 2014.09 | 7829 | 356 | 71 | 0 | 0 | 2524 | 7995 | 87889 |
| 2014.12 | 6698 | 561 | 75 | 0 | 1 | 2647 | 8674 | 86677 |
| 2015.03 | 8991 | 418 | 103 | 0 | 1 | 2518 | 8873 | 90267 |
| 2015.06 | 9725 | 691 | 126 | 0 | 16 | 2529 | 8750 | 90128 |
| 2015.09 | 9800 | 395 | 148 | 0 | 57 | 2535 | 9489 | 90266 |
| 2015.12 | 7909 | 508 | 127 | 0 | 18 | 2566 | 10066 | 85946 |
| 2016.03 | 10928 | 450 | 177 | 0 | 40 | 2373 | 8960 | 87853 |
| 2016.06 | 10452 | 575 | 232 | 0 | 38 | 2225 | 9127 | 85640 |
| 2016.09 | 9886 | 446 | 217 | 0 | 60 | 2129 | 9218 | 82481 |
| 2016.12 | 8609 | 436 | 147 | 0 | 72 | 2146 | 9840 | 79750 |
| 2017.03 | 9085 | 222 | 148 | 0 | 22 | 1966 | 9172 | 78308 |
| 2017.06 | 8965 | 180 | 132 | 0 | 31 | 1947 | 9424 | 78008 |
| 2017.09 | 8720 | 263 | 134 | 0 | 25 | 1874 | 8719 | 75680 |
| 2017.12 | 8076 | 449 | 116 | 0 | 32 | 1856 | 8735 | 73017 |
| 2018.03 | 8394 | 339 | 118 | 0 | 34 | 1781 | 8296 | 72997 |
| 2018.06 | 7928 | 144 | 124 | 0 | 23 | 1762 | 8569 | 71168 |
| 2018.09 | 7778 | 64 | 102 | 0 | 58 | 1692 | 8698 | 69317 |
| 2018.12 | 7165 | 170 | 88 | 0 | 10 | 1585 | 8392 | 64629 |
| 2019.03 | 7992 | 135 | 114 | 1 | 16 | 1510 | 8410 | 65598 |
| 2019.06 | 7959 | 238 | 124 | 1 | 8 | 1476 | 8563 | 64781 |
| 2019.09 | 8222 | 158 | 103 | 1 | 1 | 1408 | 8890 | 64177 |
| 2019.12 | 7277 | 318 | 112 | 1 | 1 | 1416 | 7963 | 59756 |

* 见第 49 页脚注。
* See footnote on page 49.

## 2.14 1 财务公司资产负债表（资产）
## Balance Sheet of Finance Companies (Assets)

单位：亿元
Unit: 100 Million Yuan

| 时间<br>Time | 国外资产<br>Foreign Assets | 储备资产<br>Reserve Assets | | | 对政府<br>债权<br>Claims on<br>Government | 对中央银行<br>债权<br>Claims on<br>Central Bank |
|---|---|---|---|---|---|---|
| | | | 准备金存款<br>Deposits with<br>Central Bank | 库存现金<br>Cash in Vault | | |
| 2012 | 98.9 | 2222.6 | 2222.6 | 0.0 | 103.7 | 1.0 |
| 2013 | 116 | 2640 | 2640 | 0 | 56 | 1 |
| 2014.03 | 124 | 2665 | 2665 | 0 | 56 | 1 |
| 2014.06 | 137 | 2811 | 2810 | 0 | 55 | 0 |
| 2014.09 | 98 | 2967 | 2967 | 0 | 51 | 0 |
| 2014.12 | 152 | 3015 | 3015 | 0 | 55 | 0 |
| 2015.03 | 137 | 2913 | 2913 | 0 | 57 | 0 |
| 2015.06 | 144 | 2115 | 2115 | 0 | 62 | 0 |
| 2015.09 | 188 | 1982 | 1982 | 0 | 76 | 0 |
| 2015.12 | 189 | 2174 | 2174 | 0 | 67 | 0 |
| 2016.03 | 250 | 1953 | 1953 | 0 | 61 | 0 |
| 2016.06 | 282 | 2060 | 2060 | 0 | 77 | 1 |
| 2016.09 | 270 | 2305 | 2305 | 0 | 70 | 70 |
| 2016.12 | 265 | 3039 | 3039 | 0 | 64 | 0 |
| 2017.03 | 264 | 2512 | 2512 | 0 | 68 | 0 |
| 2017.06 | 255 | 2535 | 2535 | 0 | 56 | 0 |
| 2017.09 | 227 | 2722 | 2722 | 0 | 56 | 0 |
| 2017.12 | 282 | 3486 | 3486 | 0 | 58 | 0 |
| 2018.03 | 206 | 2800 | 2800 | 0 | 59 | 0 |
| 2018.06 | 219 | 3040 | 3040 | 1 | 60 | 0 |
| 2018.09 | 225 | 3399 | 3399 | 0 | 69 | 0 |
| 2018.12 | 222 | 3577 | 3577 | 0 | 65 | 0 |
| 2019.03 | 191 | 2714 | 2714 | 0 | 72 | 0 |
| 2019.06 | 203 | 2744 | 2744 | 0 | 93 | 0 |
| 2019.09 | 215 | 3001 | 3000 | 1 | 88 | 0 |
| 2019.12 | 192 | 3485 | 3485 | 0 | 142 | 0 |

注：自 2008 年起，本表项目中原"央行债券"更名为"对中央银行债权"。
Note: Since 2008, the item of "Central Bank Bonds" has been renamed as "Claims on Central Bank".

## 2.14 1 财务公司资产负债表（资产）
## Balance Sheet of Finance Companies (Assets)

单位：亿元
Unit: 100 Million Yuan

| 时间<br>Time | 对其他存款性<br>公司债权 *<br>Claims on Other<br>Depository<br>Corporations* | 对其他金融性<br>公司债权 *<br>Claims on Other<br>Financial<br>Corporations* | 对非金融性<br>公司债权<br>Claims on<br>Non-financial<br>Corporations | 对其他居民<br>部门债权<br>Claims on<br>Other Resident<br>Sectors | 其他资产<br>Other Assets | 总资产<br>Total Assets |
|---|---|---|---|---|---|---|
| 2012 | 6837.6 | 511.2 | 9747.8 | 240.7 | 244.5 | 20008.0 |
| 2013 | 8890 | 518 | 11256 | 354 | 183 | 24014 |
| 2014.03 | 7519 | 692 | 11588 | 387 | 222 | 23254 |
| 2014.06 | 8026 | 943 | 12078 | 409 | 216 | 24675 |
| 2014.09 | 9557 | 1027 | 12244 | 430 | 218 | 26594 |
| 2014.12 | 12141 | 968 | 13114 | 465 | 239 | 30149 |
| 2015.03 | 9667 | 1383 | 13165 | 499 | 272 | 28092 |
| 2015.06 | 11736 | 1760 | 13825 | 523 | 292 | 30457 |
| 2015.09 | 12965 | 2348 | 14203 | 571 | 288 | 32622 |
| 2015.12 | 17973 | 2343 | 15393 | 684 | 339 | 39161 |
| 2016.03 | 13905 | 2537 | 16386 | 755 | 310 | 36158 |
| 2016.06 | 14772 | 2439 | 17529 | 818 | 298 | 38275 |
| 2016.09 | 15548 | 2971 | 17896 | 918 | 265 | 40243 |
| 2016.12 | 19733 | 2584 | 18947 | 1059 | 291 | 45982 |
| 2017.03 | 15357 | 2808 | 19894 | 1040 | 315 | 42258 |
| 2017.06 | 15401 | 3133 | 21297 | 1056 | 308 | 44039 |
| 2017.09 | 16894 | 3846 | 22064 | 1120 | 316 | 47246 |
| 2017.12 | 23390 | 3748 | 23195 | 1239 | 356 | 55755 |
| 2018.03 | 17504 | 3173 | 24431 | 1283 | 369 | 49824 |
| 2018.06 | 18698 | 3886 | 25149 | 1306 | 393 | 52751 |
| 2018.09 | 20907 | 4815 | 25808 | 1369 | 434 | 57026 |
| 2018.12 | 25376 | 3666 | 27334 | 1468 | 468 | 62177 |
| 2019.03 | 19563 | 4054 | 27663 | 1487 | 498 | 56242 |
| 2019.06 | 21634 | 3693 | 29006 | 1461 | 503 | 59337 |
| 2019.09 | 21310 | 4020 | 29877 | 1375 | 522 | 60407 |
| 2019.12 | 28289 | 3777 | 31670 | 1350 | 563 | 69467 |

* 自 2005 年起，本表采用其他存款性公司和其他金融性公司分类，其机构范围详见第 94 页 [ 注 1]。2005 年之前，存款货币银行和特定存款机构加总的数据可以替代其他存款性公司数据，其他金融机构的数据可以替代其他金融性公司数据。

* For this sheet, new classification has been adopted since 2005. Please refer to the mote 1 on page 94 for the particular institution coverage of other depository corporations and other financial corporations. To keep comparability, the data of other depository corporations before 2005 could be approximately substituted by the aggregation of deposit money banks and specific monetary institutions. Similarly, data of other financial corporations could be substituted by data of other financial institutions before 2005.

2.14 2 财务公司资产负债表（负债）
Balance Sheet of Finance Companies (Liabilities)

单位：亿元
Unit: 100 Million Yuan

| 时间<br>Time | 对非金融机构及住户负债<br>Liabilities to Non-financial Institutions & Households | 纳入广义货币的存款<br>Deposits Included in Broad Money | 企业活期存款<br>Demand Deposits of Enterprises | 企业定期存款<br>Time Deposits of Enterprises | 居民储蓄存款<br>Household Savings Deposits | 不纳入广义货币的存款<br>Deposits Excluded from Broad Money | 可转让存款<br>Transferable Deposits | 其他存款<br>Other Deposits | 其他负债<br>Other Liabilities | 对中央银行负债<br>Liabilities to Central Bank |
|---|---|---|---|---|---|---|---|---|---|---|
| 2012 | 15451.0 | 15141.0 | 7726.1 | 7414.6 | 0.2 | 302.6 | 236.1 | 66.5 | 7.5 | 97.2 |
| 2013 | 18861 | 18543 | 9519 | 9024 | 0 | 309 | 250 | 59 | 9 | 116 |
| 2014.03 | 17831 | 17528 | 8059 | 9463 | 6 | 295 | 228 | 68 | 8 | 111 |
| 2014.06 | 19034 | 18698 | 9069 | 9623 | 6 | 329 | 226 | 102 | 8 | 112 |
| 2014.09 | 20905 | 20576 | 9912 | 10658 | 5 | 322 | 196 | 125 | 8 | 106 |
| 2014.12 | 23943 | 23486 | 12739 | 10743 | 5 | 446 | 322 | 125 | 11 | 113 |
| 2015.03 | 21364 | 20741 | 9755 | 10983 | 4 | 613 | 475 | 137 | 9 | 123 |
| 2015.06 | 23648 | 23147 | 11970 | 11174 | 3 | 492 | 330 | 162 | 9 | 110 |
| 2015.09 | 25909 | 25319 | 12356 | 12961 | 2 | 581 | 364 | 217 | 9 | 110 |
| 2015.12 | 31549 | 30872 | 17150 | 13720 | 2 | 667 | 489 | 178 | 11 | 125 |
| 2016.03 | 28440 | 27798 | 13876 | 13920 | 2 | 633 | 451 | 182 | 9 | 118 |
| 2016.06 | 30266 | 29579 | 14851 | 14726 | 2 | 679 | 439 | 240 | 9 | 124 |
| 2016.09 | 32132 | 31278 | 15006 | 16269 | 2 | 847 | 528 | 319 | 8 | 143 |
| 2016.12 | 37338 | 36203 | 19687 | 16514 | 2 | 1124 | 865 | 259 | 11 | 186 |
| 2017.03 | 33082 | 32111 | 15309 | 16799 | 3 | 962 | 682 | 279 | 9 | 158 |
| 2017.06 | 34184 | 33179 | 16572 | 16603 | 4 | 984 | 713 | 271 | 21 | 182 |
| 2017.09 | 37391 | 36370 | 17604 | 18762 | 4 | 988 | 680 | 308 | 33 | 176 |
| 2017.12 | 45515 | 44086 | 23909 | 20172 | 5 | 1416 | 992 | 424 | 14 | 205 |
| 2018.03 | 39022 | 37979 | 17102 | 20872 | 5 | 1030 | 643 | 387 | 13 | 173 |
| 2018.06 | 41590 | 40611 | 19261 | 21344 | 6 | 952 | 608 | 344 | 27 | 175 |
| 2018.09 | 45695 | 44717 | 20866 | 23843 | 7 | 950 | 535 | 415 | 29 | 195 |
| 2018.12 | 50446 | 49222 | 27699 | 21516 | 7 | 1205 | 760 | 446 | 18 | 302 |
| 2019.03 | 43598 | 42661 | 21135 | 21519 | 7 | 920 | 544 | 376 | 17 | 264 |
| 2019.06 | 46118 | 45189 | 23477 | 21704 | 8 | 912 | 558 | 354 | 17 | 247 |
| 2019.09 | 47594 | 46662 | 22649 | 24006 | 8 | 916 | 495 | 420 | 16 | 209 |
| 2019.12 | 56233 | 54881 | 31964 | 22908 | 8 | 1335 | 901 | 434 | 17 | 235 |

## 2.14 2 财务公司资产负债表（负债）
## Balance Sheet of Finance Companies (Liabilities)

单位：亿元
Unit: 100 Million Yuan

| 时间<br>Time | 对其他存款性<br>公司负债 *<br>Liabilities to<br>Other Depository<br>Corporations* | 对其他金融性<br>公司负债 *<br>Liabilities to<br>Other Financial<br>Corporations* | 计入广义<br>货币的存款<br>Deposits Included<br>in Broad Money | 国外负债<br>Foreign<br>Liabilities | 债券发行<br>Bonds<br>Issue | 实收资本<br>Paid-in<br>Capital | 其他负债<br>Other<br>Liabilities | 总负债<br>Total<br>Liabilities |
|---|---|---|---|---|---|---|---|---|
| 2012 | 809.1 | 65.2 | 55.5 | 0.0 | 152.8 | 1891.1 | 1541.6 | 20008.0 |
| 2013 | 556 | 59 | 47 | 0 | 161 | 2447 | 1813 | 24014 |
| 2014.03 | 558 | 71 | 57 | 0 | 161 | 2549 | 1972 | 23254 |
| 2014.06 | 635 | 56 | 51 | 0 | 163 | 2656 | 2018 | 24675 |
| 2014.09 | 509 | 40 | 35 | 0 | 110 | 2754 | 2168 | 26594 |
| 2014.12 | 617 | 64 | 36 | 8 | 189 | 2878 | 2337 | 30149 |
| 2015.03 | 683 | 98 | 63 | 15 | 189 | 3004 | 2617 | 28092 |
| 2015.06 | 585 | 117 | 84 | 35 | 190 | 3097 | 2675 | 30457 |
| 2015.09 | 339 | 148 | 113 | 33 | 190 | 3284 | 2608 | 32622 |
| 2015.12 | 647 | 200 | 105 | 31 | 191 | 3604 | 2814 | 39161 |
| 2016.03 | 587 | 132 | 102 | 26 | 191 | 3733 | 2930 | 36158 |
| 2016.06 | 732 | 139 | 96 | 19 | 190 | 3798 | 3007 | 38275 |
| 2016.09 | 530 | 136 | 100 | 16 | 186 | 3996 | 3104 | 40243 |
| 2016.12 | 525 | 144 | 110 | 14 | 206 | 4299 | 3270 | 45982 |
| 2017.03 | 634 | 178 | 139 | 10 | 226 | 4530 | 3438 | 42258 |
| 2017.06 | 893 | 371 | 160 | 6 | 197 | 4716 | 3491 | 44039 |
| 2017.09 | 569 | 319 | 174 | 6 | 192 | 4907 | 3686 | 47246 |
| 2017.12 | 655 | 253 | 151 | 9 | 95 | 5129 | 3893 | 55755 |
| 2018.03 | 832 | 271 | 176 | 10 | 86 | 5217 | 4213 | 49824 |
| 2018.06 | 939 | 267 | 171 | 24 | 79 | 5368 | 4309 | 52751 |
| 2018.09 | 809 | 305 | 215 | 23 | 78 | 5472 | 4448 | 57026 |
| 2018.12 | 755 | 264 | 148 | 25 | 77 | 5615 | 4694 | 62177 |
| 2019.03 | 1119 | 342 | 166 | 18 | 77 | 5677 | 5147 | 56242 |
| 2019.06 | 1144 | 436 | 179 | 12 | 60 | 5816 | 5505 | 59337 |
| 2019.09 | 889 | 348 | 190 | 7 | 60 | 5901 | 5401 | 60407 |
| 2019.12 | 808 | 389 | 265 | 8 | 10 | 6122 | 5662 | 69467 |

* 见第 53 页脚注。
* See footnote on page 53.

3.1 ■ 金融统计数据报告

# 2019 年金融统计数据报告

## 一、2019 年社会融资规模增量为 25.58 万亿元

初步统计，2019 年社会融资规模增量累计为 25.58 万亿元，比上年多 3.08 万亿元（社会融资规模统计口径有所完善，详见脚注 2）。其中，对实体经济发放的人民币贷款增加 16.88 万亿元，同比多增 1.21 万亿元；对实体经济发放的外币贷款折合人民币减少 1275 亿元，同比少减 2926 亿元；委托贷款减少 9396 亿元，同比少减 6666 亿元；信托贷款减少 3467 亿元，同比少减 3508 亿元；未贴现的银行承兑汇票减少 4757 亿元，同比少减 1586 亿元；企业债券净融资 3.24 万亿元，同比多 6098 亿元；政府债券净融资 4.72 万亿元，同比少 1327 亿元；非金融企业境内股票融资 3479 亿元，同比少 127 亿元。12 月，社会融资规模增量为 2.1 万亿元，比上年同期多 1719 亿元。

从结构看，2019 年对实体经济发放的人民币贷款占同期社会融资规模的 66%，同比低 3.7 个百分点；对实体经济发放的外币贷款折合人民币占比为 –0.5%，同比高 1.4 个百分点；委托贷款占比为 –3.7%，同比高 3.4 个百分点；信托贷款占比为 –1.4%，同比高 1.7 个百分点；未贴现的银行承兑汇票占比为 –1.9%，同比高 0.9 个百分点；企业债券占比为 12.7%，同比高 1 个百分点；政府债券占比为 18.5%，同比低 3.1 个百分点；非金融企业境内股票融资占比为 1.4%，同比低 0.2 个百分点。

## 二、广义货币增长 8.7%，狭义货币增长 4.4%

12 月末，广义货币（M2）余额为 198.65 万亿元，同比增长 8.7%，增速分别比上月末和上年同期高 0.5 个和 0.6 个百分点；狭义货币（M1）余额为 57.6 万亿元，同比增长 4.4%，增速分别比上月末和上年同期高 0.9 个和 2.9 个百分点；流通中货币（M0）余额为 7.72 万亿元，同比增长 5.4%。全年净投放现金 3981 亿元。

## 三、全年人民币贷款增加 16.81 万亿元，外币贷款减少 79 亿美元

12 月末，本外币贷款余额为 158.6 万亿元，同比增长 11.9%。12 月末，人民币贷款余额为 153.11 万亿元，同比增长 12.3%，增速分别比上月末和上年同期低 0.1 个和 1.2 个百分点。

全年人民币贷款增加 16.81 万亿元，同比多增 6439 亿元。分部门看，住户部门贷款增加 7.43 万亿元，其中，短期贷款增加 1.98 万亿元，中长期贷款增加 5.45 万亿元；非金融企业及机关团体贷款增加 9.45 万亿元，其中，短期贷款增加 1.52 万亿元，中长期贷款增加 5.88 万亿元，票据融资增加 1.84 万亿元；非银行业金融机构贷款减少 933 亿元。12 月，人民币贷款增加 1.14 万亿元，同比多增 543 亿元。

12 月末，外币贷款余额为 7869 亿美元，同比下降 1%。全年外币贷款减少 79 亿美元，同比少减 352 亿美元。12 月，外币贷款减少 77 亿美元，同比多减 33 亿美元。

## 四、全年人民币存款增加 15.36 万亿元，外币存款增加 301 亿美元

12 月末，本外币存款余额为 198.16 万亿元，同比增长 8.6%。12 月末，人民币存款余额为 192.88 万亿元，同比增长 8.7%，增速分别比上月末和上年同期高 0.3 个和 0.5 个百分点。

全年人民币存款增加 15.36 万亿元，同比多增 1.96 万亿元。其中，住户存款增加 9.7 万亿元，非金融企业存款增加 3.29 万亿元，财政性存款增加 301 亿元，非银行业金融机构存款增加 1.15 万亿元。12 月，人民币存款增加 5995 亿元，同比多增 5079 亿元。

12 月末，外币存款余额为 7577 亿美元，同比增长 4.1%。全年外币存款增加 301 亿美元，同比多增 935 亿美元。12 月，外币存款增加 78 亿美元，同比多增 117 亿美元。

## 五、12 月银行间人民币市场同业拆借月加权平均利率为 2.09%，质押式债券回购月加权平均利率为 2.1%

2019 年，银行间人民币市场以拆借、现券和回购方式合计成交 1185.01 万亿元，日均成交 4.74 万亿元，日均成交同比增长 17.9%。其中，同业拆借日均成交同比增长 9.7%，现券日均成交同比增长 42.9%，质押式回购日均成交同比增长 15.2%。

12 月，同业拆借加权平均利率为 2.09%，分别比上月和上年同期低 0.2 个和 0.48 个百分点；质押式回购加权平均利率为 2.1%，分别比上月和上年同期低 0.19 个和 0.58 个百分点。

## 六、国家外汇储备余额为 3.11 万亿美元

12 月末，国家外汇储备余额为 3.11 万亿美元。12 月末，人民币汇率为 1 美元兑 6.9762 元人民币。

## 七、2019 年跨境贸易人民币结算业务发生 6.04 万亿元，直接投资人民币结算业务发生 2.78 万亿元

2019 年，以人民币进行结算的跨境货物贸易、服务贸易及其他经常项目、对外直接投资、外商直接投资分别发生 4.25 万亿元、1.79 万亿元、0.76 万亿元、2.02 万亿元。

注 1：社会融资规模增量是指一定时期内实体经济从金融体系获得的资金额。数据来源于中国人民银行、中国银行保险监督管理委员会、中国证券监督管理委员会、中央国债登记结算有限责任公司、中国银行间市场交易商协会等部门。

注 2：自 2019 年 12 月起，中国人民银行进一步完善社会融资规模统计，将"国债"和"地方政府一般债券"纳入社会融资规模统计，与原有"地方政府专项债券"合并为"政府债券"指标。指标数值为托管机构的托管面值。

注 3：自 2019 年 9 月起，中国人民银行完善"社会融资规模"中的"企业债券"统计，将"交易所企业资产支持证券"纳入"企业债券"指标；自 2018 年 9 月起，中国人民银行将"地方政府专项债券"纳入社会融资规模统计；自 2018 年 7 月起，中国人民银行完善社会融资规模统计方法，将"存款类金融机构资产支持证券"和"贷款核销"纳入社会融资规模统计，在"其他融资"项下单独列示。

注 4：文内同比数据为可比口径。

3.1 ■ Financial Statistics Data Report

# Report on Financial Statistics of 2019

**1. China's aggregate financing to the real economy (AFRE, flow) amounted to 25.58 trillion yuan in 2019**

According to preliminary statistics, AFRE (flow) reached 25.58 trillion yuan in 2019, up 3.08 trillion yuan from the previous year ( The statistics of AFRE was further adjusted since this month. Please refer to note 2 for detailed information). In particular, new RMB loans to the real economy increased by 16.88 trillion yuan, up 1.21 trillion yuan year on year; new foreign currency-denominated loans to the real economy decreased by 127.5 billion yuan, up 292.6 billion yuan year on year; new entrusted loans decreased by 939.6 billion yuan, up 666.6 billion yuan year on year; new trust loans decreased by 346.7 billion yuan, up 350.8 billion yuan year on year; undiscounted banker's acceptances decreased by 475.7 billion yuan, up 158.6 billion yuan year on year; net bond financing of enterprises rose 3.24 trillion yuan, up 609.8 billion yuan year on year; net financing of government bonds rose 4.72 trillion yuan, down 132.7 billion yuan year on year; financing by domestic non-financial companies via the domestic stock market was 347.9 billion yuan, down 12.7 billion yuan year on year. AFRE amounted to 2.1 trillion yuan in December, up 171.9 billion yuan compared with the same period of previous year.

From a structural point of view, in 2019, new RMB loans to the real economy accounted for 66 percent in the AFRE(flow), down 3.7 percentage points year on year; new foreign currency-denominated loans to the real economy accounted for minus 0.5 percent, up 1.4 percentage points year on year; new entrusted loans accounted for minus 3.7 percent, up 3.4 percentage points year on year; new trust loans accounted for minus 1.4 percent, up 1.7 percentage points year on year; new undiscounted banker's acceptances accounted for minus 1.9 percent, up 0.9 percentage point year on year; net bond financing of enterprises accounted for 12.7 percent, up 1 percentage point year on year; net financing of government bonds accounted for 18.5 percent, down 3.1 percentage points year on year; financing by domestic non-financial companies via the domestic stock market accounted for 1.4 percent, down 0.2 percentage point year on year.

**2. Broad money (M2) and narrow money (M1) rose by 8.7 percent and 4.4 percent respectively**

At end-2019, broad money (M2) stood at 198.65 trillion yuan, increased by 8.7 percent year on year, up 0.5 percentage point a month earlier and 0.6 percentage point year on year. Narrow money (M1) registered 57.6 trillion yuan, increased by 4.4 percent year on year, up 0.9 percentage point a month earlier and 2.9 percentage points year on year. Currency in circulation (M0) was 7.72 trillion yuan, increased by 5.4 percent year on year. The whole year of 2019 saw a net money injection of 398.1 billion yuan.

**3. RMB loans increased by 16.81 trillion yuan and foreign currency loans decreased by US$7.9 billion in 2019**

At end-2019, outstanding RMB and foreign currency loans registered 158.6 trillion yuan, increased by 11.9 percent year on year. Outstanding RMB loans grew by 12.3 percent year on year to 153.11 trillion yuan, down 0.1 percentage point a month earlier and 1.2 percentage points year on year.

RMB loans increased by 16.81 trillion yuan in 2019, up 643.9 billion yuan year on year. By sector, household loans increased by 7.43 trillion yuan, with short-term loans increased by 1.98 trillion yuan and medium - and long-term loans increased by 5.45 trillion yuan; loans to non-financial enterprises and other sectors increased by 9.45 trillion yuan, with short-term loans increased by 1.52 trillion yuan, medium-and long-term loans

increased by 5.88 trillion yuan, and bill financing increased by 1.84 trillion yuan; loans to non-banking financial institutions decreased by 93.3 billion yuan. For the month of December, RMB loans saw an increase of 1.14 trillion yuan, up 54.3 billion yuan year on year.

At end-2019 outstanding foreign currency loans registered US$786.9 billion, down 1 percent year on year. Foreign currency loans decreased by US$ 7.9 billion in 2019, up US$ 35.2 billion year on year and decreased by US$ 7.7 billion in December, up US$ 3.3 billion year on year.

**4. RMB deposits increased by 15.36 trillion yuan and foreign currency deposits increased by US$30.1 billion in 2019**

At end-2019, the outstanding amount of RMB and foreign currency deposits registered 198.16 trillion yuan, increased by 8.6 percent year on year. RMB deposits registered 192.88 trillion yuan, increased by 8.7 percent year on year, up 0.3 percentage point a month earlier and 0.5 percentage point year on year.

RMB deposits expanded by 15.36 trillion yuan in 2019, up 1.96 trillion yuan year on year. By sector, household deposits increased by 9.7 trillion yuan; deposits of non-financial enterprises increased by 3.29 trillion yuan; fiscal deposits increased by 30.1 billion yuan; deposits of non-banking financial institutions increased by 1.15 trillion yuan. For the month of December, RMB deposits saw an increase of 599.5 billion yuan, up 507.9 billion yuan year on year.

At end-2019, the outstanding amount of foreign currency deposits was US$757.7 billion, up 4.1 percent year on year. Foreign currency deposits increased by US$ 30.1 billion in 2019, up US$ 93.5 billion year on year and increased by US$ 7.8 billion in December, up US$ 11.7 billion year on year.

**5. The monthly weighted average interbank lending rate for December stood at 2.09 percent and the monthly weighted average interest rate on bond pledged repo stood at 2.1 percent**

In 2019, lending, spot trading and bond repo transactions in the interbank RMB market totaled 1185.01 trillion yuan. The average daily turnover was 4.74 trillion yuan, up 17.9 percent year on year. In particular, the average daily turnover of interbank lending, spot trading, and bond pledged repo increased by 9.7 percent, 42.9 percent and 15.2 percent year on year, respectively.

The monthly weighted average interbank lending rate for December stood at 2.09 percent, down 0.2 percentage point from the previous month and 0.48 percentage point year on year. The monthly weighted average interest rate on bond pledged repo registered 2.1 percent, down 0.19 percentage point from the previous month and 0.58 percentage point year on year.

**6. Official foreign exchange reserves stood at US$3.11 trillion**

At end-2019, China's foreign exchange reserves stood at US$3.11 trillion and the RMB exchange rate was 6.9762 yuan per US dollar.

**7. RMB cross-border trade settlement and RMB settlement of direct investment reached 6.04 trillion yuan and 2.78 trillion yuan respectively in 2019**

In 2019, RMB settlement in cross-border trade in goods, cross-border trade in services and other current accounts, outward FDI and inward FDI amounted to 4.25 trillion yuan, 1.79 trillion yuan, 0.76 trillion yuan and 2.02 trillion yuan respectively.

Note 1: AFRE (flow) refers to the total volume of financing provided by the financial system to the real economy during a certain period of time. In the calculation of AFRE, data are from the PBC, CBIRC, CSRC, CCDC and NAFMII.

Note 2: Since December 2019, the People's Bank of China has made further efforts to improve the statistical method of AFRE. "Treasury Bonds" and "Local Government General Bonds" have been newly introduced into AFRE and have merged with "Local Government Special Bonds" into "Government Bonds", which is recorded at face value at depositories.

Note 3: Since September 2019, the People's Bank of China has improved the statistics of "Net Financing of Corporate Bonds" in AFRE, and has incorporated "Asset-backed Securities of Non-Financial Enterprises" into "Net Financing of Corporate Bonds". Since September 2018, the People's Bank of China has incorporated "Local Government Special Bonds" into AFRE. Since July 2018, the People's Bank of China has improved the statistical method of AFRE, and has incorporated "Asset-backed Securities of Depository Financial Institutions" and "Loans Written off" into AFRE, which is reflected as a sub-item of "Other Financing".

Note 4: The year on year data are calculated on a comparative basis.

3.2 ■ 景气状况分析：2019 年四季度
Business Climate Analysis: 2019 Q4

# 工业企业生产经营指标总体回升
## Overall Business Indicators Went Up

第 114 次企业家问卷调查[1]统计显示，2019 年四季度，工业企业主要生产经营指标比上季总体回升；企业一线员工人数及工资水平均比上年有所下降。企业融资感受指数回升，成本指数持续下降。

企业景气指数[*][2]为 55.5%，比上季度上升 2.2 个百分点（见企业景气指数趋势图）。

调查的27个行业中，企业景气指数高于全国平均水平的有14个行业，分别为：（1）仪器仪表业；（2）医药制造业；（3）食饮烟业；（4）非金属矿物品业；（5）石油加工炼焦业；（6）金属矿采选业；（7）石油和天然气开采业；（8）塑料制品业；（9）电气热业；（10）其他工业；（11）有色金属冶炼及压延加工业；（12）煤炭采选业；（13）皮革毛皮羽绒业；（14）黑色金属冶炼及压延加工业。

According to the result of the 114th Entrepreneurs Questionnaire Survey, in 2019 Q4, several key indices for production and business conditions increased, employment and wage level fell. Corporate financing sentiment index rebounded, and financing cost index declined continuously.

The Climate Index of Enterprises[*][2] decreased to 55.5%, up by 2.2 percentage points from the previous quarter (See the tendency chart of enterprises climate index).

The climate indices of 14 industries out of 27 surveyed industries surpassed the national average, which includes: (1) Instruments and Meters Machinery; (2) Medical and Pharmaceutical Products; (3) Manufacture of Food, Beverage and Tobacco; (4) Nonmetal Mineral Products; (5) Petroleum Processing and Coking Products; (6) Metals Mining and Dressing; (7) Petroleum and Natural Gas Extraction; (8) Plastic Products; (9) Power, Gas and Heat Production and Supply; (10) Other Industries; (11) Smelting and Pressing of Nonferrous Metals; (12) Coal Mining and Dressing; (13) Leather, Furs, Down and Related Products; (14) Smelting and Pressing of Ferrous Metals.

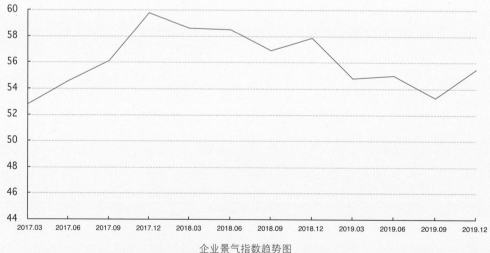

企业景气指数趋势图
The Trend of Climate Index of Enterprises

① 始自1992年的中国人民银行企业家问卷调查系统，截至2019年四季度已连续进行了114次调查。2019年四季度企业家问卷调查，共汇总有效问卷5000余份。

① The PBC Entrepreneurs Questionnaire Survey System started as of 1992 and this is the 114th Entrepreneurs Questionnaire Survey conducted in 2019 Q4. There are more than 5000 effective questionnaires for this quarter.

② 景气指数又称扩散指数（DI），是对景气调查中定性指标的量化描述，用于反映该指标所处的状态，以 % 为单位（百分化以后），其数值为 0 ~ 100。一般而言，指数上升可反映企业经营环境在改善，企业家的信心在增强，指数下降则相反。

② Climate Index or Diffusion Index (DI), is a quantitative indicator for qualitative answers to questions in the questionnaire, which is used to explain the status of the qualitative questions. Measured in percent, the index ranges from 0 to 100. Generally speaking, it shows that business condition is improving and entrepreneurs' confidence turns upward when DI ascends, and vice versa.

* 原称为"企业总体经营指数"，也称为"企业经营景气指数"。

* The former name of the "Climate Index of Enterprises" is the "General Business Condition Index".

3.3 ■ 宏观经济
Macroeconomics

# 2019 年四季度宏观经济运行监测

## China's Macroeconomic Performance in 2019 Q4

2019 年四季度，我国经济运行稳中趋缓。工业生产总体平稳，企业效益下降。投资趋缓，消费增速小幅回落，进出口持续下降，贸易顺差逐渐扩大。物价比较温和，财政收入放缓，支出力度保持平稳。

经济稳中趋缓，宏观经济热度边际回落。2019 年四季度，GDP 同比增长 6.0%，与上季度持平，比上年同期低 0.5 个百分点。企业家宏观经济热度指数为 31.9%，比上季度低 0.5 个百分点，比上年同期低 3.5 个百分点。银行家宏观经济热度指数为 30.7%，比上季度低 3.2 个百分点，比上年同期低 3.7 百分点。

工业生产总体平稳，企业效益下降。2019 年，全国规模以上工业增加值同比增长 5.7%，增速比上年同期低 0.5 个百分点。12 月，全国规模以上工业增加值同比增长 6.9%，增速比上月高 0.7 个百分点。发电量累计同比增长 3.5%，增速比上年同期低 3.3 个百分点。2019 年，全国规模以上工业企业实现利润 61996 亿元，按可比口径同比下降 3.3%，降幅比前三个季度扩大 1.2 个百分点。

固定资产投资趋缓，消费增速小幅回落。2019 年，固定资产投资（不含农户）完成 55.1 万亿元，名义同比增长 5.4%，增速比上年同期低 0.5 个百分点。其中，房地产开发投资 132194 亿元，同比增长 9.9%，增速比上年同期高 0.4 个百分点。2019 年，社会消费品零售总额 411649 亿元，名义同比增长 8.0%，增速比上年同期低 1.0 个百分点；扣除价格因素后，实际增长 6.0%，增速比上年同期低 0.9 个百分点。

进出口增速持续下降，贸易顺差逐渐扩大。2019 年，进出口总额为 4.28 万亿美元，同比下降 1.0%。其中出口 2.50 万亿美元，同比增长 0.5%，比上年同期低 9.5 个百分点；进口 2.08 万亿美元，同比下降 2.7%，比上年同期低 18.5 个百分点；贸易顺差 4219 亿美元，同比扩大 20.2%。

CPI 同比涨幅温和，上游价格涨幅回落。2019 年，CPI 同比上涨 2.9%，比上年同期高 0.8 个百分点。12 月，CPI 同比上涨 4.5%，主要受猪肉和鲜果等食品价格持续上涨影响。2019 年，PPI 同比涨幅为 –0.3%，比上年同期低 3.8 个百分点；12 月，同比涨幅为 –0.5%，比上月高 0.9 个百分点。中国人民银行监测的 CGPI 12 月同比上升 0.5%，比上月高 1.1 个百分点。

财政收入增长放缓，财政支出力度保持平稳。2019 年，全国财政收入 190382 亿元，同比增长 3.8%，增速比上年同期低 2.4 个百分点，其中税收收入 157992 亿元，同比增长 1.0%。全国财政支出 238874 亿元，同比增长 8.1%，增速比上年同期低 0.6 个百分点。2019 年，全国财政收支赤字为 48492 亿元，比上年同期多 10938 亿元。

在当前形势下，应在稳健货币政策的总基调下，综合运用数量型和价格型货币政策工具调控流动性，密切关注经济形势和就业形势的变化，增强货币政策的灵活性和前瞻性，促进国民经济持续健康发展。

In the forth quarter of 2019, economic growth became stable slow. The growth rate of industrial production kept stable, the benefit of enterprise had fallen down. The growth rate of fixed asset investment and consumption both slowed down. Growth in exports and imports continually declined, and the trade surplus expanded. Inflationary pressure was mild. Growth in fiscal revenue slowed down, and growth in fiscal expenditure kept stable.

Economic growth kept stable and macroeconomic activity index marginally declined. 2019 Q4 witnessed a GDP growth of 6.0% on a year-on-year basis, when measured in constant prices, and the same as the previous quarter, and down 0.5 percentage point compared to the corresponding period of last year. The entrepreneur macroeconomic activity index was 31.9% in 2019 Q4, down 0.5 percentage point compared to the previous quarter and down 3.5 percentage points compared to the corresponding period of last year. The banker macroeconomic activity index was 30.7%, down 3.2 percentage points compared to the previous quarter and down 3.7 percentage points compared to the corresponding period of last year.

The growth rate of industrial production kept stable, and profitability of enterprises had fallen down. The value-added of statistically large enterprises grew 5.7% on a year-on-year basis in 2019, down 0.5 percentage point compared to the same period of last year. The value-added of statistically large enterprises grew 6.9% on a year-on-year basis in December 2019, up 0.7 percentage point compared to the previous month. Power generation increased by 3.5% in 2019, down 3.3 percentage points compared to the corresponding period of last year. The profits of statistically large enterprises post 6199.6 billion yuan in 2019, which was registered a year-on-year growth rate of -3.3%, down 1.2 percentage point compared to Q1-Q3.

Growth in fixed asset investment (FAI) kept stable and consumption slowed down. Fixed asset investment (excluding those from rural households) reached 55.1 trillion yuan in 2019, a year-on-year growth of 5.4% in nominal terms, down 0.5 percentage point compared to the corresponding period of last year. Real estate development investment, which is a part of FAI, was 13.2 trillion yuan in 2019, grew 9.9% on year on year, up 0.4 percentage point compared to 2018. Retail sales of consumer goods totaled 41.2 trillion yuan, a year-on-year growth of 8.0% in nominal terms down 1.0 percentage point compared to the corresponding period of last year, and 6.0% in real terms, down 0.9 percentage point compared to the corresponding period of last year.

Growth in exports and imports declined continually, and trade surplus expanded. In 2019, exports and imports posted 4.28 trillion USD, grew by -1.0% year on year. Exports posted 2.50 trillion USD, grew by 0.5% year on year, down 9.5 percentage points compared to the corresponding period of last year. Imports posted 2.08 trillion USD, grew by -2.7% year on year, down 18.5 percentage points compared to the corresponding period of last year. The trade surplus was 421.9 billion USD, expanded by 20.2% year on year.

Year-on-year growth in CPI was mild, and the prices for upstream goods had fallen down. The year-on-year growth rate of CPI was 2.9% in 2019, up 0.8 percentage point compared to the corresponding period of last year. CPI grew by 4.5% on a year-on-year basis in December. PPI grew by -0.3% on a year-on-year basis in 2019, down 3.8 percentage points compared to the corresponding period of last year. PPI grew by -0.5% on a year-on-year basis in December, up 0.9 percentage point compared to last month. The growth rate in CGPI was 0.5% on a year-on-year basis in December, up 1.1 percentage point compared to last month.

Growth in fiscal revenue slowed down, growth in fiscal expenditure kept stable. Fiscal revenue registered 19.0 trillion yuan in 2019, grew by 3.8% on a year-on-year basis, down 2.4 percentage points compared to the corresponding period of last year. Tax revenue, a component of fiscal revenue, posted 15.8 trillion yuan, which grew by 1.0% on a year-on-year basis. Fiscal expenditures registered 23.9 trillion yuan, grew by 8.1% on a year-on-year basis, down 0.6 percentage points compared to the corresponding period of last year. Fiscal deficit was 4849.2 billion yuan in 2019, 1093.8 billion yuan more than the corresponding period of last year.

Against the background, the PBC should continue its sound monetary policy, use appropriate pricing and quantity tools for monetary policy, pay close attention to changes in economy and employment, enhanced flexibility and forward-looking of the monetary policy, in order to realize the sustainable and health development of national economy.

4.1 ■ 全国银行间同业拆借交易统计表
Statistics of Interbank Lending

单位：亿元，%
Unit: 100 Million Yuan，%

| 时间<br>Time | 1 天<br>1-day | | 7 天<br>7-day | | 14 天<br>14-day | |
|---|---|---|---|---|---|---|
| | 交易量<br>Trading<br>Volume | 加权平均利率<br>Weighted<br>Average<br>Interest<br>Rate | 交易量<br>Trading<br>Volume | 加权平均利率<br>Weighted<br>Average<br>Interest<br>Rate | 交易量<br>Trading<br>Volume | 加权平均利率<br>Weighted<br>Average<br>Interest<br>Rate |
| 2012 | 402814 | | 41934 | | 12068 | |
| 2013 | 289636 | | 44024 | | 11579 | |
| 2014 | 294983 | | 61061 | | 11767 | |
| 2015 | 539953 | | 76974 | | 15305 | |
| 2016 | 839763 | | 92765 | | 12771 | |
| | | | | | | |
| 2017.01 | 50192 | 2.22 | 6982 | 2.71 | 1814 | 3.15 |
| 2017.02 | 62629 | 2.38 | 5150 | 2.93 | 904 | 3.30 |
| 2017.03 | 67691 | 2.51 | 6244 | 3.16 | 1026 | 3.53 |
| 2017.04 | 53821 | 2.56 | 4989 | 3.18 | 761 | 3.41 |
| 2017.05 | 47751 | 2.79 | 6267 | 3.24 | 729 | 3.83 |
| 2017.06 | 55703 | 2.85 | 6910 | 3.30 | 661 | 3.92 |
| 2017.07 | 48944 | 2.73 | 6593 | 3.26 | 444 | 3.80 |
| 2017.08 | 54286 | 2.88 | 6633 | 3.41 | 613 | 3.96 |
| 2017.09 | 59760 | 2.78 | 7094 | 3.50 | 1736 | 4.07 |
| 2017.10 | 47104 | 2.71 | 6327 | 3.36 | 416 | 4.02 |
| 2017.11 | 63922 | 2.79 | 7995 | 3.44 | 807 | 3.99 |
| 2017.12 | 68003 | 2.71 | 9337 | 3.46 | 2838 | 4.18 |
| | | | | | | |
| 2018.01 | 93171 | 2.69 | 10728 | 3.17 | 1060 | 3.89 |
| 2018.02 | 73939 | 2.61 | 7741 | 3.26 | 1509 | 3.96 |
| 2018.03 | 103998 | 2.66 | 8921 | 3.39 | 771 | 4.00 |
| 2018.04 | 73557 | 2.67 | 8430 | 3.57 | 487 | 4.05 |
| 2018.05 | 105699 | 2.63 | 8905 | 3.31 | 711 | 3.73 |
| 2018.06 | 87492 | 2.62 | 9190 | 3.51 | 610 | 3.88 |
| 2018.07 | 110556 | 2.39 | 8821 | 3.18 | 563 | 3.00 |
| 2018.08 | 141082 | 2.23 | 8799 | 3.03 | 1116 | 2.76 |
| 2018.09 | 120855 | 2.52 | 7417 | 3.33 | 2704 | 3.19 |
| 2018.10 | 107791 | 2.35 | 7110 | 3.20 | 1021 | 2.71 |
| 2018.11 | 127077 | 2.43 | 8521 | 3.17 | 1265 | 2.73 |
| 2018.12 | 110241 | 2.46 | 8361 | 3.57 | 1062 | 3.54 |
| | | | | | | |
| 2019.01 | 133759 | 2.07 | 8504 | 3.19 | 735 | 2.89 |
| 2019.02 | 103760 | 2.12 | 8277 | 3.03 | 895 | 2.63 |
| 2019.03 | 138424 | 2.35 | 9415 | 3.20 | 1388 | 2.93 |
| 2019.04 | 137262 | 2.35 | 10236 | 3.18 | 1641 | 3.02 |
| 2019.05 | 139085 | 2.17 | 7904 | 3.23 | 917 | 2.70 |
| 2019.06 | 116137 | 1.60 | 6241 | 3.17 | 351 | 2.94 |
| 2019.07 | 129006 | 2.00 | 8527 | 3.08 | 884 | 2.65 |
| 2019.08 | 105474 | 2.60 | 8283 | 3.20 | 768 | 2.85 |
| 2019.09 | 94081 | 2.47 | 8746 | 3.16 | 2328 | 2.97 |
| 2019.10 | 85192 | 2.49 | 8094 | 3.13 | 788 | 2.88 |
| 2019.11 | 101685 | 2.22 | 7359 | 3.05 | 537 | 2.88 |
| 2019.12 | 102337 | 1.98 | 9016 | 3.01 | 667 | 3.21 |

## 4.1 ■ 全国银行间同业拆借交易统计表
## Statistics of Interbank Lending

单位：亿元，%
Unit: 100 Million Yuan，%

| 时间<br>Time | 21 天<br>21-day | | 1 个月<br>1-month | | 2 个月<br>2-month | |
|---|---|---|---|---|---|---|
| | 交易量<br>Trading<br>Volume | 加权平均利率<br>Weighted<br>Average<br>Interest<br>Rate | 交易量<br>Trading<br>Volume | 加权平均利率<br>Weighted<br>Average<br>Interest<br>Rate | 交易量<br>Trading<br>Volume | 加权平均利率<br>Weighted<br>Average<br>Interest<br>Rate |
| 2012 | 2370 | | 4476 | | 1626 | |
| 2013 | 1828 | | 5070 | | 1034 | |
| 2014 | 899 | | 4665 | | 1237 | |
| 2015 | 1372 | | 4243 | | 1006 | |
| 2016 | 2209 | | 4463 | | 2129 | |
| 2017.01 | 588 | 3.81 | 687 | 3.69 | 428 | 4.22 |
| 2017.02 | 194 | 3.68 | 316 | 4.15 | 271 | 4.34 |
| 2017.03 | 140 | 4.20 | 421 | 4.39 | 930 | 4.51 |
| 2017.04 | 63 | 4.03 | 466 | 4.13 | 447 | 4.35 |
| 2017.05 | 38 | 4.20 | 270 | 4.13 | 229 | 4.67 |
| 2017.06 | 64 | 4.50 | 365 | 4.91 | 224 | 5.11 |
| 2017.07 | 69 | 4.13 | 365 | 3.89 | 207 | 4.20 |
| 2017.08 | 46 | 3.93 | 392 | 3.67 | 247 | 4.24 |
| 2017.09 | 219 | 4.18 | 294 | 4.19 | 437 | 4.73 |
| 2017.10 | 22 | 4.25 | 216 | 4.16 | 449 | 4.44 |
| 2017.11 | 580 | 4.10 | 570 | 4.03 | 448 | 4.70 |
| 2017.12 | 1103 | 4.03 | 716 | 4.80 | 747 | 5.22 |
| 2018.01 | 226 | 4.23 | 264 | 4.32 | 347 | 4.78 |
| 2018.02 | 319 | 4.16 | 309 | 4.11 | 445 | 4.43 |
| 2018.03 | 115 | 4.68 | 246 | 4.48 | 296 | 4.75 |
| 2018.04 | 116 | 4.34 | 412 | 3.95 | 289 | 4.18 |
| 2018.05 | 180 | 3.96 | 984 | 3.78 | 349 | 4.21 |
| 2018.06 | 132 | 4.60 | 151 | 4.35 | 179 | 4.84 |
| 2018.07 | 61 | 3.46 | 274 | 3.16 | 249 | 3.46 |
| 2018.08 | 121 | 2.89 | 521 | 2.75 | 289 | 3.00 |
| 2018.09 | 1243 | 2.81 | 381 | 3.40 | 750 | 3.18 |
| 2018.10 | 461 | 2.76 | 564 | 2.90 | 211 | 3.07 |
| 2018.11 | 492 | 2.75 | 408 | 2.88 | 505 | 3.05 |
| 2018.12 | 674 | 3.04 | 524 | 3.46 | 296 | 3.95 |
| 2019.01 | 393 | 3.03 | 381 | 2.95 | 225 | 3.41 |
| 2019.02 | 74 | 2.60 | 311 | 2.76 | 548 | 2.77 |
| 2019.03 | 186 | 2.98 | 674 | 2.97 | 277 | 2.90 |
| 2019.04 | 257 | 2.90 | 395 | 2.91 | 177 | 3.11 |
| 2019.05 | 127 | 2.95 | 228 | 3.01 | 349 | 3.05 |
| 2019.06 | 71 | 3.11 | 320 | 3.31 | 231 | 3.51 |
| 2019.07 | 92 | 2.66 | 504 | 2.75 | 96 | 3.38 |
| 2019.08 | 91 | 2.85 | 192 | 3.26 | 174 | 3.21 |
| 2019.09 | 870 | 3.04 | 488 | 3.23 | 336 | 3.32 |
| 2019.10 | 137 | 2.96 | 393 | 3.17 | 200 | 3.40 |
| 2019.11 | 61 | 2.94 | 285 | 3.39 | 729 | 3.17 |
| 2019.12 | 269 | 3.30 | 390 | 3.30 | 273 | 3.48 |

## 4.1 ■ 全国银行间同业拆借交易统计表
## Statistics of Interbank Lending

单位：亿元，%
Unit: 100 Million Yuan，%

| 时间<br>Time | 3 个月<br>3-month | | 4 个月<br>4-month | | 6 个月<br>6-month | |
|---|---|---|---|---|---|---|
| | 交易量<br>Trading<br>Volume | 加权平均利率<br>Weighted<br>Average<br>Interest<br>Rate | 交易量<br>Trading<br>Volume | 加权平均利率<br>Weighted<br>Average<br>Interest<br>Rate | 交易量<br>Trading<br>Volume | 加权平均利率<br>Weighted<br>Average<br>Interest<br>Rate |
| 2012 | 1170 | | 81 | | 379 | |
| 2013 | 1748 | | 67 | | 119 | |
| 2014 | 1670 | | 60 | | 100 | |
| 2015 | 2445 | | 120 | | 146 | |
| 2016 | 3477 | | 263 | | 510 | |
| 2017.01 | 199 | 4.23 | 34 | 4.26 | 51 | 4.35 |
| 2017.02 | 189 | 4.51 | 203 | 4.47 | 20 | 4.53 |
| 2017.03 | 133 | 4.87 | 18 | 4.64 | 23 | 4.63 |
| 2017.04 | 129 | 4.55 | 11 | 4.62 | 39 | 4.43 |
| 2017.05 | 175 | 4.86 | 11 | 4.70 | 20 | 4.96 |
| 2017.06 | 249 | 5.14 | 24 | 5.09 | 33 | 4.91 |
| 2017.07 | 158 | 4.57 | 11 | 4.46 | 36 | 4.55 |
| 2017.08 | 156 | 4.66 | 32 | 4.47 | 26 | 4.71 |
| 2017.09 | 100 | 4.93 | 4 | 4.89 | 12 | 4.87 |
| 2017.10 | 206 | 4.81 | 58 | 4.57 | 22 | 4.89 |
| 2017.11 | 286 | 5.18 | 24 | 5.12 | 81 | 4.86 |
| 2017.12 | 200 | 5.59 | 46 | 5.31 | 14 | 5.29 |
| 2018.01 | 232 | 5.18 | 90 | 5.03 | 77 | 5.20 |
| 2018.02 | 243 | 4.88 | 82 | 5.05 | 45 | 5.17 |
| 2018.03 | 238 | 5.42 | 32 | 5.10 | 99 | 5.25 |
| 2018.04 | 802 | 4.33 | 145 | 4.24 | 133 | 4.52 |
| 2018.05 | 431 | 4.51 | 12 | 4.73 | 38 | 4.70 |
| 2018.06 | 161 | 5.40 | 20 | 4.84 | 78 | 4.85 |
| 2018.07 | 463 | 3.81 | 71 | 3.61 | 76 | 3.70 |
| 2018.08 | 525 | 3.46 | 32 | 3.47 | 65 | 3.56 |
| 2018.09 | 231 | 4.32 | 12 | 3.79 | 95 | 3.90 |
| 2018.10 | 929 | 3.24 | 571 | 3.10 | 135 | 3.50 |
| 2018.11 | 567 | 3.59 | 59 | 3.38 | 48 | 3.94 |
| 2018.12 | 312 | 4.45 | 88 | 3.76 | 108 | 3.90 |
| 2019.01 | 414 | 3.82 | 140 | 2.94 | 22 | 3.53 |
| 2019.02 | 256 | 3.68 | 161 | 2.95 | 93 | 3.02 |
| 2019.03 | 360 | 4.00 | 63 | 2.97 | 39 | 3.33 |
| 2019.04 | 846 | 3.26 | 113 | 3.18 | 35 | 3.36 |
| 2019.05 | 660 | 3.42 | 17 | 3.19 | 34 | 3.27 |
| 2019.06 | 302 | 3.79 | 29 | 3.44 | 33 | 3.60 |
| 2019.07 | 489 | 3.44 | 16 | 3.33 | 20 | 3.77 |
| 2019.08 | 323 | 3.68 | 21 | 3.43 | 19 | 3.44 |
| 2019.09 | 289 | 3.78 | 18 | 3.63 | 36 | 3.23 |
| 2019.10 | 328 | 3.91 | 46 | 3.40 | 33 | 3.26 |
| 2019.11 | 425 | 3.73 | 21 | 3.82 | 81 | 3.63 |
| 2019.12 | 319 | 4.04 | 18 | 3.59 | 28 | 3.67 |

## 4.1 ■ 全国银行间同业拆借交易统计表
### Statistics of Interbank Lending

单位：亿元，%
Unit: 100 Million Yuan，%

| 时间<br>Time | 9 个月<br>9-month | | 1 年<br>1-year | | 交易量合计 | 加权平均利率 |
|---|---|---|---|---|---|---|
| | 交易量<br>Trading<br>Volume | 加权平均利率<br>Weighted<br>Average<br>Interest<br>Rate | 交易量<br>Trading<br>Volume | 加权平均利率<br>Weighted<br>Average<br>Interest<br>Rate | Trading<br>Volume | Weighted<br>Average<br>Interest<br>Rate |
| 2012 | 29 | | 97 | | 467044 | |
| 2013 | 2 | | 83 | | 355190 | |
| 2014 | 22 | | 163 | | 376626 | |
| 2015 | 17 | | 553 | | 642135 | |
| 2016 | 259 | | 522 | | 959131 | |
| 2017.01 | 1 | 4.25 | 90 | 4.67 | 61066 | 2.36 |
| 2017.02 | 15 | 4.31 | 14 | 4.60 | 69905 | 2.47 |
| 2017.03 | 10 | 4.65 | 25 | 4.64 | 76661 | 2.62 |
| 2017.04 | 11 | 4.67 | 31 | 4.78 | 60767 | 2.65 |
| 2017.05 | 9 | 4.97 | 17 | 4.36 | 55514 | 2.88 |
| 2017.06 | 10 | 5.20 | 42 | 5.26 | 64285 | 2.94 |
| 2017.07 | 14 | 4.81 | 30 | 4.89 | 56871 | 2.82 |
| 2017.08 | 11 | 4.86 | 19 | 4.85 | 62461 | 2.96 |
| 2017.09 | 6 | 5.01 | 15 | 5.34 | 69678 | 2.92 |
| 2017.10 | 3 | 5.01 | 12 | 5.04 | 54835 | 2.82 |
| 2017.11 | 9 | 5.08 | 8 | 4.86 | 74730 | 2.92 |
| 2017.12 | 5 | 5.27 | 28 | 5.32 | 83037 | 2.91 |
| 2018.01 | 18 | 5.23 | 71 | 5.34 | 106283 | 2.78 |
| 2018.02 | 37 | 5.26 | 41 | 5.46 | 84710 | 2.73 |
| 2018.03 | 52 | 5.23 | 56 | 5.45 | 114825 | 2.74 |
| 2018.04 | 33 | 4.85 | 45 | 5.14 | 84450 | 2.81 |
| 2018.05 | 36 | 4.69 | 104 | 4.86 | 117448 | 2.72 |
| 2018.06 | 19 | 4.93 | 82 | 5.18 | 98113 | 2.73 |
| 2018.07 | 6 | 4.13 | 53 | 4.02 | 121193 | 2.47 |
| 2018.08 | 44 | 3.54 | 59 | 3.68 | 152655 | 2.29 |
| 2018.09 | 14 | 4.40 | 33 | 4.43 | 133735 | 2.59 |
| 2018.10 | 13 | 3.77 | 22 | 4.37 | 118827 | 2.42 |
| 2018.11 | 5 | 4.62 | 33 | 4.32 | 138981 | 2.49 |
| 2018.12 | 47 | 3.90 | 53 | 4.25 | 121766 | 2.57 |
| 2019.01 | 8 | 3.45 | 52 | 3.86 | 144633 | 2.15 |
| 2019.02 | 8 | 3.27 | 85 | 3.68 | 114468 | 2.20 |
| 2019.03 | 23 | 3.50 | 50 | 3.67 | 150897 | 2.42 |
| 2019.04 | 15 | 3.68 | 91 | 3.42 | 151069 | 2.43 |
| 2019.05 | 84 | 3.29 | 130 | 3.50 | 149536 | 2.24 |
| 2019.06 | 5 | 3.70 | 15 | 3.72 | 123735 | 1.70 |
| 2019.07 | 11 | 3.57 | 19 | 3.75 | 139664 | 2.08 |
| 2019.08 | 8 | 3.27 | 2 | 4.12 | 115354 | 2.65 |
| 2019.09 | 4 | 3.43 | 17 | 3.80 | 107214 | 2.55 |
| 2019.10 | 5 | 3.31 | 26 | 3.39 | 95241 | 2.56 |
| 2019.11 | 7 | 3.56 | 23 | 4.12 | 111214 | 2.29 |
| 2019.12 | 2 | 4.14 | 28 | 4.15 | 113346 | 2.09 |

4.2 ■ 全国银行间质押式回购交易统计表
Statistics of Interbank Pledged Repo

单位：亿元，%
Unit: 100 Million Yuan，%

| 时间<br>Time | 1 天<br>1-day | | 7 天<br>7-day | | 14 天<br>14-day | |
|---|---|---|---|---|---|---|
| | 交易量<br>Trading<br>Volume | 加权平均利率<br>Weighted<br>Average<br>Interest<br>Rate | 交易量<br>Trading<br>Volume | 加权平均利率<br>Weighted<br>Average<br>Interest<br>Rate | 交易量<br>Trading<br>Volume | 加权平均利率<br>Weighted<br>Average<br>Interest<br>Rate |
| 2012 | 1109323 | | 172165 | | 47390 | |
| 2013 | 1201735 | | 196620 | | 64787 | |
| 2014 | 1669081 | | 300413 | | 96061 | |
| 2015 | 3700895 | | 461541 | | 114361 | |
| 2016 | 4861135 | | 618755 | | 138334 | |
| 2017.01 | 264508 | 2.24 | 42838 | 2.67 | 22797 | 3.33 |
| 2017.02 | 287141 | 2.44 | 50053 | 3.08 | 13838 | 3.59 |
| 2017.03 | 405358 | 2.59 | 59949 | 3.51 | 20181 | 4.47 |
| 2017.04 | 346259 | 2.65 | 48919 | 3.36 | 16365 | 3.78 |
| 2017.05 | 381767 | 2.78 | 59981 | 3.29 | 17262 | 4.03 |
| 2017.06 | 446443 | 2.85 | 73710 | 3.49 | 18930 | 4.40 |
| 2017.07 | 421857 | 2.78 | 74549 | 3.32 | 14810 | 3.99 |
| 2017.08 | 458893 | 2.96 | 77543 | 3.54 | 16813 | 4.18 |
| 2017.09 | 458094 | 2.84 | 61700 | 3.41 | 38821 | 4.60 |
| 2017.10 | 355495 | 2.75 | 59513 | 3.37 | 14355 | 4.21 |
| 2017.11 | 473470 | 2.82 | 77143 | 3.49 | 16378 | 4.37 |
| 2017.12 | 447983 | 2.73 | 77846 | 3.86 | 26009 | 5.35 |
| 2018.01 | 462802 | 2.70 | 81105 | 3.23 | 14793 | 4.16 |
| 2018.02 | 298454 | 2.60 | 57077 | 3.09 | 29302 | 4.07 |
| 2018.03 | 490196 | 2.68 | 79215 | 3.33 | 23288 | 4.59 |
| 2018.04 | 370736 | 2.86 | 81666 | 3.59 | 17505 | 4.68 |
| 2018.05 | 455390 | 2.65 | 78832 | 3.22 | 17147 | 3.79 |
| 2018.06 | 425911 | 2.62 | 86074 | 3.46 | 19327 | 4.66 |
| 2018.07 | 545183 | 2.34 | 69676 | 2.74 | 12928 | 3.01 |
| 2018.08 | 661308 | 2.18 | 67747 | 2.57 | 14228 | 2.80 |
| 2018.09 | 492925 | 2.50 | 51496 | 2.69 | 39666 | 3.42 |
| 2018.10 | 479507 | 2.33 | 59300 | 2.66 | 12548 | 2.84 |
| 2018.11 | 600094 | 2.41 | 79599 | 2.70 | 14573 | 2.79 |
| 2018.12 | 500152 | 2.43 | 68357 | 3.22 | 28860 | 4.69 |
| 2019.01 | 630661 | 2.04 | 58535 | 2.58 | 26319 | 3.04 |
| 2019.02 | 427065 | 2.15 | 56512 | 2.64 | 19196 | 2.70 |
| 2019.03 | 579491 | 2.38 | 70527 | 2.85 | 21149 | 3.18 |
| 2019.04 | 591981 | 2.38 | 72584 | 2.75 | 24665 | 3.07 |
| 2019.05 | 600153 | 2.20 | 61450 | 2.68 | 15821 | 2.83 |
| 2019.06 | 525712 | 1.57 | 56339 | 2.55 | 16911 | 3.01 |
| 2019.07 | 664404 | 2.07 | 66926 | 2.66 | 14222 | 2.80 |
| 2019.08 | 608335 | 2.62 | 71830 | 2.79 | 14229 | 2.88 |
| 2019.09 | 541640 | 2.48 | 56792 | 2.71 | 41189 | 3.06 |
| 2019.10 | 488763 | 2.52 | 72170 | 2.76 | 11740 | 2.95 |
| 2019.11 | 621747 | 2.23 | 63031 | 2.70 | 12578 | 2.75 |
| 2019.12 | 621195 | 1.96 | 78612 | 2.69 | 20246 | 3.02 |

## 4.2 ■ 全国银行间质押式回购交易统计表
## Statistics of Interbank Pledged Repo

单位：亿元，%
Unit: 100 Million Yuan，%

| 时间<br>Time | 21 天<br>21-day | | 1 个月<br>1-month | | 2 个月<br>2-month | |
|---|---|---|---|---|---|---|
| | 交易量<br>Trading<br>Volume | 加权平均利率<br>Weighted<br>Average<br>Interest<br>Rate | 交易量<br>Trading<br>Volume | 加权平均利率<br>Weighted<br>Average<br>Interest<br>Rate | 交易量<br>Trading<br>Volume | 加权平均利率<br>Weighted<br>Average<br>Interest<br>Rate |
| 2012 | 9913 | | 13155 | | 8120 | |
| 2013 | 14263 | | 24745 | | 8264 | |
| 2014 | 16051 | | 22896 | | 6722 | |
| 2015 | 11337 | | 18661 | | 5372 | |
| 2016 | 21404 | | 23673 | | 7801 | |
| 2017.01 | 6743 | 4.36 | 8453 | 4.03 | 3529 | 4.57 |
| 2017.02 | 2048 | 4.10 | 1459 | 4.21 | 2277 | 4.35 |
| 2017.03 | 3740 | 4.71 | 5667 | 4.82 | 2795 | 4.94 |
| 2017.04 | 2040 | 4.22 | 1554 | 4.15 | 1220 | 4.29 |
| 2017.05 | 2309 | 4.30 | 3016 | 4.40 | 2797 | 4.64 |
| 2017.06 | 2682 | 5.01 | 3101 | 5.14 | 2446 | 5.22 |
| 2017.07 | 1185 | 4.21 | 941 | 4.21 | 738 | 4.20 |
| 2017.08 | 1720 | 4.25 | 1431 | 4.08 | 1324 | 4.21 |
| 2017.09 | 5841 | 5.04 | 3883 | 4.96 | 3760 | 4.79 |
| 2017.10 | 3447 | 4.42 | 822 | 4.40 | 1254 | 4.37 |
| 2017.11 | 9916 | 4.47 | 1645 | 4.47 | 1720 | 4.62 |
| 2017.12 | 14637 | 4.88 | 4954 | 5.71 | 3183 | 5.77 |
| 2018.01 | 11214 | 4.62 | 3592 | 4.33 | 3668 | 4.67 |
| 2018.02 | 10942 | 4.34 | 5838 | 4.58 | 2092 | 4.31 |
| 2018.03 | 13771 | 4.79 | 2128 | 4.98 | 2749 | 4.86 |
| 2018.04 | 10703 | 4.68 | 2577 | 4.12 | 1543 | 4.23 |
| 2018.05 | 11985 | 4.50 | 2176 | 3.86 | 1497 | 4.25 |
| 2018.06 | 10791 | 4.68 | 2139 | 5.19 | 1700 | 5.09 |
| 2018.07 | 9656 | 4.00 | 3036 | 3.30 | 770 | 3.37 |
| 2018.08 | 9587 | 3.63 | 2674 | 2.71 | 858 | 3.05 |
| 2018.09 | 9473 | 3.50 | 6676 | 3.42 | 1808 | 3.33 |
| 2018.10 | 7111 | 3.15 | 1818 | 3.13 | 686 | 3.73 |
| 2018.11 | 7012 | 2.92 | 2634 | 2.74 | 1886 | 2.92 |
| 2018.12 | 12801 | 3.99 | 6651 | 4.05 | 2045 | 4.03 |
| 2019.01 | 13652 | 3.23 | 8869 | 3.20 | 5259 | 3.25 |
| 2019.02 | 6213 | 2.89 | 710 | 2.95 | 1730 | 2.89 |
| 2019.03 | 9247 | 3.08 | 5620 | 3.19 | 1082 | 3.16 |
| 2019.04 | 9628 | 2.99 | 3018 | 3.12 | 1574 | 3.09 |
| 2019.05 | 8132 | 2.92 | 1857 | 3.00 | 1202 | 3.08 |
| 2019.06 | 8937 | 3.27 | 3768 | 3.89 | 740 | 4.16 |
| 2019.07 | 8467 | 2.87 | 2556 | 3.17 | 514 | 3.50 |
| 2019.08 | 7054 | 2.94 | 2235 | 3.07 | 526 | 3.40 |
| 2019.09 | 10980 | 3.13 | 4581 | 3.10 | 2086 | 3.36 |
| 2019.10 | 6291 | 2.91 | 2392 | 3.20 | 616 | 3.34 |
| 2019.11 | 6277 | 2.87 | 2349 | 3.01 | 1066 | 3.23 |
| 2019.12 | 9369 | 3.09 | 5666 | 3.36 | 1561 | 3.47 |

4.2 ■ 全国银行间质押式回购交易统计表
## Statistics of Interbank Pledged Repo

单位：亿元，%
Unit: 100 Million Yuan，%

| 时间<br>Time | 3 个月<br>3-month | | 4 个月<br>4-month | | 6 个月<br>6-month | |
|---|---|---|---|---|---|---|
| | 交易量<br>Trading Volume | 加权平均利率<br>Weighted Average Interest Rate | 交易量<br>Trading Volume | 加权平均利率<br>Weighted Average Interest Rate | 交易量<br>Trading Volume | 加权平均利率<br>Weighted Average Interest Rate |
| 2012 | 4421 | | 612 | | 804 | |
| 2013 | 7068 | | 613 | | 1045 | |
| 2014 | 9854 | | 1214 | | 1464 | |
| 2015 | 10193 | | 768 | | 849 | |
| 2016 | 9346 | | 679 | | 743 | |
| 2017.01 | 475 | 4.57 | 192 | 4.27 | 95 | 4.27 |
| 2017.02 | 557 | 4.51 | 440 | 4.47 | 185 | 4.47 |
| 2017.03 | 868 | 4.86 | 507 | 4.61 | 350 | 4.78 |
| 2017.04 | 272 | 4.40 | 41 | 4.64 | 147 | 4.63 |
| 2017.05 | 592 | 4.86 | 107 | 4.84 | 90 | 4.96 |
| 2017.06 | 1468 | 5.13 | 287 | 5.31 | 71 | 5.07 |
| 2017.07 | 713 | 4.35 | 539 | 4.40 | 241 | 4.52 |
| 2017.08 | 382 | 4.48 | 68 | 4.50 | 54 | 4.55 |
| 2017.09 | 774 | 4.59 | 166 | 4.74 | 190 | 4.71 |
| 2017.10 | 249 | 4.70 | 90 | 4.71 | 42 | 4.75 |
| 2017.11 | 708 | 4.76 | 388 | 5.01 | 70 | 5.03 |
| 2017.12 | 1388 | 5.55 | 707 | 5.42 | 159 | 5.43 |
| 2018.01 | 863 | 4.85 | 48 | 5.14 | 26 | 5.17 |
| 2018.02 | 665 | 4.49 | 89 | 4.90 | 24 | 5.03 |
| 2018.03 | 541 | 4.80 | 287 | 4.94 | 77 | 4.90 |
| 2018.04 | 666 | 4.37 | 173 | 4.34 | 53 | 4.59 |
| 2018.05 | 908 | 4.54 | 489 | 4.44 | 19 | 4.58 |
| 2018.06 | 648 | 4.63 | 343 | 4.48 | 33 | 4.58 |
| 2018.07 | 617 | 3.93 | 248 | 4.09 | 31 | 4.26 |
| 2018.08 | 829 | 3.23 | 98 | 3.43 | 85 | 3.40 |
| 2018.09 | 539 | 3.12 | 239 | 3.31 | 151 | 3.78 |
| 2018.10 | 647 | 3.22 | 137 | 3.25 | 27 | 3.95 |
| 2018.11 | 410 | 3.37 | 488 | 3.36 | 18 | 3.82 |
| 2018.12 | 366 | 3.87 | 248 | 3.74 | 109 | 3.64 |
| 2019.01 | 599 | 3.24 | 307 | 3.24 | 8 | 3.45 |
| 2019.02 | 319 | 2.91 | 363 | 3.14 | 26 | 3.48 |
| 2019.03 | 481 | 3.08 | 125 | 3.28 | 66 | 3.00 |
| 2019.04 | 877 | 3.00 | 69 | 3.21 | 18 | 3.69 |
| 2019.05 | 625 | 3.15 | 172 | 3.12 | 78 | 3.31 |
| 2019.06 | 307 | 3.60 | 207 | 3.33 | 213 | 3.41 |
| 2019.07 | 614 | 3.16 | 186 | 3.23 | 204 | 3.27 |
| 2019.08 | 434 | 3.11 | 298 | 3.20 | 50 | 3.32 |
| 2019.09 | 399 | 3.30 | 74 | 3.31 | 126 | 3.36 |
| 2019.10 | 196 | 3.46 | 373 | 3.16 | 150 | 3.31 |
| 2019.11 | 644 | 3.33 | 342 | 3.26 | 130 | 3.21 |
| 2019.12 | 466 | 3.49 | 248 | 3.38 | 263 | 3.22 |

## 4.2 全国银行间质押式回购交易统计表
### Statistics of Interbank Pledged Repo

单位：亿元，%
Unit: 100 Million Yuan，%

| 时间<br>Time | 9个月<br>9-month | | 1年<br>1-year | | 交易量合计 | 加权平均利率 |
|---|---|---|---|---|---|---|
| | 交易量<br>Trading Volume Interest Rate | 加权平均利率<br>Weighted Average | 交易量<br>Trading Volume Interest Rate | 加权平均利率<br>Weighted Average | Trading Volume Interest Rate | Weighted Average |
| 2012 | 89 | | 182 | | 1366174 | |
| 2013 | 234 | | 384 | | 1519757 | |
| 2014 | 123 | | 311 | | 2124191 | |
| 2015 | 60 | | 73 | | 4324109 | |
| 2016 | 84 | | 740 | | 5682693 | |
| 2017.01 | 34 | 4.16 | 166 | 4.56 | 349831 | 2.48 |
| 2017.02 | 30 | 4.40 | 4 | 4.55 | 358030 | 2.61 |
| 2017.03 | 479 | 4.82 | 6 | 4.93 | 499901 | 2.84 |
| 2017.04 | 6 | 4.74 | 35 | 4.82 | 416858 | 2.80 |
| 2017.05 | 6 | 5.01 | 1 | 5.10 | 467927 | 2.92 |
| 2017.06 | 12 | 5.04 | 7 | 5.04 | 549157 | 3.03 |
| 2017.07 | 9 | 4.52 | 4 | 4.63 | 515587 | 2.90 |
| 2017.08 | 7 | 4.69 | 9 | 4.71 | 558244 | 3.09 |
| 2017.09 | 30 | 4.80 | 13 | 4.89 | 573273 | 3.07 |
| 2017.10 | 6 | 4.88 | 14 | 4.92 | 435286 | 2.91 |
| 2017.11 | 18 | 4.98 | 26 | 5.10 | 581482 | 3.00 |
| 2017.12 | 140 | 5.44 | 24 | 5.20 | 577029 | 3.11 |
| 2018.01 | 3 | 5.26 | 14 | 5.28 | 578129 | 2.88 |
| 2018.02 | 3 | 5.18 | 6 | 5.29 | 404493 | 2.87 |
| 2018.03 | 26 | 4.75 | 7 | 5.12 | 612286 | 2.90 |
| 2018.04 | 3 | 4.92 | 24 | 5.21 | 485648 | 3.10 |
| 2018.05 | 1 | 5.28 | 1 | 5.39 | 568444 | 2.82 |
| 2018.06 | 69 | 5.12 | 12 | 5.01 | 547048 | 2.89 |
| 2018.07 | 10 | 5.15 | 7 | 4.23 | 642163 | 2.43 |
| 2018.08 | 20 | 3.39 | 4 | 3.89 | 757437 | 2.25 |
| 2018.09 | 1 | 3.80 | 1 | 3.75 | 602974 | 2.60 |
| 2018.10 | 0 | 5.20 | 1 | 3.65 | 561781 | 2.39 |
| 2018.11 | 2 | 3.88 | 2 | 4.14 | 706717 | 2.46 |
| 2018.12 | 12 | 3.65 | 4 | 3.80 | 619606 | 2.68 |
| 2019.01 | 7 | 4.17 | 8 | 4.01 | 744225 | 2.16 |
| 2019.02 | 1 | 3.00 | 2 | 3.78 | 512138 | 2.24 |
| 2019.03 | 10 | 3.22 | 3 | 3.34 | 687801 | 2.47 |
| 2019.04 | 6 | 4.49 | 6 | 3.74 | 704427 | 2.46 |
| 2019.05 | 6 | 4.43 | 4 | 3.71 | 689500 | 2.27 |
| 2019.06 | 4 | 9.71 | 8 | 4.63 | 613147 | 1.74 |
| 2019.07 | 57 | 3.72 | 15 | 3.69 | 758165 | 2.15 |
| 2019.08 | 11 | 2.97 | — | — | 705002 | 2.65 |
| 2019.09 | 3 | 4.62 | 1 | 20.00 | 657870 | 2.56 |
| 2019.10 | 6 | 5.51 | 2 | 7.01 | 582698 | 2.57 |
| 2019.11 | 98 | 3.15 | 7 | 3.47 | 708270 | 2.29 |
| 2019.12 | 10 | 3.44 | 5 | 3.43 | 737642 | 2.10 |

4.3 ■ 国内各类债券发行统计表
## Statistics of Debt Securities Issue

单位：亿元
Unit: 100 Million Yuan

| 时间<br>Time | 国债<br>Government<br>Securities | 中央银行票据<br>Central Bank<br>Bills | 金融债券<br>Financial Bonds | 公司信用类债券<br>Corporate<br>Debenture Bonds | 各类债券合计<br>Total |
|---|---|---|---|---|---|
| 2015 | 59408 | 0 | 102095 | 67235 | 228738 |
| 2016 | 91086 | 0 | 182152 | 82387 | 356037 |
| 2017.01 | 1360 | 0 | 13316 | 2206 | 16882 |
| 2017.02 | 1846 | 0 | 23077 | 2212 | 27135 |
| 2017.03 | 6199 | 0 | 26408 | 6036 | 38714 |
| 2017.04 | 6084 | 0 | 18322 | 5199 | 29655 |
| 2017.05 | 8076 | 0 | 17071 | 2809 | 28035 |
| 2017.06 | 8697 | 0 | 23177 | 3992 | 35901 |
| 2017.07 | 11479 | 0 | 20488 | 6648 | 38730 |
| 2017.08 | 13987 | 0 | 21860 | 6633 | 42545 |
| 2017.09 | 7317 | 0 | 27257 | 6300 | 40973 |
| 2017.10 | 7053 | 0 | 18023 | 4786 | 29873 |
| 2017.11 | 8013 | 0 | 24206 | 5621 | 37891 |
| 2017.12 | 2772 | 0 | 24850 | 3908 | 31530 |
| 2018.01 | 1900 | 0 | 18564 | 4258 | 24796 |
| 2018.02 | 1486 | 0 | 17182 | 2998 | 21716 |
| 2018.03 | 4009 | 0 | 29254 | 8732 | 42082 |
| 2018.04 | 6269 | 0 | 20570 | 8918 | 35838 |
| 2018.05 | 7002 | 0 | 26045 | 4374 | 37506 |
| 2018.06 | 9188 | 0 | 26359 | 4853 | 40407 |
| 2018.07 | 10943 | 0 | 16842 | 6445 | 34285 |
| 2018.08 | 12525 | 0 | 22843 | 8261 | 43709 |
| 2018.09 | 11059 | 0 | 26026 | 5821 | 42933 |
| 2018.10 | 6055 | 0 | 19736 | 5955 | 31798 |
| 2018.11 | 3348 | 0 | 27056 | 8734 | 39205 |
| 2018.12 | 4495 | 0 | 23580 | 8557 | 36685 |
| 2019.01 | 5880 | 0 | 16396 | 10677 | 32972 |
| 2019.02 | 5242 | 0 | 15715 | 3525 | 24482 |
| 2019.03 | 8036 | 0 | 27690 | 10877 | 46668 |
| 2019.04 | 6926 | 0 | 19950 | 10175 | 37076 |
| 2019.05 | 7429 | 0 | 23184 | 6203 | 36846 |
| 2019.06 | 12838 | 0 | 20035 | 6992 | 39905 |
| 2019.07 | 9144 | 0 | 21157 | 9232 | 39587 |
| 2019.08 | 9939 | 0 | 24165 | 9959 | 44132 |
| 2019.09 | 6177 | 0 | 22059 | 9488 | 37748 |
| 2019.10 | 4687 | 0 | 18433 | 8862 | 32024 |
| 2019.11 | 4829 | 0 | 25134 | 10389 | 40412 |
| 2019.12 | 4062 | 0 | 25443 | 10680 | 40220 |

注：公司信用类债券包括非金融企业债务融资工具、企业债券及公司债、可转债等。自2015年起，金融债券数据中包含同业存单数据。

Note: Corporate debenture bonds include non-financial enterprise financing instruments, enterprise bonds, corporate bonds, convertible bonds, etc.. NCDs have been included in financial bonds since 2015.

#### 4.4 ■ 国内各类债券余额统计表
#### Statistics of Debt Securities Outstanding

单位：亿元
Unit: 100 Million Yuan

| 时间<br>Time | 国债<br>Government<br>Securities | 中央银行票据<br>Central Bank<br>Bills | 金融债券<br>Financial Bonds | 公司信用类债券<br>Corporate<br>Debenture Bonds | 国际机构债券<br>International<br>Institution Bonds | 各类债券合计<br>Total |
|---|---|---|---|---|---|---|
| 2015 | 154524 | 4222 | 184596 | 144329 | 31 | 487816 |
| 2016 | 225734 | 0 | 236499 | 175180 | 537 | 637950 |
| 2017.01 | 226400 | 0 | 239113 | 178280 | 537 | 644329 |
| 2017.02 | 226209 | 0 | 248762 | 176996 | 537 | 652504 |
| 2017.03 | 229141 | 0 | 255817 | 177843 | 607 | 663408 |
| 2017.04 | 235080 | 0 | 258552 | 178646 | 657 | 672935 |
| 2017.05 | 241253 | 0 | 256017 | 176338 | 735 | 674343 |
| 2017.06 | 247825 | 0 | 260855 | 176420 | 724 | 685824 |
| 2017.07 | 257926 | 0 | 265802 | 178363 | 839 | 702931 |
| 2017.08 | 262346 | 0 | 269847 | 179691 | 913 | 712798 |
| 2017.09 | 267832 | 0 | 272811 | 181165 | 1008 | 722816 |
| 2017.10 | 272800 | 0 | 272592 | 182043 | 998 | 728433 |
| 2017.11 | 278779 | 0 | 276525 | 182964 | 1013 | 739281 |
| 2017.12 | 281538 | 0 | 278301 | 183252 | 1013 | 744104 |
| 2018.01 | 281544 | 0 | 277554 | 187010 | 1088 | 747197 |
| 2018.02 | 281719 | 0 | 281140 | 187556 | 1138 | 751553 |
| 2018.03 | 283535 | 0 | 287321 | 190946 | 1195 | 762996 |
| 2018.04 | 288838 | 0 | 288806 | 193115 | 1277 | 772036 |
| 2018.05 | 291566 | 0 | 295336 | 193842 | 1337 | 782081 |
| 2018.06 | 298075 | 0 | 296566 | 194525 | 1366 | 790532 |
| 2018.07 | 306073 | 0 | 298285 | 195540 | 1421 | 801318 |
| 2018.08 | 314725 | 0 | 300772 | 198366 | 1501 | 815364 |
| 2018.09 | 323833 | 0 | 303057 | 198023 | 1428 | 826340 |
| 2018.10 | 326865 | 0 | 307302 | 198419 | 1470 | 834055 |
| 2018.11 | 326618 | 0 | 316174 | 201705 | 1537 | 846033 |
| 2018.12 | 330069 | 0 | 322585 | 205603 | 1550 | 859807 |
| 2019.01 | 331769 | 0 | 326134 | 219143 | 1540 | 878586 |
| 2019.02 | 336116 | 15 | 325832 | 219257 | 1540 | 882759 |
| 2019.03 | 339528 | 15 | 330940 | 222772 | 1611 | 894865 |
| 2019.04 | 343961 | 15 | 332809 | 226312 | 1636 | 904733 |
| 2019.05 | 347817 | 15 | 338174 | 227477 | 1611 | 915094 |
| 2019.06 | 354685 | 40 | 339900 | 229694 | 1631 | 925949 |
| 2019.07 | 361112 | 40 | 341488 | 231957 | 1686 | 936284 |
| 2019.08 | 366171 | 90 | 345587 | 235021 | 1686 | 948555 |
| 2019.09 | 369948 | 140 | 349168 | 236143 | 1681 | 957080 |
| 2019.10 | 371819 | 200 | 352700 | 237908 | 1669 | 964295 |
| 2019.11 | 373535 | 210 | 358083 | 241323 | 1659 | 974809 |
| 2019.12 | 377273 | 220 | 364622 | 246176 | 1659 | 989950 |

注：本表含在境内发行的美元债券，公司信用类债券包括非金融企业债务融资工具、企业债券及公司债、可转债等。自2015年起，金融债券数据中包含同业存单数据。

Note: The sheet include the dollar bonds issued in the territory. Corporate debenture bonds include non-financial enterprise financing instruments, enterprise bonds, corporate bonds, convertible bonds, etc.. NCDs have been included in financial bonds since 2015.

4.5 ■ 人民币汇率统计表
## Statistics of Exchange Rate

单位：外币／元人民币
Unit: USD，HKD，100JPY and EURO/RMB

| 时间<br>Time | 美元<br>USD | | 港元<br>HKD | |
|---|---|---|---|---|
| | 平均汇率<br>（美元／人民币）<br>Average<br>Exchange Rate<br>(USD/RMB) | 期末汇率<br>（美元／人民币）<br>End-of-period<br>Exchange Rate<br>(USD/RMB) | 平均汇率<br>（港元／人民币）<br>Average<br>Exchange Rate<br>(HKD/RMB) | 期末汇率<br>（港元／人民币）<br>End-of-period<br>Exchange Rate<br>(HKD/RMB) |
| 2012 | | 6.2855 | | 0.8109 |
| 2013 | | 6.0969 | | 0.7862 |
| 2014 | | 6.1190 | | 0.7889 |
| 2015 | | 6.4936 | | 0.8378 |
| 2016 | | 6.9370 | | 0.8945 |
| 2017.01 | 6.8918 | 6.8588 | 0.8886 | 0.8842 |
| 2017.02 | 6.8713 | 6.8750 | 0.8855 | 0.8858 |
| 2017.03 | 6.8932 | 6.8993 | 0.8876 | 0.8878 |
| 2017.04 | 6.8845 | 6.8931 | 0.8856 | 0.8858 |
| 2017.05 | 6.8827 | 6.8633 | 0.8840 | 0.8808 |
| 2017.06 | 6.8019 | 6.7744 | 0.8723 | 0.8679 |
| 2017.07 | 6.7654 | 6.7283 | 0.8664 | 0.8616 |
| 2017.08 | 6.6736 | 6.6010 | 0.8533 | 0.8436 |
| 2017.09 | 6.5634 | 6.6369 | 0.8400 | 0.8497 |
| 2017.10 | 6.6154 | 6.6397 | 0.8477 | 0.8513 |
| 2017.11 | 6.6186 | 6.6034 | 0.8480 | 0.8458 |
| 2017.12 | 6.5942 | 6.5342 | 0.8440 | 0.8359 |
| 2018.01 | 6.4364 | 6.3339 | 0.8231 | 0.8099 |
| 2018.02 | 6.3162 | 6.3294 | 0.8075 | 0.8086 |
| 2018.03 | 6.3220 | 6.2881 | 0.8063 | 0.8013 |
| 2018.04 | 6.2975 | 6.3393 | 0.8024 | 0.8079 |
| 2018.05 | 6.3758 | 6.4144 | 0.8123 | 0.8175 |
| 2018.06 | 6.4556 | 6.6166 | 0.8227 | 0.8431 |
| 2018.07 | 6.7034 | 6.8165 | 0.8542 | 0.8685 |
| 2018.08 | 6.8433 | 6.8246 | 0.8718 | 0.8695 |
| 2018.09 | 6.8445 | 6.8792 | 0.8730 | 0.8800 |
| 2018.10 | 6.9264 | 6.9646 | 0.8837 | 0.8877 |
| 2018.11 | 6.9351 | 6.9357 | 0.8857 | 0.8868 |
| 2018.12 | 6.8853 | 6.8632 | 0.8805 | 0.8762 |
| 2019.01 | 6.7897 | 6.7025 | 0.8659 | 0.8546 |
| 2019.02 | 6.7364 | 6.6901 | 0.8584 | 0.8523 |
| 2019.03 | 6.7093 | 6.7335 | 0.8548 | 0.8578 |
| 2019.04 | 6.7151 | 6.7286 | 0.8560 | 0.8578 |
| 2019.05 | 6.8524 | 6.8992 | 0.8731 | 0.8791 |
| 2019.06 | 6.8820 | 6.8747 | 0.8793 | 0.8797 |
| 2019.07 | 6.8752 | 6.8841 | 0.8802 | 0.8798 |
| 2019.08 | 7.0879 | 7.0214 | 0.9033 | 0.8956 |
| 2019.09 | 7.0785 | 7.0729 | 0.9033 | 0.9020 |
| 2019.10 | 7.0702 | 7.0533 | 0.9016 | 0.9000 |
| 2019.11 | 7.0177 | 7.0298 | 0.8963 | 0.8980 |
| 2019.12 | 7.0128 | 6.9762 | 0.8984 | 0.8958 |

注：本表汇率为中国外汇交易中心对外公布的人民币汇率中间价。
Note: The exchange rate is the CNY central parity rate released by the China Foreign Exchange Trade System.

## 4.5 ■ 人民币汇率统计表
## Statistics of Exchange Rate

单位：外币／元人民币
Unit: USD，HKD，100JPY and EURO/RMB

| 时间<br>Time | 日元<br>JPY | | 欧元<br>EURO | |
|---|---|---|---|---|
| | 平均汇率<br>（100 日元／人民币）<br>Average<br>Exchange Rate<br>(100JPY/RMB) | 期末汇率<br>（100 日元／人民币）<br>End-of-period<br>Exchange Rate<br>(100JPY/RMB) | 平均汇率<br>（欧元／人民币）<br>Average<br>Exchange Rate<br>(EURO/RMB) | 期末汇率<br>（欧元／人民币）<br>End-of-period<br>Exchange Rate<br>(EURO/RMB) |
| 2012 | | 7.3049 | | 8.3176 |
| 2013 | | 5.7771 | | 8.4189 |
| 2014 | | 5.1371 | | 7.4556 |
| 2015 | | 5.3875 | | 7.0952 |
| 2016 | | 5.9591 | | 7.3068 |
| 2017.01 | 5.9939 | 6.0596 | 7.3179 | 7.3821 |
| 2017.02 | 6.0788 | 6.1307 | 7.3085 | 7.2589 |
| 2017.03 | 6.1043 | 6.1766 | 7.3668 | 7.3721 |
| 2017.04 | 6.2655 | 6.2023 | 7.3829 | 7.4945 |
| 2017.05 | 6.1331 | 6.1995 | 7.6042 | 7.6760 |
| 2017.06 | 6.1367 | 6.0485 | 7.6389 | 7.7496 |
| 2017.07 | 6.0174 | 6.0879 | 7.7898 | 7.9059 |
| 2017.08 | 6.0762 | 5.9780 | 7.8855 | 7.8525 |
| 2017.09 | 5.9272 | 5.9089 | 7.8143 | 7.8233 |
| 2017.10 | 5.8592 | 5.8700 | 7.7845 | 7.7333 |
| 2017.11 | 5.8643 | 5.8945 | 7.7643 | 7.8252 |
| 2017.12 | 5.8373 | 5.7883 | 7.8019 | 7.8023 |
| 2018.01 | 5.7951 | 5.8216 | 7.8414 | 7.8553 |
| 2018.02 | 5.8235 | 5.8872 | 7.7866 | 7.7355 |
| 2018.03 | 5.9612 | 5.9066 | 7.7975 | 7.7378 |
| 2018.04 | 5.8603 | 5.7967 | 7.7417 | 7.6714 |
| 2018.05 | 5.8097 | 5.8986 | 7.5344 | 7.4814 |
| 2018.06 | 5.8698 | 5.9914 | 7.5397 | 7.6515 |
| 2018.07 | 6.0191 | 6.1398 | 7.8345 | 7.9799 |
| 2018.08 | 6.1668 | 6.1542 | 7.9083 | 7.9646 |
| 2018.09 | 6.1207 | 6.0705 | 7.9788 | 8.0111 |
| 2018.10 | 6.1587 | 6.1590 | 7.9526 | 7.9008 |
| 2018.11 | 6.1219 | 6.1153 | 7.8824 | 7.8991 |
| 2018.12 | 6.1279 | 6.1887 | 7.8309 | 7.8473 |
| 2019.01 | 6.2346 | 6.1478 | 7.7553 | 7.6981 |
| 2019.02 | 6.0964 | 6.0321 | 7.6363 | 7.6082 |
| 2019.03 | 6.0358 | 6.0867 | 7.5869 | 7.5607 |
| 2019.04 | 6.0148 | 6.0255 | 7.5440 | 7.5256 |
| 2019.05 | 6.2388 | 6.3019 | 4.7549 | 7.6833 |
| 2019.06 | 6.3745 | 6.3816 | 7.7759 | 7.8170 |
| 2019.07 | 6.3530 | 6.3401 | 7.7179 | 7.6803 |
| 2019.08 | 6.6845 | 6.6163 | 7.8661 | 7.8225 |
| 2019.09 | 6.6085 | 6.5699 | 7.8083 | 7.7538 |
| 2019.10 | 6.5291 | 6.4827 | 7.8335 | 7.8676 |
| 2019.11 | 6.4486 | 6.4186 | 7.7577 | 7.7406 |
| 2019.12 | 6.4236 | 6.4086 | 7.7895 | 7.8155 |

注：本表汇率为中国外汇交易中心对外公布的人民币汇率中间价。
Note: The exchange rate is the CNY central parity rate released by the China Foreign Exchange Trade System.

4.6 ■ 国内股票市场统计表
## Statistics of Stock Market

| 时间<br>Time | 股票筹资额<br>（亿元）<br>Equity<br>Financing<br>(100 Million<br>Yuan) | 成交金额<br>（亿元）<br>Turnover of<br>Trading<br>(100 Million<br>Yuan) | 期末总股本<br>（亿股）<br>Volume<br>Issued<br>at the End of Period<br>(100 Million<br>Shares) | 期末市价总值<br>（亿元）<br>Total Market<br>Capitalization<br>at the End of Period<br>(100 Million<br>Yuan) | 期末上市公司数<br>（家）<br>Number of<br>Listed Company<br>at the End<br>of Period | 期末收盘指数 (Index) | |
|---|---|---|---|---|---|---|---|
| | | | | | | 上证综合指数<br>Shanghai Stock<br>Exchange<br>Composite<br>Index | 深证成分指数<br>Shenzhen Stock<br>Exchange<br>Componet<br>Index |
| 2012 | 4131 | 314583 | 31834 | 230358 | 2494 | 2269 | 9116 |
| 2013 | 3867 | 468072 | 33822 | 239077 | 2489 | 2116 | 8122 |
| 2014 | 7060 | 742385 | 36795 | 372547 | 2613 | 3235 | 11015 |
| 2015 | 11321 | 2550538 | 43015 | 531304 | 2827 | 3539 | 12665 |
| 2016 | 14510 | 1273845 | 48750 | 507686 | 3052 | 3104 | 10177 |
| | | | | | | | |
| 2017.01 | 1740 | 67642 | 49348 | 517248 | 3105 | 3159 | 10052 |
| 2017.02 | 572 | 80836 | 49506 | 538212 | 3137 | 3242 | 10391 |
| 2017.03 | 965 | 115943 | 49757 | 539588 | 3185 | 3223 | 10429 |
| 2017.04 | 1235 | 92082 | 50177 | 527481 | 3223 | 3155 | 10235 |
| 2017.05 | 549 | 81304 | 50891 | 513613 | 3261 | 3117 | 9865 |
| 2017.06 | 552 | 84759 | 51837 | 534322 | 3297 | 3192 | 10530 |
| 2017.07 | 609 | 97612 | 52384 | 542177 | 3326 | 3273 | 10505 |
| 2017.08 | 666 | 117672 | 52624 | 561973 | 3362 | 3361 | 10817 |
| 2017.09 | 1330 | 115101 | 52844 | 569301 | 3399 | 3349 | 11087 |
| 2017.10 | 934 | 79400 | 53044 | 579121 | 3426 | 3393 | 11368 |
| 2017.11 | 1452 | 112035 | 53325 | 564016 | 3462 | 3317 | 10944 |
| 2017.12 | 1139 | 80238 | 53747 | 567086 | 3485 | 3307 | 11040 |
| | | | | | | | |
| 2018.01 | 1137 | 114890 | 53987 | 585573 | 3500 | 3481 | 11160 |
| 2018.02 | 379 | 64393 | 54201 | 561646 | 3512 | 3259 | 10829 |
| 2018.03 | 507 | 103299 | 54370 | 559519 | 3522 | 3169 | 10869 |
| 2018.04 | 574 | 82388 | 54586 | 542533 | 3531 | 3082 | 10324 |
| 2018.05 | 465 | 89887 | 55150 | 544220 | 3539 | 3095 | 10296 |
| 2018.06 | 354 | 69820 | 55914 | 504217 | 3547 | 2847 | 9379 |
| 2018.07 | 1278 | 77787 | 56651 | 506208 | 3551 | 2876 | 9179 |
| 2018.08 | 826 | 65795 | 56811 | 475702 | 3557 | 2725 | 8465 |
| 2018.09 | 369 | 49745 | 57016 | 486616 | 3568 | 2821 | 8401 |
| 2018.10 | 239 | 52376 | 57172 | 446534 | 3573 | 2603 | 7483 |
| 2018.11 | 359 | 78105 | 57603 | 453623 | 3581 | 2588 | 7682 |
| 2018.12 | 340 | 53253 | 57581 | 434924 | 3584 | 2494 | 7240 |
| | | | | | | | |
| 2019.01 | 633 | 65541 | 58028 | 448886 | 3600 | 2585 | 7479 |
| 2019.02 | 119 | 88923 | 58147 | 524862 | 3606 | 2941 | 9032 |
| 2019.03 | 253 | 186267 | 58309 | 562856 | 3617 | 3091 | 9907 |
| 2019.04 | 353 | 168851 | 58429 | 555258 | 3627 | 3078 | 9675 |
| 2019.05 | 1437 | 98311 | 58794 | 522966 | 3639 | 2899 | 8923 |
| 2019.06 | 863 | 87474 | 59322 | 536297 | 3648 | 2979 | 9178 |
| 2019.07 | 649 | 91583 | 59799 | 540503 | 3682 | 2933 | 9327 |
| 2019.08 | 286 | 98646 | 60287 | 539710 | 3697 | 2886 | 9366 |
| 2019.09 | 321 | 113548 | 60432 | 545836 | 3708 | 2905 | 9446 |
| 2019.10 | 323 | 76695 | 60565 | 552694 | 3723 | 2929 | 9635 |
| 2019.11 | 759 | 85305 | 60809 | 546887 | 3751 | 2872 | 9582 |
| 2019.12 | 866 | 113015 | 61720 | 592935 | 3777 | 3050 | 10431 |

## 5.1 ■ 中央银行基准利率
## Benchmark Interest Rates of Central Bank

单位：%（年利率）
Unit: % p.a.

| 项目／日期 | Items/Date | 2002.02.21 | 2003.12.21 | 2004.03.25 | 2005.03.17 | 2008.01.01 | 2008.11.27 | 2008.12.23 | 2010.10.20 | 2010.12.26 |
|---|---|---|---|---|---|---|---|---|---|---|
| 准备金账户 * | Reserve Account* | | | | | | | | | |
| 法定准备金 | Reserve Requirements | 1.89 | 1.89 | 1.89 | 1.89 | — | 1.62 | — | 1.62 | 1.62 |
| 超额储备 | Excess Reserves | 1.89 | 1.62 | 1.62 | 0.99 | — | 0.72 | — | 0.72 | 0.72 |
| 对金融机构贷款 | Loans to Financial Institution | | | | | | | | | |
| 20 天以内 | Less than 20 days | 2.70 | 2.70 | 3.33 | 3.33 | 4.14 | 3.06 | 2.79 | 2.79 | 3.25 |
| 3 个月以内 | 3 months or less | 2.97 | 2.97 | 3.60 | 3.60 | 4.41 | 3.33 | 3.06 | 3.06 | 3.55 |
| 6 个月以内 | 6 months or less | 3.15 | 3.15 | 3.78 | 3.78 | 4.59 | 3.51 | 3.24 | 3.24 | 3.75 |
| 1 年 | 1 year | 3.24 | 3.24 | 3.87 | 3.87 | 4.68 | 3.60 | 3.33 | 3.33 | 3.85 |
| 再贴现 | Rediscount | 2.97 | 2.97 | 3.24 | 3.24 | 4.32 | 2.97 | 1.80 | 1.80 | 2.25 |

* 2003 年 12 月准备金账户分为法定准备金和超额储备两个账户。
* As of December 2003, reserve account was divided into reserve requirements and excess reserves.

5.2 ■ 金融机构：人民币法定存款基准利率
Financial Institutions: Official Benchmark Rates of RMB Deposits

单位：%（年利率）
Unit: % p.a.

| 项目／日期 | Items/Date | 2012.07.06 | 2014.11.22 | 2015.03.01 | 2015.05.11 | 2015.06.28 | 2015.08.26 | 2015.10.24 |
|---|---|---|---|---|---|---|---|---|
| 活期 | Demand | 0.35 | 0.35 | 0.35 | 0.35 | 0.35 | 0.35 | 0.35 |
| 定期 | Time | | | | | | | |
| 3 个月 | 3 months | 2.10 | 2.35 | 2.10 | 1.85 | 1.60 | 1.35 | 1.10 |
| 6 个月 | 6 months | 2.80 | 2.55 | 2.30 | 2.05 | 1.80 | 1.55 | 1.30 |
| 1 年 | 1 year | 3.00 | 2.75 | 2.50 | 2.25 | 2.00 | 1.75 | 1.50 |
| 2 年 | 2 years | 3.75 | 3.35 | 3.10 | 2.85 | 2.60 | 2.35 | 2.10 |
| 3 年 | 3 years | 4.25 | 4.00 | 3.75 | 3.50 | 3.25 | 3.00 | 2.75 |
| 5 年 | 5 years | 4.75 | 4.00 | — | — | — | — | — |

## 5.3 ■ 金融机构：人民币法定贷款基准利率
### Financial Institutions: Official Benchmark Rates of RMB Loans

单位：%（年利率）
Unit: % p.a.

| 项目／日期　　　　Items/Date | 2012.07.06 | 2014.11.22 | 2015.03.01 | 2015.05.11 | 2015.06.28 | 2015.08.26 | 2015.10.24 |
|---|---|---|---|---|---|---|---|
| 短期贷款<br>Short-term | | | | | | | |
| 1年以内（含1年）within 1 year(including 1 year) | 6.00 | 5.60 | 5.35 | 5.10 | 4.85 | 4.60 | 4.35 |
| 中长期贷款<br>Medium- and long-term | | | | | | | |
| 1～5年（含5年）1~5 years(including 5 years) | 6.15 | 6.00 | 5.75 | 5.50 | 5.25 | 5.00 | 4.75 |
| 5年以上　　　　over 5 years | 6.55 | 6.15 | 5.90 | 5.65 | 5.40 | 5.15 | 4.90 |

注：自2014年11月22日起，金融机构人民币贷款基准利率期限档次简并为1年以内（含1年）、1～5年（含5年）和5年以上三个档次。
Note: Since November 22, 2014, the terms of official benchmark rates of RMB loans to financial institutions have merged into three:within 1 year
　　　(including 1 year), 1~5 years(including 5 years), over 5 years.

6.1 ■ 2018 年资金流量表（金融交易账户）

## Flow of Funds Statement, 2018(Financial Transactions Accounts)

| 部门 / 交易项目 | 顺序号 | 住户 Households 运用 Uses | 住户 Households 来源 Sources | 非金融企业 Non-financial Corporations 运用 Uses | 非金融企业 Non-financial Corporations 来源 Sources | 政府 General Government 运用 Uses | 政府 General Government 来源 Sources | 金融机构 Financial Institutions 运用 Uses | 金融机构 Financial Institutions 来源 Sources |
|---|---|---|---|---|---|---|---|---|---|
| 净金融投资 | 1 | 55348 | | -79875 | | -46515 | | 74253 | |
| 资金运用合计 | 2 | 135701 | | -4163 | | 19147 | | 185604 | |
| 资金来源合计 | 3 | | 80353 | | 75712 | | 65663 | | 111350 |
| 通货 | 4 | 1969 | | 231 | | 51 | | | 2563 |
| 存款 | 5 | 77092 | | 11724 | | 16168 | | -12 | 105210 |
| 活期存款 | 6 | 18712 | | -766 | | 254 | | | 18200 |
| 定期存款 | 7 | 54633 | | 22350 | | 19532 | | | 96516 |
| 财政存款 | 8 | | | | | -596 | | | -596 |
| 外汇存款 | 9 | -221 | | -4011 | | -13 | | -180 | -4184 |
| 其他存款 | 10 | 3968 | | -5849 | | -3010 | | 168 | -4726 |
| 证券公司客户保证金 | 11 | -366 | | -565 | | -64 | | -181 | -1229 |
| 贷款 | 12 | | 78514 | | 49160 | | 4448 | 125268 | -6124 |
| 短期贷款与票据融资 | 13 | | 24947 | | 23401 | | | 48348 | |
| 中长期贷款 | 14 | | 49533 | | 50075 | | | 99607 | |
| 外汇贷款 | 15 | | 2 | | -2246 | | 33 | -2854 | 43 |
| 委托贷款 | 16 | | 4260 | | -18364 | | -2043 | -16554 | -363 |
| 其他贷款 | 17 | | -228 | | -3705 | | 6458 | -3279 | -5804 |
| 未贴现的银行承兑汇票 | 18 | | | -6343 | -6343 | | | -6343 | -6343 |
| 保险准备金 | 19 | 22155 | | 1071 | | | 12117 | | 11109 |
| 金融机构往来 | 20 | | | | | | | 8283 | 2201 |
| 存款准备金 | 21 | | | | | | | -9970 | -9610 |
| 债券 | 22 | 1047 | | 1049 | 18298 | 1049 | 48532 | 106833 | 45350 |
| 政府债券 | 23 | 843 | | -4 | | -40 | 48532 | 43066 | |
| 金融债券 | 24 | 28 | | 6 | | 533 | | 45659 | 45350 |
| 中央银行债券 | 25 | | | | | | | 7 | |
| 企业债券 | 26 | 176 | | 1048 | 18298 | 556 | | 18102 | |
| 股票 | 27 | 1694 | | 3174 | 6758 | 297 | | 1447 | 2696 |
| 证券投资基金份额 | 28 | 5601 | | 8637 | | 981 | | 2771 | 18784 |
| 库存现金 | 29 | | | | | | | -516 | -491 |
| 中央银行贷款 | 30 | | | | | | | 9592 | 9592 |
| 其他（净） | 31 | 26511 | 1840 | -33845 | 1799 | 665 | 136 | -52398 | -62842 |
| 直接投资 | 32 | | | 6384 | 13466 | | | | |
| 其他对外债权债务 | 33 | | | 4320 | 3175 | | 430 | -423 | 482 |
| 国际储备资产 | 34 | | | | | | | 1250 | |
| 国际收支错误与遗漏 | 35 | | | | -10601 | | | | |

单位：亿元人民币
Unit: 100 Million of RMB Yuan

| 国内合计 All Domestic Sectors | | 国 外 The Rest of the World | | 总 计 Total | | No. | Sectors Items |
|---|---|---|---|---|---|---|---|
| 运用 Uses | 来源 Sources | 运用 Uses | 来源 Sources | 运用 Uses | 来源 Sources | | |
| 3211 | | -3211 | | 0 | | 1 | Net financial investment |
| 336289 | | 21413 | | 357702 | | 2 | Financial uses |
| | 333078 | | 24624 | | 357702 | 3 | Financial sources |
| 2251 | 2563 | 312 | | 2563 | 2563 | 4 | Currency |
| 104973 | 105210 | 643 | 405 | 105615 | 105615 | 5 | Deposits |
| 18200 | 18200 | | | 18200 | 18200 | 6 | Demand deposits |
| 96516 | 96516 | | | 96516 | 96516 | 7 | Time deposits |
| -596 | -596 | | | -596 | -596 | 8 | Fiscal deposits |
| -4424 | -4184 | 646 | 405 | -3779 | -3779 | 9 | Foreign exchange deposits |
| -4723 | -4726 | -3 | | -4726 | -4726 | 10 | Other deposits |
| -1177 | -1229 | -52 | | -1229 | -1229 | 11 | Customer margin of securities companies |
| 125268 | 125998 | 1913 | 1184 | 127181 | 127181 | 12 | Loans |
| 48348 | 48348 | | | 48348 | 48348 | 13 | Short-term loans & Bills financing |
| 99607 | 99607 | | | 99607 | 99607 | 14 | Medium-and long-term loans |
| -2854 | -2168 | 1913 | 1228 | -941 | -941 | 15 | Foreign exchange loans |
| -16554 | -16510 | | -44 | -16554 | -16554 | 16 | Designated loans |
| -3279 | -3279 | | | -3279 | -3279 | 17 | Other loans |
| -12686 | -12686 | | | -12686 | -12686 | 18 | Undiscounted bankers' acceptance bills |
| 23226 | 23226 | | | 23226 | 23226 | 19 | Insurance technical reserves |
| 8283 | 2201 | 1360 | 7442 | 9643 | 9643 | 20 | Inter-financial institutions accounts |
| -9970 | -9610 | 360 | | -9610 | -9610 | 21 | Required and excessive reserves |
| 109979 | 112180 | 5115 | 2915 | 115095 | 115095 | 22 | Bonds |
| 43865 | 48532 | 4623 | -44 | 48488 | 48488 | 23 | Government and public bonds |
| 46227 | 45350 | 465 | 1341 | 46691 | 46691 | 24 | Financial bonds |
| 7 | | | 7 | 7 | 7 | 25 | Central bank bonds |
| 19881 | 18298 | 28 | 1610 | 19908 | 19908 | 26 | Corporate bonds |
| 6612 | 9454 | 4015 | 1172 | 10626 | 10626 | 27 | Shares |
| 17989 | 18784 | 795 | | 18784 | 18784 | 28 | Securities investment funds shares |
| -516 | -491 | | -25 | -516 | -516 | 29 | Cash in vault |
| 9592 | 9592 | | | 9592 | 9592 | 30 | Central bank loans |
| -59067 | -59067 | | | -59067 | -59067 | 31 | Miscellaneous (net) |
| 6384 | 13466 | 13466 | 6384 | 19850 | 19850 | 32 | Foreign direct investment |
| 3897 | 4087 | 4087 | 3897 | 7985 | 7985 | 33 | Other foreign assets and debts |
| 1250 | | | 1250 | 1250 | 1250 | 34 | International reserve assets |
| | -10601 | -10601 | | -10601 | -10601 | 35 | Errors and omissions in the BOP |

## 7.1 5000 户企业主要财务指标
## Major Financial Indicators of 5000 Principal Enterprises

上年同期 =100 单位：%
Previous Year=100 Unit: %

| 时间<br>Time | 货币资金<br>Monetary Funds | 存货<br>Inventories | 流动资产<br>Current<br>Assets | 固定资产<br>净额<br>Net Fixed<br>Assets | 短期借款<br>Short-term<br>Borrowing |
|---|---|---|---|---|---|
| 2012 | -0.1 | 5.1 | 6.8 | 6.4 | 14.8 |
| 2013 | 2.2 | 8.2 | 7.7 | 8.7 | 9.4 |
| 2014 | 13.3 | 2.5 | 7.3 | 6.0 | -1.0 |
| 2015 | 9.9 | -3.4 | 3.5 | 1.3 | 4.9 |
| 2016 | 6.8 | 4.2 | 7.3 | 3.4 | 5.8 |
| 2017.01 | 3.6 | 5.4 | 6.6 | 3.2 | 6.3 |
| 2017.02 | 9.2 | 6.5 | 8.5 | 3.2 | 6.3 |
| 2017.03 | 8.5 | 8.2 | 8.5 | 2.5 | 6.1 |
| 2017.04 | 8.7 | 8.7 | 9.2 | 2.5 | 7.3 |
| 2017.05 | 10.8 | 7.7 | 9.1 | 2.8 | 8.0 |
| 2017.06 | 8.6 | 7.5 | 8.8 | 2.9 | 6.5 |
| 2017.07 | 10.7 | 6.8 | 9.2 | 2.7 | 6.2 |
| 2017.08 | 9.2 | 7.0 | 9.1 | 2.8 | 6.5 |
| 2017.09 | 9.4 | 8.0 | 9.9 | 3.0 | 6.9 |
| 2017.10 | 10.1 | 7.8 | 9.9 | 2.8 | 5.6 |
| 2017.11 | 9.9 | 8.0 | 9.3 | 2.5 | 4.1 |
| 2017.12 | 10.8 | 6.4 | 8.9 | 3.0 | 3.1 |
| 2018.01 | 15.9 | 5.7 | 10.1 | 2.5 | 2.3 |
| 2018.02 | 9.2 | 6.1 | 8.6 | 2.7 | 3.1 |
| 2018.03 | 7.6 | 4.6 | 7.6 | 3.4 | 2.3 |
| 2018.04 | 8.2 | 3.3 | 8.0 | 3.0 | 1.7 |
| 2018.05 | 8.0 | 4.5 | 8.5 | 3.0 | 0.1 |
| 2018.06 | 8.2 | 4.9 | 8.6 | 2.8 | 0.8 |
| 2018.07 | 8.0 | 6.7 | 8.7 | 3.3 | 1.1 |
| 2018.08 | 8.2 | 6.9 | 8.4 | 3.1 | -0.8 |
| 2018.09 | 5.2 | 5.3 | 6.8 | 4.1 | -1.2 |
| 2018.10 | 5.9 | 6.0 | 6.7 | 4.1 | -1.0 |
| 2018.11 | 4.9 | 4.7 | 6.1 | 3.9 | -1.2 |
| 2018.12 | 4.7 | 3.3 | 5.1 | 4.2 | -1.7 |
| 2019.01 | 2.6 | 2.7 | 4.2 | 4.8 | -2.0 |
| 2019.02 | 4.9 | 1.6 | 4.0 | 4.5 | -3.1 |
| 2019.03 | 7.8 | 0.9 | 5.0 | 4.6 | -2.4 |
| 2019.04 | 7.0 | 3.0 | 3.7 | 4.7 | -3.7 |
| 2019.05 | 5.6 | 2.6 | 3.5 | 4.5 | -3.6 |
| 2019.06 | 7.4 | 1.3 | 4.1 | 4.9 | -3.1 |
| 2019.07 | 6.6 | 0.6 | 3.1 | 4.4 | -4.6 |
| 2019.08 | 6.9 | 0.0 | 2.9 | 4.4 | -3.7 |
| 2019.09 | 7.0 | 0.1 | 2.8 | 3.9 | -1.9 |
| 2019.10 | 5.8 | -0.9 | 2.5 | 3.3 | -2.3 |
| 2019.11 | 6.9 | -1.2 | 3.0 | 4.0 | -1.5 |
| 2019.12 | 4.8 | 1.0 | 3.4 | 1.9 | -1.4 |

## 7.1 5000 户企业主要财务指标
## Major Financial Indicators of 5000 Principal Enterprises

上年同期 =100 单位：%
Previous Year=100  Unit: %

| 时间<br>Time | 流动负债<br>合计<br>Total Current<br>Liabilities | 长期负债<br>合计<br>Total Long-term<br>Liabilities | 所有者权益<br>合计<br>Owner's Equity | 产品销售<br>收入<br>Sales Revenue | 工业总产值<br>（现价）<br>Industrial Output<br>(Current Price) |
|---|---|---|---|---|---|
| 2012 | 9.0 | 10.2 | 7.3 | 4.6 | 4.4 |
| 2013 | 9.1 | 10.3 | 6.7 | 4.7 | 3.3 |
| 2014 | 6.7 | 7.0 | 7.4 | 2.8 | -0.7 |
| 2015 | 6.0 | 5.1 | 3.7 | -8.2 | -7.7 |
| 2016 | 6.8 | 3.2 | 6.8 | 1.2 | 1.5 |
| 2017.01 | 5.8 | 4.5 | 7.3 | 7.9 | 12.9 |
| 2017.02 | 7.3 | 4.6 | 7.6 | 20.3 | 22.5 |
| 2017.03 | 6.7 | 4.5 | 7.9 | 18.7 | 21.6 |
| 2017.04 | 7.2 | 4.2 | 7.5 | 17.5 | 19.2 |
| 2017.05 | 6.8 | 4.2 | 7.2 | 16.9 | 18.4 |
| 2017.06 | 6.6 | 3.8 | 7.0 | 16.0 | 18.3 |
| 2017.07 | 6.5 | 3.8 | 7.5 | 15.8 | 18.1 |
| 2017.08 | 5.7 | 4.3 | 8.3 | 15.8 | 18.0 |
| 2017.09 | 6.6 | 4.0 | 8.7 | 15.9 | 17.3 |
| 2017.10 | 6.2 | 3.3 | 9.2 | 16.0 | 17.1 |
| 2017.11 | 5.4 | 2.7 | 10.6 | 15.2 | 16.4 |
| 2017.12 | 4.3 | 2.1 | 11.3 | 13.5 | 15.7 |
| 2018.01 | 5.5 | 1.1 | 11.3 | 21.3 | 18.1 |
| 2018.02 | 4.8 | -0.7 | 11.8 | 8.4 | 10.6 |
| 2018.03 | 3.8 | -0.4 | 12.1 | 7.7 | 7.8 |
| 2018.04 | 3.6 | -0.4 | 12.5 | 9.2 | 8.9 |
| 2018.05 | 3.8 | 0.2 | 13.0 | 9.3 | 9.5 |
| 2018.06 | 4.2 | 0.9 | 12.4 | 9.3 | 8.9 |
| 2018.07 | 4.2 | 1.5 | 12.4 | 9.4 | 8.8 |
| 2018.08 | 4.4 | 1.1 | 11.8 | 9.3 | 8.8 |
| 2018.09 | 4.1 | 0.6 | 11.4 | 8.7 | 8.7 |
| 2018.10 | 3.9 | 0.8 | 11.2 | 8.8 | 9.2 |
| 2018.11 | 3.8 | 0.9 | 9.8 | 8.4 | 8.3 |
| 2018.12 | 3.2 | 2.7 | 8.3 | 7.9 | 7.4 |
| 2019.01 | 2.5 | 4.6 | 7.9 | 1.3 | -0.8 |
| 2019.02 | 1.8 | 6.0 | 7.4 | 1.5 | 0.5 |
| 2019.03 | 3.2 | 8.2 | 7.0 | 5.2 | 3.8 |
| 2019.04 | 2.5 | 8.6 | 6.6 | 3.9 | 3.3 |
| 2019.05 | 2.9 | 7.8 | 6.3 | 3.4 | 2.3 |
| 2019.06 | 3.6 | 7.2 | 6.6 | 3.2 | 2.8 |
| 2019.07 | 3.3 | 6.6 | 6.0 | 3.3 | 2.9 |
| 2019.08 | 2.8 | 7.4 | 6.0 | 2.6 | 2.9 |
| 2019.09 | 2.7 | 7.6 | 5.6 | 1.2 | 2.0 |
| 2019.10 | 2.6 | 7.4 | 5.5 | 2.6 | 2.3 |
| 2019.11 | 3.0 | 7.9 | 5.7 | 2.5 | 2.6 |
| 2019.12 | 2.0 | 9.5 | 5.5 | 1.7 | 2.2 |

注： 2015 年 5 月调整企业财务调查指标，停用"固定资产合计"，"固定资产净额"是指固定资产合计减去累计折旧和减值准备后的净额。

Note: Since May 2015, the item of "Total Fixed Assets" has been replaced by "Net Fixed Assets", which equals nominal fixed assets, minus accumulated depreciation and allowance for impairment of fixed assets.

7.2 ■ 5000 户企业主要财务分析指标
## Major Financial Analytical Indicators of 5000 Principal Enterprises

上年同期 =100 单位：%
Previous Year=100　Unit:　%

| 时间<br>Time | 货币资金占用系数<br>Ratio of Monetary<br>Funds to Sales | 流动比率<br>Ratio of<br>Liquidity | 资产负债比率<br>Liabilities/Assets<br>Ratio | 流动资产<br>周转率<br>Turn-over Ratio of<br>Liquid Assets | 工业产品<br>销售率<br>Industrial Products<br>Sales Ratio | 销售成本<br>利润率<br>Ratio of Profits<br>to Sales Expenses |
|---|---|---|---|---|---|---|
| 2012 | 13.4 | 102.1 | 61.5 | 1.8 | 110.9 | 6.1 |
| 2013 | 13.1 | 100.9 | 62.1 | 1.9 | 112.6 | 5.4 |
| 2014 | 14.5 | 101.5 | 61.9 | 1.7 | 116.5 | 5.7 |
| 2015 | 17.3 | 99.0 | 62.4 | 1.5 | 116.2 | 4.6 |
| 2016 | 18.2 | 99.9 | 62.0 | 1.4 | 115.8 | 6.0 |
| 2017.01 | 17.5 | 101.0 | 61.9 | 1.3 | 111.8 | 8.1 |
| 2017.02 | 18.4 | 101.8 | 61.8 | 1.3 | 113.8 | 7.2 |
| 2017.03 | 17.8 | 102.3 | 61.7 | 1.4 | 112.8 | 8.3 |
| 2017.04 | 17.5 | 102.5 | 61.8 | 1.4 | 113.2 | 7.9 |
| 2017.05 | 17.3 | 102.6 | 61.8 | 1.4 | 113.3 | 7.6 |
| 2017.06 | 17.0 | 102.5 | 61.6 | 1.4 | 113.4 | 8.0 |
| 2017.07 | 16.9 | 103.1 | 61.5 | 1.4 | 112.9 | 7.8 |
| 2017.08 | 17.0 | 104.2 | 61.3 | 1.4 | 113.0 | 7.8 |
| 2017.09 | 17.0 | 105.7 | 61.1 | 1.4 | 113.2 | 8.0 |
| 2017.10 | 17.0 | 106.4 | 60.9 | 1.4 | 112.9 | 8.1 |
| 2017.11 | 17.1 | 107.0 | 60.6 | 1.4 | 112.6 | 8.1 |
| 2017.12 | 17.6 | 104.8 | 60.2 | 1.5 | 112.5 | 8.0 |
| 2018.01 | 16.6 | 106.0 | 60.2 | 1.4 | 112.9 | 9.9 |
| 2018.02 | 18.3 | 106.1 | 59.8 | 1.3 | 110.5 | 8.3 |
| 2018.03 | 17.5 | 106.7 | 59.6 | 1.4 | 112.0 | 8.9 |
| 2018.04 | 17.2 | 107.3 | 59.6 | 1.4 | 112.4 | 8.7 |
| 2018.05 | 17.0 | 107.7 | 59.5 | 1.4 | 112.1 | 8.9 |
| 2018.06 | 16.7 | 107.3 | 59.5 | 1.4 | 112.9 | 9.4 |
| 2018.07 | 16.5 | 107.9 | 59.4 | 1.4 | 112.7 | 9.3 |
| 2018.08 | 16.6 | 108.4 | 59.3 | 1.4 | 112.8 | 9.1 |
| 2018.09 | 16.5 | 108.5 | 59.2 | 1.4 | 113.2 | 9.2 |
| 2018.10 | 16.4 | 109.5 | 58.9 | 1.5 | 112.6 | 8.9 |
| 2018.11 | 16.4 | 109.6 | 58.9 | 1.5 | 112.7 | 8.8 |
| 2018.12 | 17.0 | 107.8 | 58.9 | 1.5 | 112.4 | 8.3 |
| 2019.01 | 16.7 | 107.8 | 59.0 | 1.4 | 115.0 | 8.7 |
| 2019.02 | 18.9 | 108.5 | 58.7 | 1.3 | 111.3 | 7.1 |
| 2019.03 | 17.9 | 108.7 | 58.9 | 1.4 | 113.4 | 8.1 |
| 2019.04 | 17.7 | 108.8 | 58.9 | 1.4 | 113.2 | 8.2 |
| 2019.05 | 17.3 | 108.7 | 58.8 | 1.4 | 113.5 | 8.3 |
| 2019.06 | 17.2 | 107.9 | 58.9 | 1.4 | 113.3 | 8.7 |
| 2019.07 | 16.9 | 107.9 | 58.8 | 1.4 | 113.0 | 8.4 |
| 2019.08 | 17.2 | 108.7 | 58.7 | 1.4 | 112.4 | 8.2 |
| 2019.09 | 17.5 | 108.8 | 58.7 | 1.4 | 112.2 | 8.3 |
| 2019.10 | 16.9 | 109.4 | 58.3 | 1.5 | 112.4 | 8.1 |
| 2019.11 | 17.2 | 109.8 | 58.3 | 1.5 | 111.7 | 7.9 |
| 2019.12 | 17.6 | 108.5 | 58.3 | 1.5 | 111.4 | 7.7 |

7.3 ■ 5000 户企业景气扩散指数 *

## Diffusion Indices of Business Survey of 5000 Principal Enterprises*

单位：%
Unit: %

| 时间<br>Time | 宏观经济热度指数<br>Macro-economy Index | 企业景气指数<br>Business Climate Index | 设备能力利用水平<br>Production Capacity Utilization | 产成品库存水平<br>Inventory Level | 国内订货水平<br>Domestic Order Level | 出口产品订单<br>Overseas Order Level | 资金周转状况<br>Funds Turnover | 销货款回笼情况<br>Cash Inflow from Sales | 银行贷款掌握状况<br>Lending Attitude of Bank | 企业盈利情况<br>Profitability | 产品销售价格水平<br>Price Level of Sales | 原材料购进价格水平<br>Price Level of Raw Materials | 固定资产投资情况<br>Fixed Assets Investment |
|---|---|---|---|---|---|---|---|---|---|---|---|---|---|
| 2012 | 31.6 | 61.8 | 40.0 | 45.5 | 47.7 | 47.1 | 59.7 | 63.8 | 38.6 | 53.1 | 46.4 | 60.7 | 49.6 |
| 2013 | 34.7 | 58.1 | 41.2 | 44.9 | 49.4 | 48.7 | 57.3 | 60.9 | 45.7 | 57.6 | 46.5 | 57.3 | 52.2 |
| 2014 | 31.1 | 54.5 | 40.4 | 43.5 | 46.5 | 48.9 | 54.3 | 59.2 | 44.9 | 55.0 | 43.0 | 51.5 | 49.0 |
| 2015.03 | 29.2 | 52.8 | 39.0 | 44.1 | 42.5 | 46.8 | 54.2 | 59.1 | 45.1 | 51.0 | 41.5 | 49.9 | 46.2 |
| 2015.06 | 29.3 | 51.8 | 39.2 | 43.7 | 46.3 | 49.3 | 53.4 | 57.4 | 45.7 | 52.8 | 43.3 | 51.8 | 48.0 |
| 2015.09 | 24.5 | 49.4 | 37.2 | 42.8 | 43.3 | 48.1 | 52.5 | 56.5 | 45.7 | 51.1 | 39.1 | 47.3 | 47.4 |
| 2015.12 | 22.7 | 48.4 | 36.9 | 43.0 | 42.5 | 43.6 | 52.0 | 55.8 | 45.7 | 50.5 | 39.2 | 46.2 | 46.0 |
| 2016.03 | 21.1 | 46.7 | 35.2 | 44.3 | 39.1 | 41.0 | 52.4 | 55.6 | 46.1 | 47.2 | 39.5 | 47.6 | 43.2 |
| 2016.06 | 24.4 | 48.3 | 36.8 | 45.3 | 46.6 | 46.5 | 52.5 | 55.8 | 46.1 | 52.7 | 45.6 | 54.9 | 46.1 |
| 2016.09 | 25.2 | 50.3 | 37.7 | 45.2 | 46.0 | 46.9 | 53.4 | 57.3 | 46.2 | 54.7 | 46.9 | 56.7 | 46.9 |
| 2016.12 | 27.8 | 52.6 | 40.1 | 46.2 | 49.9 | 45.6 | 54.6 | 59.0 | 46.6 | 57.1 | 51.7 | 63.1 | 47.4 |
| 2017.03 | 31.3 | 52.8 | 38.7 | 46.8 | 44.0 | 41.7 | 56.3 | 60.0 | 46.4 | 49.9 | 53.6 | 68.0 | 45.4 |
| 2017.06 | 34.0 | 54.6 | 41.1 | 46.6 | 50.6 | 50.4 | 55.8 | 60.5 | 45.8 | 56.1 | 50.7 | 62.9 | 48.4 |
| 2017.09 | 35.9 | 55.5 | 41.3 | 46.8 | 50.2 | 49.6 | 56.7 | 61.3 | 45.4 | 57.6 | 52.5 | 65.4 | 49.8 |
| 2017.12 | 38.6 | 59.8 | 43.8 | 47.7 | 53.0 | 48.5 | 58.8 | 63.8 | 46.7 | 61.5 | 56.1 | 68.6 | 50.9 |
| 2018.03 | 38.9 | 58.6 | 41.4 | 47.8 | 47.6 | 45.0 | 58.7 | 63.8 | 46.4 | 56.7 | 52.9 | 66.1 | 48.2 |
| 2018.06 | 40.1 | 58.5 | 43.7 | 47.6 | 52.7 | 50.8 | 57.8 | 62.7 | 45.6 | 59.7 | 52.1 | 64.8 | 50.8 |
| 2018.09 | 37.2 | 56.9 | 42.5 | 46.7 | 49.6 | 48.5 | 57.0 | 62.8 | 45.8 | 58.9 | 51.0 | 64.3 | 51.0 |
| 2018.12 | 35.4 | 57.9 | 43.6 | 47.0 | 50.1 | 45.5 | 58.1 | 63.1 | 46.4 | 58.7 | 50.8 | 63.1 | 50.5 |
| 2019.03 | 34.1 | 54.8 | 41.4 | 46.6 | 44.2 | 42.9 | 58.6 | 62.8 | 47.8 | 52.3 | 47.0 | 58.8 | 47.1 |
| 2019.06 | 34.5 | 55.0 | 42.8 | 46.4 | 48.8 | 46.3 | 57.8 | 62.3 | 48.4 | 56.6 | 47.3 | 58.7 | 48.7 |
| 2019.09 | 32.4 | 53.3 | 41.4 | 46.0 | 47.0 | 44.5 | 57.8 | 61.8 | 48.0 | 55.3 | 45.7 | 56.3 | 49.7 |
| 2019.12 | 31.9 | 55.5 | 42.7 | 46.5 | 49.1 | 43.2 | 59.0 | 63.7 | 49.0 | 57.3 | 47.6 | 57.1 | 50.0 |

\* 通过对企业经营者进行问卷调查，得出对问题回答的三种结果，即上升、持平、下降各占总数的比重，然后利用上升的比重减去下降的比重，用其差额来反映景气状况的水平和趋势。

\* Diffusion Index on Business Survey: based on the questionnaire sent to enterprise managers, proportions are calculated for the positive, unchanged and negative answers respectively. The diffusion index and its trend are reflected in the difference of the shares between the positive and negative answers.

注：2013 年二季度对问卷内容进行了重新修订，本表中发布的数据也相应调整。具体为：（1）停止发布"能源供应状况""原材料供应状况"、"产品销售情况"以及"设备投资情况"；（2）新增发布"宏观经济热度指数"和"原材料购进价格指数"；（3）修改"产成品库存水平指数"计算方法，新指数 = 100 − 原指数，本表中已对 2013 年二季度以前公布的历史数据进行调整。

Note: The questionnaire for PBC Entrepreneurs Survey was revised and certain adjustments were made to the table as of 2013Q2, including: (1) Indices of Energy Supply, Raw Material Supply and Products Sales were not compiled; (2) Indices of Macro-economy and Price Level of Raw Materials were added; (3) Compilation method was adjusted for Inventory Level Index, while the new index equals 100 minus the original index. All the historical data in the table was re-calculated accordingly.

8.1 ■ 主要物价指数
Major Price Indices

以上年同月为100
Previous Corresponding Month=100

| 时间<br>Time | 零售物价指数<br>Retail Price<br>Index | 居民消费价格指数<br>Consumer Price<br>Index | 企业商品价格指数<br>Corporate Goods Price Index | | |
| --- | --- | --- | --- | --- | --- |
| | | | 总指数<br>Overall Index | 投资品<br>Capital Goods | 消费品<br>Consumer Goods |
| 2012 | 102.0 | 102.6 | 98.4 | 98.0 | 101.4 |
| 2013 | 101.4 | 102.6 | 99.3 | 99.0 | 101.4 |
| 2014 | 101.0 | 102.0 | 95.6 | 95.2 | 98.4 |
| 2015 | 100.1 | 101.4 | 92.7 | 91.8 | 100.3 |
| 2016 | 100.7 | 102.0 | 106.8 | 107.3 | 101.8 |
| 2017.01 | 101.9 | 102.5 | 108.5 | 109.1 | 102.4 |
| 2017.02 | 100.7 | 100.8 | 109.3 | 110.2 | 101.3 |
| 2017.03 | 100.7 | 100.9 | 108.4 | 109.3 | 100.6 |
| 2017.04 | 100.9 | 101.2 | 106.8 | 107.6 | 100.3 |
| 2017.05 | 101.1 | 101.5 | 106.2 | 106.9 | 99.8 |
| 2017.06 | 100.9 | 101.5 | 106.1 | 106.8 | 100.0 |
| 2017.07 | 100.7 | 101.4 | 105.8 | 106.5 | 99.9 |
| 2017.08 | 101.1 | 101.8 | 106.7 | 107.4 | 100.4 |
| 2017.09 | 101.0 | 101.6 | 106.9 | 107.7 | 100.4 |
| 2017.10 | 101.3 | 101.9 | 106.8 | 107.5 | 100.7 |
| 2017.11 | 101.3 | 101.7 | 105.3 | 105.9 | 100.5 |
| 2017.12 | 101.4 | 101.8 | 104.4 | 104.8 | 100.5 |
| 2018.01 | 101.3 | 101.5 | 103.9 | 104.3 | 100.2 |
| 2018.02 | 102.0 | 102.9 | 103.4 | 103.6 | 101.1 |
| 2018.03 | 101.4 | 102.1 | 102.7 | 102.8 | 100.6 |
| 2018.04 | 101.4 | 101.8 | 102.8 | 103.0 | 100.3 |
| 2018.05 | 101.5 | 101.8 | 103.6 | 103.9 | 100.6 |
| 2018.06 | 101.8 | 101.9 | 104.1 | 104.4 | 100.9 |
| 2018.07 | 102.2 | 102.1 | 103.9 | 104.1 | 101.5 |
| 2018.08 | 102.3 | 102.3 | 103.3 | 103.5 | 101.6 |
| 2018.09 | 102.6 | 102.5 | 103.2 | 103.3 | 101.9 |
| 2018.10 | 102.8 | 102.5 | 102.8 | 102.9 | 101.6 |
| 2018.11 | 102.2 | 102.2 | 101.8 | 101.8 | 101.2 |
| 2018.12 | 101.4 | 101.9 | 100.3 | 100.1 | 100.6 |
| 2019.01 | 101.0 | 101.7 | 99.5 | 99.3 | 100.1 |
| 2019.02 | 101.0 | 101.5 | 99.7 | 99.5 | 100.2 |
| 2019.03 | 101.9 | 102.3 | 100.6 | 100.4 | 101.5 |
| 2019.04 | 102.0 | 102.5 | 101.1 | 100.8 | 102.6 |
| 2019.05 | 102.1 | 102.7 | 100.7 | 100.3 | 103.0 |
| 2019.06 | 101.8 | 102.7 | 99.8 | 99.4 | 102.9 |
| 2019.07 | 101.8 | 102.8 | 99.7 | 99.3 | 102.9 |
| 2019.08 | 101.8 | 102.8 | 99.3 | 98.7 | 103.7 |
| 2019.09 | 101.9 | 103.0 | 98.9 | 98.2 | 104.7 |
| 2019.10 | 102.2 | 103.8 | 98.9 | 98.0 | 106.4 |
| 2019.11 | 103.0 | 104.5 | 99.4 | 98.4 | 107.6 |
| 2019.12 | 103.4 | 104.5 | 100.5 | 99.6 | 107.8 |

## 8.2 企业商品价格指数
## Corporate Goods Price Indices(CGPI)

以 1993 年 12 月为 100
December 1993=100

| 时间<br>Time | 总指数<br>Overall<br>Index | 农产品<br>Agricultural<br>Product | 矿产品<br>Minning<br>Product | 煤、油、电<br>Coal, Oil and<br>Electricity | 加工业产品<br>Processed<br>Product |
|---|---|---|---|---|---|
| 2012 | 151.9 | 227.6 | 228.0 | 283.4 | 120.0 |
| 2013 | 150.8 | 236.0 | 223.5 | 279.2 | 118.7 |
| 2014 | 144.1 | 230.2 | 201.8 | 250.9 | 114.8 |
| 2015 | 133.5 | 238.0 | 176.7 | 213.1 | 107.0 |
| 2016 | 142.6 | 246.3 | 198.5 | 236.9 | 113.8 |
| 2017.01 | 144.1 | 254.1 | 200.6 | 241.9 | 114.5 |
| 2017.02 | 144.9 | 251.9 | 204.3 | 242.6 | 115.4 |
| 2017.03 | 145.1 | 245.8 | 208.2 | 243.1 | 115.8 |
| 2017.04 | 144.4 | 242.7 | 204.7 | 242.2 | 115.4 |
| 2017.05 | 143.7 | 237.0 | 201.3 | 241.0 | 115.2 |
| 2017.06 | 143.3 | 234.5 | 199.7 | 238.0 | 115.1 |
| 2017.07 | 143.4 | 234.5 | 200.6 | 235.2 | 115.5 |
| 2017.08 | 144.9 | 237.2 | 207.3 | 237.8 | 116.5 |
| 2017.09 | 146.1 | 238.2 | 209.4 | 240.8 | 117.6 |
| 2017.10 | 147.2 | 239.0 | 208.7 | 243.7 | 118.4 |
| 2017.11 | 147.8 | 239.2 | 207.8 | 247.6 | 118.8 |
| 2017.12 | 148.8 | 242.8 | 209.6 | 250.3 | 119.4 |
| 2018.01 | 149.7 | 248.5 | 211.8 | 253.6 | 119.7 |
| 2018.02 | 149.8 | 253.8 | 212.2 | 254.5 | 119.5 |
| 2018.03 | 148.9 | 244.6 | 211.5 | 252.6 | 119.2 |
| 2018.04 | 148.4 | 238.3 | 209.4 | 253.5 | 119.1 |
| 2018.05 | 148.8 | 235.8 | 209.8 | 257.3 | 119.4 |
| 2018.06 | 149.2 | 234.3 | 209.5 | 259.9 | 119.7 |
| 2018.07 | 149.1 | 234.8 | 208.7 | 260.3 | 119.5 |
| 2018.08 | 149.7 | 238.5 | 214.6 | 260.9 | 119.9 |
| 2018.09 | 150.8 | 243.1 | 220.9 | 263.6 | 120.5 |
| 2018.10 | 151.4 | 242.3 | 222.2 | 266.8 | 120.8 |
| 2018.11 | 150.5 | 238.9 | 223.0 | 263.3 | 120.4 |
| 2018.12 | 149.2 | 240.4 | 221.0 | 254.1 | 119.6 |
| 2019.01 | 148.9 | 244.3 | 221.7 | 250.0 | 119.3 |
| 2019.02 | 149.3 | 251.1 | 224.0 | 251.8 | 119.1 |
| 2019.03 | 149.8 | 253.7 | 225.7 | 255.3 | 119.2 |
| 2019.04 | 150.0 | 254.9 | 228.5 | 255.0 | 119.4 |
| 2019.05 | 149.8 | 252.9 | 231.6 | 256.2 | 119.2 |
| 2019.06 | 148.9 | 251.1 | 235.2 | 253.3 | 118.5 |
| 2019.07 | 148.6 | 252.2 | 239.6 | 249.6 | 118.3 |
| 2019.08 | 148.6 | 258.1 | 240.9 | 246.9 | 118.1 |
| 2019.09 | 149.2 | 265.6 | 240.4 | 246.4 | 118.4 |
| 2019.10 | 149.7 | 271.8 | 238.8 | 247.5 | 118.5 |
| 2019.11 | 149.6 | 276.9 | 236.0 | 247.7 | 118.1 |
| 2019.12 | 149.9 | 281.5 | 236.4 | 249.0 | 118.1 |

9 ■ 主要经济金融指标图
Charts of Major Economic & Financial Indicators

工业增加值当月同比增长变化图
Growth Changes of Industrial Value-added

单位：%
Unit：%

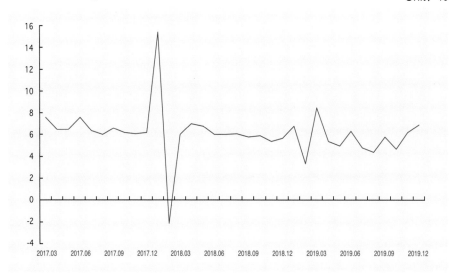

社会消费品零售总额当月同比增长变化图
Growth Changes of Retail Sales of Consumer Goods

单位：%
Unit：%

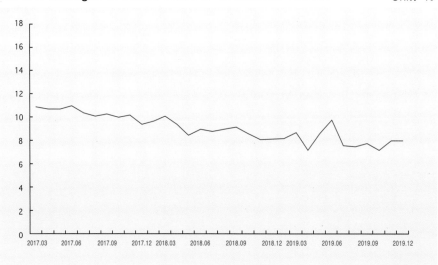

## 进出口增长变化图
## Growth Changes of Import & Export

单位：%
Unit：%

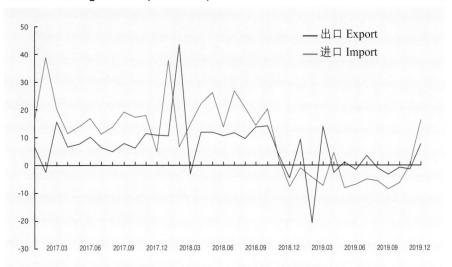

## 货币供应量增长率图
## Money Supply Growth Rate

单位：%
Unit：%

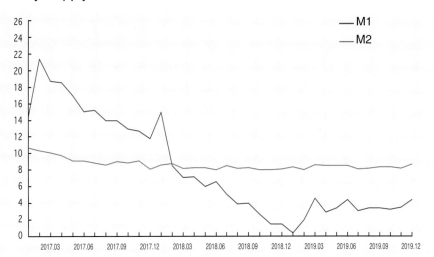

2019 年四季度末其他存款性公司金融资产分布图
## Assets Distribution of Other Depository Corporations (End of 2019 Q4)

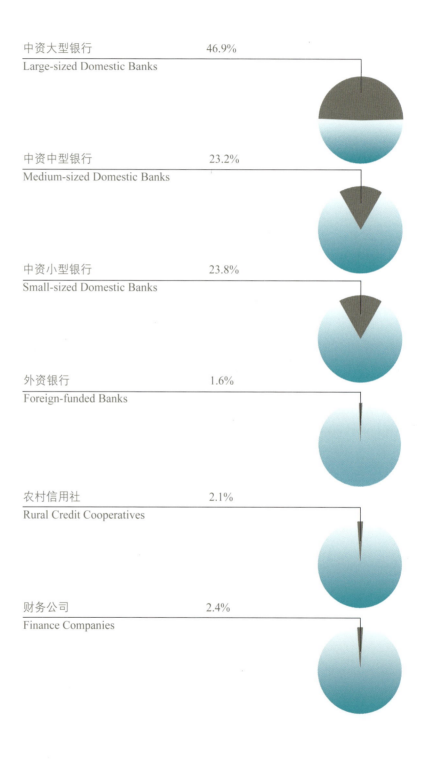

中资大型银行 46.9%
Large-sized Domestic Banks

中资中型银行 23.2%
Medium-sized Domestic Banks

中资小型银行 23.8%
Small-sized Domestic Banks

外资银行 1.6%
Foreign-funded Banks

农村信用社 2.1%
Rural Credit Cooperatives

财务公司 2.4%
Finance Companies

1 年期储蓄利率与居民消费价格指数涨幅对比图                        单位：%
One-year Savings Interest Rate and CPI Growth Rate          Unit：%

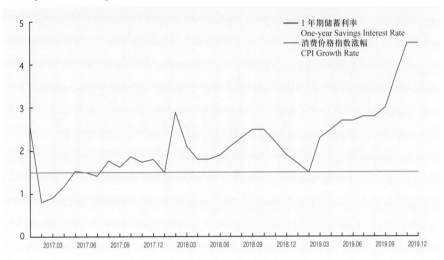

主要物价指数                                              以上年同期为100
Major Price Indices                              Previous Corresponding Month = 100

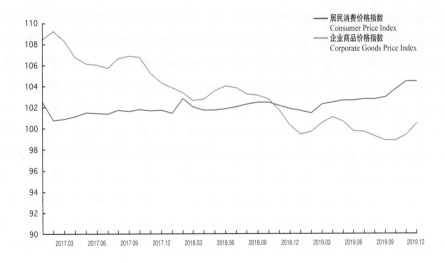

5000 户企业经营景气指数高于全国平均水平的主要行业
（2019 年四季度）

Indices above the National Average Level of Business Conditions of
Major Industries among 5000 Principal Enterprises （2019 Q4）

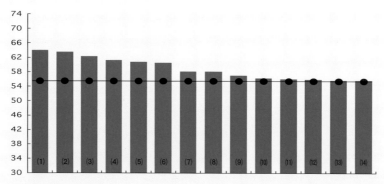

(1) 仪器仪表业；(2) 医药制造业；(3) 食饮烟业；(4) 非金属矿物品业；(5) 石油加工炼焦业；(6) 金属矿采选业；(7) 石油和天然气开采业；(8) 塑料制品业；(9) 电气热业；(10) 其他工业；(11) 有色金属冶炼及压延加工业；(12) 煤炭采选业；(13) 皮革毛皮羽绒业；(14) 黑色金属冶炼及压延加工业。

(1) Instruments and Meters Machinery; (2) Medical and Pharmaceutical Products; (3) Manufacture of Food, Beverage and Tobacco; (4) Nonmetal Mineral Products; (5) Petroleum Processing and Coking Products; (6) Metals Mining and Dressing; (7) Petroleum and Natural Gas Extraction; (8) Plastic Products; (9) Power, Gas and Heat Production and Supply; (10) Other Industries; (11) Smelting and Pressing of Nonferrous Metals; (12) Coal Mining and Dressing; (13) Leather, Furs, Down and Related Products; (14) Smelting and Pressing of Ferrous Metals.

5000 户企业货币资金与存货趋势图

Growth Changes of Monetary Funds
and Inventories of 5000 Principal
Enterprises

以上年同期为100
Previous Corresponding Period = 100

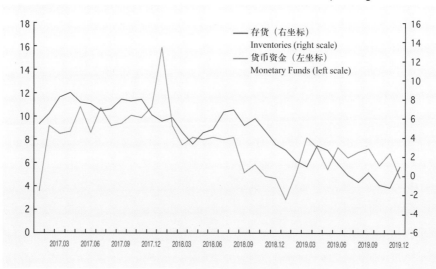

上海银行间同业拆放利率
Shibor

单位：%

Unit：%

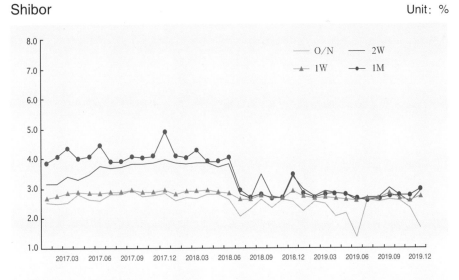

同业拆借、质押式回购月加权平均利率
Monthly Weighted Average Interest Rate of Interbank
Lending and Pledged Repo

单位：%

Unit：%

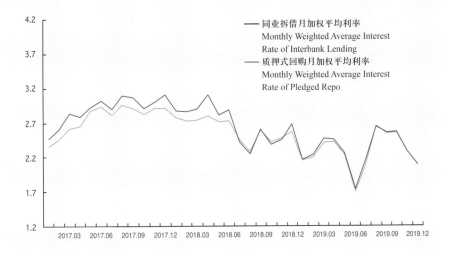

中债国债收益率曲线
# Chinabond Yield Curves of Government Securities

单位：%
Unit：%

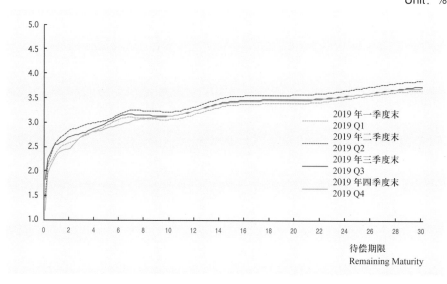

待偿期限
Remaining Maturity

中债国债、中短期票据收益率
# Chinabond Yield of Government Securities and Medium/
Short-term Notes

单位：%
Unit：%

## 10 ■ 主要指标的概念及定义

1 ■ **名义GDP** 按市场价格计算的国内生产总值。

**国内生产总值** 按市场价格计算的国内生产总值的简称。它是一个国家（地区）所有常住单位在一定时期内生产活动的最终成果。在实际核算中，国内生产总值的三种表现形式为三种计算方法，即生产法、收入法和支出法，三种计算方法分别从不同的方面反映国内生产总值及其构成。

**三大产业** 根据社会生产活动历史发展的顺序对产业结构进行划分，产品直接取自自然界的部门称为第一产业，对初级产品进行再加工的部门称为第二产业，为生产和消费提供各种服务的部门称为第三产业。

**工业增加值** 指工业在报告期内以货币表现的工业生产活动的最终成果。

**国有及国有控股企业** 指国有企业加上国有控股企业。国有企业（过去的全民所有制工业或国营工业）是指企业全部资产归国家所有，并按《中华人民共和国企业法人登记管理条例》规定登记注册的非公司制的经济组织，包括国有企业、国有独资公司和国有联营企业。1957年以前的公私合营和私营工业，后均改造为国营工业，1992年改为国有工业，这部分工业的资料不单独分列时，均包括在国有企业内。国有控股企业是对混合所有制经济的企业进行的国有控股分类，它是指这些企业的全部资产中国有资产（股份）相对其他所有者中的任何一个所有者占资（股）最多的企业。该分组反映了国有经济控股情况。

**集体企业** 指企业资产归集体所有，并按《中华人民共和国企业法人登记管理条例》规定登记注册的经济组织，是社会主义公有制经济的组成部分。它包括城乡所有使用集体投资举办的企业，以及部分个人通过集资自愿放弃所有权并依法经工商行政管理机关认定为集体所有制的企业。

1 ■ **Nominal GDP** Nominal GDP is the Gross Domestic Product measured on the basis of current price.

**Gross Domestic Product** refers to Gross Domestic Product calculated at market price, which is all the final products of all resident units (enterprises and self-employed individuals) of a country (or region) during a certain period of time. In the practice of national accounting, Gross Domestic Product is calculated by three approaches, i. e. product approach, income approach, and expenditure approach, respectively to reflect Gross Domestic Product and its composition from different aspects.

**Three Industries** industry structure has been classified according to the historical sequence of development. Primary industry refers to extraction of natural resources, secondary industry involves processing of primary products, and tertiary industry provides services of various kinds for production and consumption.

**Industrial Value-added** refers to final results of industrial production of industry in money terms during reference period.

**State-owned and State-holding Enterprises** refer to state-owned enterprises plus state-holding enterprises. State-owned enterprises (originally known as state-run enterprises with ownership by the whole society) are non-corporate economic entities registered in accordance with the *Regulation of the People's Republic of China on the Management of Registration of Legal Enterprises*, where all assets are owned by the state. Included in this category are state-owned enterprises, state-funded corporations and state-owned joint-operation enterprises. Joint state-private industries and private industries, which existed before 1957, were transformed into state-run industries since 1957, and into state-owned industries after 1992. Statistics on those enterprises are included in the state-owned industries instead of grouping them separately. State-holding enterprises are a sub-classification of enterprises with mixed ownership, referring to enterprises where the percentage of state assets (or shares by the state) is larger than any other single share holder of the same enterprise. This sub-classification illustrates the control of the state assets.

**Collective Enterprises** refer to economic entities registered in accordance with the *Regulation of the People's Republic of China on the Management of Registration of Legal Enterprises,* where assets are owned collectively. Collective enterprises constitute an integral part of the socialist economy with public ownership. They include urban and rural enterprises invested collectively, and some enterprises registered in industrial and commercial administration agency as collective units where funds are pooled together by individuals who voluntarily give up their rights of ownership.

## 10 ■Concepts and Definitions for Major Indicators

**港、澳、台商投资企业**　指企业注册登记类型中的港、澳、台资合资、合作、独资经营企业和股份有限公司之和。

**Enterprises with Funds from Hong Kong, Macao and Taiwan**　refer to all industrial enterprises registered as the joint-venture cooperative, sole(exclusive) investment industrial enterprises and limited liability corporations with funds from Hong Kong, Macao and Taiwan.

**外商投资企业**　指企业注册登记类型中的中外合资、合作经营企业，外资企业和外商投资股份有限公司之和。

**Foreign Funded Enterprises**　refer to all industrial enterprises registered as the joint-venture, cooperative, sole(exclusive) investment industrial enterprises and limited liability corporations with foreign funds.

**城镇居民可支配收入**　指居民家庭在支付个人所得税后余下的实际收入，即实际收入减去个人所得税、家庭副业生产支出和记账补贴后的余额。

**Disposable Income of Urban Households**　equals the actual income deducted by the personal income tax, that is the remainder of the actual income deducted by the personal income tax, the expenditure of the sideline production of households and the subsidies paid for sample-data-collecting.

**全社会固定资产投资**　固定资产投资额是以货币表现的建造和购置固定资产活动的工作量。全社会固定资产投资包括国有经济单位投资、城乡集体经济单位投资、各种经济类型的单位投资和城乡居民个人投资。

**Total Investment in Fixed Assets**　value of investment in fixed assets refers to construction and purchase of fixed assets in money terms. Total investment in fixed assets includes investment by state-owned units, urban and rural collective units, and units of various other kinds of ownership and individual investment by urban and rural residents.

**基本建设投资**　指企业、事业、行政单位以扩大生产能力或工程效益为主要目的的新建、扩建工程及有关工作，包括工厂、矿山、铁路、桥梁、港口、农田水利、商店、住宅、学校、医院等工程的建造和机器设备、车辆、船舶、飞机等的购置。

**Capital Construction Investment**　refers to investment in new projects or an addition to existing facilities for the purposes of enlarging production capacity or improving efficiency, which includes construction of plants, mines, railways, bridges, harbors, water conservation facilities, stores, residential facilities, schools, hospitals, and purchase of machinery and equipment, vehicles, ships, and planes.

**基本建设投资额**　指以货币表现的基本建设完成的工作量。它是根据工程的实际进度按预算价格（预算价格是编制施工图预算时所用的价格）计算的工作量，没有形成工程实体的建筑材料和没有开始安装的设备，都不计算投资完成额。

**Value of Construction Investment**　refers to completion of capital construction in money terms. It is calculated at budget prices according to the actual completion of the project and therefore, construction materials and equipment not put into operation are not included.

**更新改造投资**　更新改造指国有企业、事业单位对原有设施进行固定资产更新和技术改造，以及相应配套的工程和有关工作（不包括大修理和维护工程）。更新改造投资是以货币表现的更新改造完成的工作量。

**Technical Upgrading and Transformation**　refers to the investment in projects to renew, modernize or replace existing assets and related supplementary projects (excluding major repairs and maintenance projects), which is presented in money terms.

## 10 ■ 主要指标的概念及定义

**社会消费品零售额**　指各种经济类型的批发和零售贸易业、餐饮业、制造业和其他行业对城乡居民和社会集团的消费品零售额。这个指标反映通过各种商品流通渠道向居民和社会集团供应的满足他们生活需要的消费品，是研究人民生活水平、社会消费品购买力、货币流通等问题的重要指标。

**进出口总额**　指实际进出我国境内的货物总金额。进出口总额用于观察一个国家在对外贸易方面的总规模。我国规定出口货物按离岸价格统计，进口货物按到岸价格统计。

**净出口**　指出口与进口的差额。

**外商直接投资**　指外国企业和经济组织或个人（包括华侨、港澳台胞以及我国在境外注册的企业）按我国有关政策、法规，用现汇、实物、技术等在我国境内开办外商独资企业，与我国境内的企业或经济组织共同举办中外合资经营企业、合作经营企业或合作开发资源的投资（包括外商投资收益的再投资），以及经政府有关部门批准的项目投资总额内，企业从境外借入的资金。

**外汇储备**　指一国政府所拥有的全部外汇，其表现形式可以是在国外银行的存款、外国国库券和长短期债券，以及在国际收支发生逆差时可以动用的债权。

**Value of Retail Sales of Consumer Goods**　refers to the sum of retail sales of consumer goods by wholesale and retail industry, catering, manufacturing establishments and establishments in other industries of different types of ownership to urban and rural households and institutions, as well as retail sales by farmers to non-agricultural households. Illustrating the supply of consumer goods through various channels to households and institutions to meet their demands, this is an important indicator for the study of issues on people's livelihood, on the purchasing power of consumer goods and on the circulation of money.

**The Total Value of Imports and Exports at Customs**　refers to the value of commodities imported into and exported from the boundary of China. The indicator of the total value of imports and exports at customs can be used to observe the total size of external trade in a country. Under the stipulation of Chinese government, exports are calculated on FOB basis, while imports are on CIF basis.

**Net Export**　refers to the difference between the value of exports and imports.

**Direct Investment by Foreign Business**　refers to the investment inside China by foreign enterprises and economic organizations or individuals (including overseas Chinese, compatriots in Hong Kong, Macao and Taiwan, and Chinese enterprises registered abroad), following the relevant policies and laws of China, for the establishment of wholly foreign-owned enterprises, by means of convertible currencies, supplies, technique and so on and the establishment of joint venture enterprises, contractual joint ventures or co-operative exploration of resources with enterprises or economic organization in China (including re-investment of profits from foreign businessmen's enterprises), and the funds that enterprises borrow from abroad in the total investment of projects which are approved by the relevant department of the government.

**Foreign Exchange Reserves**　refer to the total amount of foreign exchange held by the government of one country which can be in the form of the bank deposits abroad, treasury bonds, short-term and long-term bonds of foreign countries and the claims on nonresidents which can be utilized as the financing resources should the balance of payments deficits arise.

10 ■ Concepts and Definitions for Major Indicators

2 ■金融机构信贷收支表（人民币）

对金融机构信贷收支表的说明

　　金融机构范围包括中国人民银行、中国工商银行、中国农业银行、中国银行、中国建设银行、国家开发银行、中国进出口银行、中国农业发展银行、交通银行、中信银行、中国光大银行、华夏银行、广发银行、平安银行、招商银行、上海浦东发展银行、兴业银行、中国民生银行、恒丰银行、浙商银行、渤海银行、城市商业银行、城市信用社、农村信用社、农村商业银行、农村合作银行、外资银行、财务公司、信托投资公司、金融租赁公司、中国邮政储蓄银行、村镇银行 *。

[ 注 1 ] 对 2006 年货币统计报表的说明

　　自 2006 年起，中国人民银行按照国际货币基金组织《货币与金融统计手册》对货币金融统计制度进行了修订。2006 年一季度及以后各期数据与历史数据不完全可比。修订的主要内容包括以下三个方面：

　　①在机构分类上，将金融性公司划分为存款性公司和其他金融性公司，存款性公司划分为货币当局和其他存款性公司。货币当局为中国人民银行，其他存款性公司包括四大国有商业银行、其他国有银行、股份制商业银行、合作金融机构、中国邮政储蓄银行、财务公司。

　　②根据金融性公司新分类，开始编制其他存款性公司资产负债表；将中央银行资产负债表、其他存款性公司资产负债表合并，编制存款性公司概览。存款性公司概览同原银行概览相比，不包含信托投

2 ■ Sources and Uses of Credit Funds of Financial Institutions (RMB)

Notes to the Sheet of the Sources and Uses of Credit Funds of Financial Institutions

Financial Institutions include the People's Bank of China, Industrial and Commercial Bank of China, Agricultural Bank of China, Bank of China, China Construction Bank, China Development Bank, Export-Import Bank of China, Agricultural Development Bank of China, Bank of Communications, CITIC Bank, China Everbright Bank, Hua Xia Bank, Guangdong Development Bank, Ping An Bank, China Merchants Bank, Shanghai Pudong Development Bank, Industrial Bank Co., Ltd., China Minsheng Banking Corporation, Evergrowing Bank, China Zheshang Bank, China Bohai Bank, Urban Commercial Banks, Urban Credit Cooperatives, Rural Credit Cooperatives, Rural Commercial Banks, Rural Cooperative Banks, Foreign-funded Bank, Finance Companies, Trust and Investment Companies, Financial Leasing Companies and Postal Savings Bank of China, Rural Banks*.

Note 1: Introduction to 2006 Revision of Monetary Statistics

Since 2006, the People's Bank of China has revised the system of monetary and financial statistics in line with the IMF *Manual on Monetary and Financial Statistics*. As from the first quarter of 2006, the monetary statistics thereafter are not fully comparable with historical statistics.The revision includes the following 3 aspects:

① To reclassify the Financial Corporations as the depository corporations and other financial corporations. Depository corporations are sub-divided into categories of the monetary authority and other depository corporations. The monetary authority is the People's Bank of China; other depository corporations include 4 Major State-owned Commercial Banks, Other State-owned Banks, Joint Stock Commercial Banks, Cooperative Financial Institutions, Postal Savings Bank of China, Finance Companies.

② The balance sheet of other depository corporations has been compiled according to the new classification of the financial corporations since 2006. Depository corporations survey is the consolidation of the balance sheets of the monetary authority and the other depositary corporations. The

---

\* 自 2009 年 1 月起，金融机构范围包括村镇银行。
\* As of January 2009, Rural Banks were included in the coverage of financial institutions.

# 10 ■ 主要指标的概念及定义

资公司和金融租赁公司。自 2006 年开始不再编制银行概览、货币概览、存款货币银行资产负债表和特定存款机构资产负债表。

③调整部分报表项目。如将中央银行资产负债表中的"对存款货币银行债权""对特定存款机构债权""对其他金融机构债权"调整为"对其他存款性公司债权"和"对其他金融性公司债权"两项，将"储备货币"项下的"金融机构存款"三个子项调整为"其他存款性公司存款""其他金融性公司存款"等。

## 1. 货币当局

中国人民银行。

## 2. 其他存款性公司

(1) 四大国有商业银行：中国工商银行、中国农业银行、中国银行、中国建设银行。

(2) 其他国有银行：国家开发银行、中国进出口银行、中国农业发展银行。

(3) 股份制商业银行：交通银行、中信银行、中国光大银行、华夏银行、广发银行、平安银行、招商银行、上海浦东发展银行、兴业银行、中国民生银行、恒丰银行、浙商银行、渤海银行、农村商业银行、城市商业银行、外资商业银行。

(4) 合作金融机构：城市信用社、农村信用社、农村合作银行。

(5) 中国邮政储蓄银行。

(6) 财务公司。

main distinction between depository corporations survey and banking survey lies in the fact that data of trust and investment companies and financial leasing companies are not included in the depository corporations survey. Since 2006, the banking survey, monetary survey, balance sheet of monetary authorities, balance sheet of deposit money banks, balance sheet of specific depository institutions will no longer be compiled.

③ Adjust some items of all relevant statistical sheets. Examples: reclassify the 3 balance sheet items of the central bank— "claims on deposit money banks" "claims on specific depository institutions" and "claims on other financial institutions" to "claims on other depository corporations" and "claims on other financial corporations". Reclassify the 3 sub-items of "deposits of financial institutions" under "reserve money" to "deposits of other depository corporations" and "deposits of other financial corporations", etc..

## 1. Monetary Authority

The People's Bank of China.

## 2. Other Depository Corporations

(1) 4 Major State-owned Commercial Banks: Industrial and Commercial Bank of China, Agricultural Bank of China, Bank of China, China Construction Bank.

(2) Other State-owned Banks: China Development Bank, Export-Import Bank of China, Agricultural Development Bank of China.

(3) Joint Stock Commercial Banks: Bank of Communications, CITIC Bank, China Everbright Bank, Hua Xia Bank, Guangdong Development Bank, Ping An Bank, China Merchants Bank, Shanghai Pudong Development Bank, Industrial Bank, China Minsheng Banking Corporation, Evergrowing Bank, China Zheshang Bank, China Bohai Bank, Rural Commercial Banks, Urban Commercial Banks, Foreign-funded Commercial Banks.

(4) Cooperative Financial Institutions: Urban Credit Cooperatives, Rural Credit Cooperatives, Rural Cooperative Banks.

(5) Postal Savings Bank of China.

(6) Finance Companies.

## 10 Concepts and Definitions for Major Indicators

### 3．其他金融性公司

(1) 保险公司和养老基金（企业年金）。

(2) 信托投资公司。

(3) 金融租赁公司。

(4) 资产管理公司。

(5) 汽车金融服务公司。

(6) 金融担保公司。

(7) 证券公司。

(8) 投资基金。

(9) 证券交易所。

(10) 其他金融辅助机构。

### ［注2］ 对2010年货币统计报表的说明

自2010年1月起，中国人民银行按照国际货币基金组织《货币与金融统计手册》的概念、定义和分类，以中国境内各金融机构的本、外币业务统计数据为基础编制货币统计报表。

#### 主要变动

1．由于金融机构分组、会计科目的变动，对2009年12月末数据进行了修正。

2．调整其他存款性公司机构分组方法。

增设"中资大型银行资产负债表""中资中型银行资产负债表"和"中资小型银行资产负债表"。终止"国有商业银行资产负债表""股份制商业银行资产负债表""政策性银行资产负债表""城市商业银行资产负债表""中国邮政储蓄银行资产负债表"。

### 3. Other Financial Corporations

(1) Insurance Companies and Pension Fund (enterprise annuities).

(2) Financial Trust and Investment Companies.

(3) Financial Leasing Companies.

(4) Asset Management Companies.

(5) Auto Financing Companies.

(6) Financial Guarantee Companies.

(7) Securities Companies.

(8) Investment Funds.

(9) Stock Exchange.

(10) Other Financial Auxiliary Institutions.

### Note 2: Introduction to 2010 Revision of Monetary Statistics

As of January 2010, monetary and financial statistics are compiled based on the RMB and foreign currency statistical data of domestically operating financial institutions, in line with the concept, definition and classification of the IMF *Manual of Monetary and Financial Statistics*, by the People's Bank of China.

#### Major Revisions

1. Statistical data of December 2009 is adjusted as a result of the change in institutional classification and accounting items.

2. Classification of other depository corporations is adjusted.

Newly added balance sheets are compiled for: "Large-sized Domestic Banks" "Medium-sized Domestic Banks" and "Small-sized Domestic Banks". Original balance sheets are suspended for: "State-owned Commercial Banks" "Joint Stock Commercial Banks" "Policy Banks" "Urban Commercial Banks" and "Postal Savings Bank of China".

# 10 ■ 主要指标的概念及定义

中资大型银行：本外币资产总量超过 2 万亿元的中资银行（以 2008 年末各金融机构本外币资产总额为参考标准）。

中资中型银行：本外币资产总量小于 2 万亿元且大于 3000 亿元的中资银行。

中资小型银行：本外币资产总量小于 3000 亿元的中资银行。

3. 修订后的金融机构分组如下：

(1) 货币当局：中国人民银行。

(2) 其他存款性公司。

①中资大型银行：中国工商银行、中国建设银行、中国农业银行、中国银行、国家开发银行、交通银行、中国邮政储蓄银行。

②中资中型银行：招商银行、中国农业发展银行、上海浦东发展银行、中信银行、兴业银行、中国民生银行、中国光大银行、华夏银行、中国进出口银行、广发银行、平安银行、北京银行、上海银行、江苏银行。

③中资小型银行：恒丰银行、浙商银行、渤海银行、小型城市商业银行、农村商业银行、农村合作银行、村镇银行。

④外资商业银行。

⑤城市信用社。

⑥农村信用社。

⑦财务公司。

(3) 其他金融性公司。

Large-sized Domestic Banks: refer to all the domestic banks with the total RMB and foreign currency asset volume more than 2 trillion yuan (as of year-end 2008).

Medium-sized Domestic Banks: refer to all the domestic banks with the total RMB and foreign currency asset volume more than 300 billion yuan but less than 2 trillion yuan.

Small-sized Domestic Banks: refer to all the domestic banks with the total RMB and foreign currency asset volume less than 300 billion yuan.

3. Classification of Financial Institutions:

(1) Monetary Authority: the People's Bank of China.

(2) Other Depository Corporations.

① Large-sized Domestic Banks: Industrial and Commercial Bank of China, China Construction Bank, Agricultural Bank of China, Bank of China, China Development Bank, Bank of Communications, Postal Savings Bank of China.

② Medium-sized Domestic Banks: China Merchants Bank, Agricultural Development Bank of China, Shanghai Pudong Development Bank, CITIC Bank, Industrial Bank Co., Ltd., China Minsheng Banking Corporations, China Everbright Bank, Huaxia Bank, Export-Import Bank of China, Guangdong Development Bank, Ping An Bank, Bank of Beijing, Bank of Shanghai, Bank of Jiangsu.

③ Small-sized Domestic Banks: Evergrowing Bank, China Zheshang Bank, China Bohai Bank, Small-sized Urban Commercial Banks, Rural Commercial Banks, Rural Cooperative Banks, Rural Banks.

④ Foreign-funded Commercial Banks.

⑤ Urban Credit Cooperatives.

⑥ Rural Credit Cooperatives.

⑦ Finance Companies.

(3) Other Financial Corporations.

## 10 ■ Concepts and Definitions for Major Indicators

①保险公司和养老基金（企业年金）。

②信托投资公司。

③金融租赁公司。

④金融资产管理公司。

⑤汽车金融服务公司。

⑥金融担保公司。

⑦证券公司。

⑧投资基金。

⑨证券交易所。

⑩其他金融辅助机构。

**主要指标解释**

### 2.1 ■ 货币当局资产负债表

1. **国外资产**：中国人民银行控制的以人民币计值的国家外汇储备、货币黄金及在国际金融机构的头寸和以外汇缴存的人民币存款准备金。

2. **对政府债权**：中国人民银行持有的政府债券。

3. **对其他存款性公司债权**：中国人民银行对其他存款性公司发放的贷款、再贴现、持有的其他存款性公司发行的金融债券及从其他存款性公司买入的返售证券等。

4. **对其他金融性公司债权**：中国人民银行对其他金融性公司发放的贷款，办理的再贴现以及持有的其他金融性公司发行的债券等。

5. **对非金融性公司债权**：中国人民银行为支持老、少、边、穷地区发展而发放的专项贷款等。

① Insurance Companies and Pension Fund (Enterprise Annuities).

② Financial Trust and Investment Companies.

③ Financial Leasing Companies.

④ Asset Management Companies.

⑤ Auto Financing Companies.

⑥ Financial Guarantee Companies.

⑦ Securities Companies.

⑧ Investment Funds.

⑨ Stock Exchange.

⑩ Other Financial Auxiliary Institutions.

**Major Indicators**

### 2.1 ■ Statistical Composition of the Balance Sheet of Monetary Authorities

1. **Foreign Assets:** mainly include Renminbi equivalent value of the state foreign exchange reserves, monetary gold and position of the People's Bank of China with international financial institutions, as well as the RMB required reserves in foreign currencies.

2. **Claims on Government:** holding of government bonds by the People's Bank of China.

3. **Claims on Other Depository Corporations:** financing by the People's Bank of China in forms of lending, rediscounting, repos and etc., to other depository corporations,and purchased bonds issued by other depository corporations.

4. **Claims on Other Financial Corporations:** financing by the People's Bank of China in forms of lending and rediscounting, etc. to other financial corporations,and purchased bonds issued by other financial corporations.

5. **Claims on Non-financial Corporations:** earmarked loan of the People's Bank of China to poor,remote,and minorities areas for economic development.

# 10 ■ 主要指标的概念及定义

6. 其他资产：在本表中未作分类的资产。

7. 储备货币：中国人民银行发行的货币，金融机构在中国人民银行的准备金存款。

8. 发行债券：中国人民银行发行的债券。

9. 国外负债：以人民币计值的中国人民银行对非居民的负债，主要包括国际金融机构在中国人民银行的存款等。

10. 政府存款：各级政府在中国人民银行的财政性存款。

11. 自有资金：中国人民银行信贷基金。

12. 其他负债：在本表中未作分类的负债。

## 2.2 ■ 其他存款性公司资产负债表

1. 国外资产：其他存款性公司以人民币计值的对非居民的债权，主要包括库存外币现金、存放境外同业、拆放境外同业、境外有价证券投资、境外贷款等。

2. 储备资产：其他存款性公司存放在中国人民银行的准备金存款及库存现金。

3. 对政府债权：其他存款性公司持有的政府债券。

4. 对中央银行债权：其他存款性公司持有中国人民银行发行的债券及其他债权。

5. 对其他存款性公司债权：其他存款性公司持有的本机构以外的其他存款性公司以本币和外币计值的可转让存款、贷款、股票及其他股权、金融衍生工具等。

6. **Other Assets:** the assets not classified in the sheet.

7. **Reserve Money:** currency issued by the People's Bank of China and reserve requirements of financial insitutions.

8. **Bond Issue:** bonds issued by the People's Bank of China.

9. **Foreign Liabilities:** RMB equivalent value of non-resident claims on the People's Bank of China, mainly including deposits of international organizations with the People's Bank of China.

10. **Government Deposits:** treasury deposits of fiscal departments at various levels with the People's Bank of China.

11. **Self-owned Funds:** credit funds of the People's Bank of China.

12. **Other Liabilities:** the liabilities not classified in the sheet.

## 2.2 ■ Statistical Composition of the Balance Sheet of Other Depository Corporations (ODCs)

1. **Foreign Assets:** claims of other depository corporations on non-residents in Renminbi equivalent value, including cash in vaults, deposits with and lendings to foreign banks, overseas portfolio investments and overseas lending.

2. **Reserve Assets:** reserve requirements account with the People's Bank of China and cash in vaults.

3. **Claims on Government:** government bonds purchased by other depository corporations.

4. **Claims on Central Bank:** central bank bonds purchased by other depository corporations, and other claims on central bank.

5. **Claims on Other Depository Corporations:** claims of other depository corporations (ODCs)on other ODCs denominated in Renminbi or in foreign currencies, including transferrable deposits, loans,shares and other equities and financial derivatives, etc..

## 10 ■ Concepts and Definitions for Major Indicators

6. 对其他金融性公司债权：其他存款性公司存放和拆放给其他金融性公司的款项及持有其他金融性公司发行的债券等。

7. 对非金融性公司债权：其他存款性公司对非金融性公司发放的贷款、票据融资和对非金融性公司的投资等。

8. 对其他居民部门债权：其他存款性公司对其他居民部门发放的贷款等。

9. 其他资产：在本表中未作分类的资产。

10. 对非金融机构及住户负债：其他存款性公司吸收的非金融机构及住户的活期存款、定期存款、储蓄存款、外汇存款及其他负债。

11. 对中央银行负债：其他存款性公司向中国人民银行借入的款项，包括再贷款、再贴现、债券回购等。

12. 对其他存款性公司负债：其他存款性公司从其他存款性公司吸收的存款和拆入款等。

13. 对其他金融性公司负债：其他存款性公司从其他金融性公司吸收的存款和拆入款项等。

14. 国外负债：其他存款性公司以人民币计值的对非居民的负债，如非居民外汇存款、境外筹资和国外同业往来等。

15. 债券发行：其他存款性公司为筹措资金而发行的债券等。

16. 实收资本：其他存款性公司实际收到出资人投入公司的资本。

17. 其他负债：在本表中未作分类的负债。

**6. Claims on Other Financial Corporations:** deposits with and lending to other financial corporations by other depository corporations and purchased bonds issued by these financial corporations.

**7. Claims on Non-financial Corporations:** loans to, notes on discount to and investment in non-financial corporations by other depository corporations.

**8. Claims on Other Resident Sectors:** loans to other resident sectors by other depository corporations.

**9. Other Assets:** the assets not classified in the sheet.

**10. Liabilities to Non-financial Institutions & Households Sectors:** deposits of non-financial & households sectors with other depository corporations, including demand deposits, time deposits and saving deposits, foreign exchange savings and other liabilities.

**11. Liabilities to Central Bank:** borrowing from the People's Bank of China in forms of borrowing, rediscounting, repos and etc., by other depository corporations.

**12. Liabilities to Other Depository Corporations:** deposits of and borrowing from other ODCs by other depository corporations.

**13. Liabilities to Other Financial Corporations:** deposits of and borrowing from other financial corporations.

**14. Foreign Liabilities:** liabilities of other depository corporations to non-residents in Renminbi equivalent value, including foreign exchange deposit of non-resident, external borrowing, and inter-bank transactions with foreign banks.

**15. Bonds Issue:** bonds issued by other depository corporations.

**16. Paid-up Capital:** capital contributed actually by the investors to other depository corporations.

**17. Other Liabilities:** the liabilities not classified in the sheet.

# 10 ■主要指标的概念及定义

## 2.3 ■ 存款性公司概览及货币供应量

将汇总的货币当局资产负债表与汇总的其他存款性公司资产负债表合并，编制存款性公司概览。

广义货币为存款性公司概览中的货币和准货币，现阶段我国货币供应量分为以下三个层次：

**M0**：流通中现金；
**M1**：货币，M0 + 活期存款；
**M2**：M1 + 准货币。

自 2001 年 6 月起，准货币中含证券公司存放在金融机构的客户保证金。

## 3 ■ 金融市场

金融市场指资金供给者和资金需求者从事资金融通活动的场所。

**同业拆借**　指与全国银行间同业拆借中心联网的金融机构之间通过同业中心的交易系统进行的无担保资金融通行为。拆借期限最短为 1 天，最长为 1 年。交易中心按 1 天、7 天、14 天、21 天、1 个月、2 个月、3 个月、4 个月、6 个月、9 个月、1 年共 11 个品种计算和公布加权平均利率。

**质押式回购**　指交易双方进行的以债券为权利质押的一种短期资金融通业务，指资金融入方（正回购方）在将债券出质给资金融出方（逆回购方）融入资金的同时，双方约定在将来某一日期由正回购方按约定回购利率计算的资金额向逆回购方返还资金，逆回购解除出质债券上质权的融资行为。质押式回购的期限为 1 天到 365 天，交易系统按 1 天、7 天、14 天、21 天、1 个月、2 个月、3 个月、4 个月、6 个月、9 个月、1 年共 11 个品种统计公布质押式回购的成交量和成交价。

## 2.3 ■ Depository Corporations Survey and Money Supply

Depository corporations survey is the consolidation of the balance sheets of the monetary authorities and other depository corporations.

Broad money is the money and the quasi-money of the depository corporations. There are three indicators of money stock at current stage in China:

**M0**: currency in circulation;
**M1**: or money, M0 + demand deposits;
**M2**: M1 + quasi-money.

Effective June 2001, other deposits would include margin account of security companies maintained with financial institutions.

## 3 ■ Financial Markets

Financial markets are markets in which financing activities occur between supplier and demander.

**Interbank Lending**　refers to no-guarantee financing business which is dealt through the trading system of the CFETS by and among financial institutions which link the CFETS via the network. For interbank lending, the shortest term is 1 day, and the longest term is 1 year. The CFETS is responsible for calculating and publicating the weighted average rates in accord with a total of 11 terms including 1 day, 7 days, 14 days, 21 days, 1 month, 2 months, 3 months, 4 months, 6 months, 9 months, and 1 year.

**Pledged Repo**　a type of short-term financing business where bonds are used by both trading parties as a pledge of rights. It refers to a financing act in which borrower (positive repo party), pledges bonds to lender (reverse repo party) for funds, and at the same time two parties agree upon that when at a future date positive repo party returns the amount of funds calculated at the specified repo rate to the reverse repo party, the reverse repo party shall lift the pledged rights on the pledged bonds. The terms of pledged repo range from 1 day to 365 days. Through the trading system, the trading volume and price of pledged repo is publicly released as a total of 11 terms including 1 day, 7 days, 14 days, 21 days, 1 month, 2 months, 3 months, 4 months, 6 months, 9 months and 1 year.

## 10 ■ Concepts and Definitions for Major Indicators

**债券** 以票据形式筹集资金而发行的、承诺按一定利率付息和一定期限偿还本金的书面债务证书。包括国债、中央银行票据、金融债券、公司信用类债券等。

**国债** 政府发行的债券。

**金融债券** 除中央银行以外的金融机构发行的债券。

**公司信用类债券** 非金融企业发行的债券，包括非金融企业债务融资工具、企业债券以及公司债、可转债等。

**Shibor** 上海银行间同业拆放利率，以位于上海的全国银行间同业拆借中心为技术平台计算、发布并命名，是由信用等级较高的银行组成报价团自主报出的人民币同业拆出利率计算确定的算术平均利率，是单利、无担保、批发性利率。目前，对社会公布的 Shibor 品种包括隔夜、1 周、2 周、1 个月、3 个月、6 个月、9 个月及 1 年。

**中债国债收益率曲线** 以全国银行间市场发行的人民币计价的固定利率国债为样本券，期限自隔夜至 50 年的收益率曲线。样本券发行人为中华人民共和国财政部。

**中债中短期票据收益率曲线（AAA 级）** 以全国银行间市场发行的人民币计价的固定利率中期票据、短期融资券、超短期融资券和非公开定向债务融资工具为样本券，期限自隔夜至 15 年的收益率曲线。样本券发行人为主体信用评级为 AAA 级的非金融机构。

**Bonds** negotiable and bearer instruments which give the holder the unconditional right to a fixed or contractually determined variable interest on a specified date or dates. They include government securities, central bank bills, financial bonds, and corporate debenture bonds.

**Government Securities** securities issued by the government.

**Financial Bonds** bonds issued by the financial institutions excluding the central bank.

**Corporate Debenture Bonds** bonds issued by the non-financial corporate businesses and include non-financial enterprise financing instruments, enterprise bonds, corporate bonds, convertible bonds, etc..

**Shibor** Shanghai Interbank Offered Rate is calculated, announced and named on the technological platform of the National Interbank Funding Center in Shanghai. It is a simple, no-guarantee, wholesale interest rate calculated by arithmetically averaging all the interbank RMB lending rates offered by the price quotation group of banks with a high credit rating. Currently, the Shibor consists of eight maturities: overnight, 1 week, 2 weeks, 1 month, 3 months, 6 months, 9 months and 1 year.

**Chinabond Yield Curve of Government Securities** the yield curve with sample securities of CNY-denominated fixed-rate treasury bond with Yield-to-Maturity from O/N to 50 years in national interbank market. The issuer of the sample securities is Ministry of Finance of People's Republic of China.

**Chinabond Yield Curve of Medium/Short-term Notes (AAA)** the yield curve with sample securities of CNY-denominated fixed-rate Medium-term notes, Short-term financing bonds, Super Short-term commercial paper and Privately placed debt-financing instruments with Yield-to-Maturity from O/N to 15 years in national interbank market. The issuer of the sample securities are non-financial institutions with credit rating of AAA.

# 10 ■主要指标的概念及定义

## 4 ■资金流量表主要指标的概念及定义

**资金流量表（金融交易账户）**① 用矩阵账户的表现形式，反映国民经济各机构部门之间，以及国内与国外之间所发生的金融交易的流量。该账户将国民经济所有的机构单位分为五大机构部门：住户、非金融企业、政府、金融机构和国外，列在矩阵账户的宾栏；将发生在这五大机构部门之间的所有金融交易按交易发生时所采用的金融工具的形式进行分类，列在矩阵账户的主栏；按照资金流量核算原则，采用复式记账法，以交易价格记录所有金融交易流量的价值；在每一个机构部门下，设来源与运用，反映各机构部门在各种金融资产与负债上的变化。

**住户部门** 由城镇住户和农村住户构成，含个体经营户。该部门主要从事最终消费活动及自我使用为目的的生产活动，也从事少量的以营利为目的的生产活动。

**非金融企业部门** 由所有从事非金融生产活动，并以营利为目的的常住独立核算的法人企业单位组成。

**政府部门** 由中央政府、各级地方政府、机关团体和社会保障基金组成。该部门为公共和个人消费提供非营利性产出，并承担对国民收入和财富进行再分配的职责。

**金融部门** 由主要从事金融中介或相关辅助性金融活动的金融性公司和准公司组成。该部门提供银行、保险、证券业等金融服务。

## 4 ■Flow of Funds Statement's Concepts and Definitions for major Indicators

**Flow of Funds Statement (Financial Transactions Accounts)**① being presented in matrix format. Flow of Funds Accounts encompass all financial transactions among domestic sectors and between these sectors and the rest of the world. In the accounts, all institutional units are grouped under five sectors: households, non-financial corporations, general government, financial institutions and the rest of the world, and all financial transactions are mainly classified by financial instruments. The financial transactions and sectors are listed on the rows and columns of the matrix respectively. The double entry flow of funds accounting is based on an accrual basis. All flows are measured according to the transaction prices. The terms sources and uses are employed to reflect the changes in financial assets and financial liabilities of each sector.

**Households** include urban and rural households with individually-owned enterprises also included. The sector is mainly engaged in final consumption and self-serving production. Some of them are also engaged in profit-making production.

**Non-financial Corporations** consist of resident corporate units which are market producers and whose principal activity is the production of goods and non-financial services.

**General Government** includes central government, local government, government organization and social security funds. They produce and supply non-market output for collective and individual consumption and they also assume responsibilities for redistributing national income and wealth.

**Financial Institutions** include financial corporations and financial institutions, which are primarily involved in financial intermediation and related auxiliary financial activities. They supply financial service including banking, insurance, and securities.

---

① 目前有些金融交易尚无法统计，如股权、商业信用和某些应收应付项目等。
① Some financial transactions are not accounted temporarily, such as equity, trade credit, some accounts receivable/payable.

## 10 ■ Concepts and Definitions for Major Indicators

国外部门 与国内机构单位发生金融交易的所有非常住机构单位。

**The Rest of the World** non-resident units which have financial transactions with resident units.

资金运用合计 各部门资金运用之和。

**Financial Uses** are the total amounts in the uses column of each sector.

资金来源合计 为各部门资金来源之和。

**Financial Sources** are the total amounts in the sources column of each sector.

净金融投资 资金运用合计与资金来源合计的差额。

**Net Financial Investment** is the differences between financial uses and financial sources.

通货① 以现金形式存在于市场流通领域中的货币，包括辅币和纸币。

**Currency**① notes and coins in circulation.

存款 以各种形式存在存款类金融机构的存款，包括活期存款、定期存款、财政存款、外汇存款和其他存款等。

**Deposits** include all types of deposits of depository financial institutions, including demand deposits, time deposits, fiscal deposits, foreign exchange deposits and others.

活期存款 没有约定期限、随时可提取使用的存款。

**Demand Deposits** deposits which can be withdrawn on demand.

定期存款 约定存期、利率，到期支取本息的存款。

**Time Deposits** deposits that are subject to a fixed term and interest rate, which can be withdrawn principal and interest after the specified term.

财政存款 财政部门存放在银行业金融机构的各项财政资金。

**Fiscal Deposits** deposits of government sector in the banking financial institutions.

外汇存款 境内各机构部门在境内金融机构及国外的外币存款，以及国外部门在国内金融机构的外币存款。

**Foreign Exchange Deposits** foreign exchange denominated deposits of non-financial residents with domestic financial institutions and the rest of world, and those of non-residents with domestic financial institutions.

其他存款 未包括在以上存款中的其他存款，如委托存款、信托存款等。

**Other Deposits** deposits which are not classified above, such as designated deposits, trust deposits, etc..

---

① 现在还无法统计人民币在国外流通的以及外币在国内流通的货币数量。
① RMB circulated in foreign countries and the domestically circulated foreign currencies are not accounted temporarily.

# 10 ■ 主要指标的概念及定义

**贷款** 指金融机构发放的各类贷款，包括短期贷款、票据融资、中长期贷款、外汇贷款、委托贷款和其他贷款等。

**Loans** all transactions in loans, including short-term loans, bills financing, medium-term and long-term loans, foreign exchange loans, designated loans and other loans.

**短期贷款与票据融资** 指金融机构发放的短期贷款和票据融资。其中，短期贷款指金融机构提供的期限在 1 年以内（含 1 年）的贷款；票据融资指银行业金融机构通过对客户持有的商业汇票、银行承兑汇票等票据进行贴现提供的融资。

**Short-term Loans and Bills Financing** provided by financial institutions with a short-term maturity(usually within one year or one year) are short-term loans; bills financing means that the financial institutions offer the funds to the clients by discounting the commercial paper, bankers' acceptance bills, and other papers held by the clients.

**中长期贷款** 金融机构为企业和住户等部门提供的期限在 1 年以上的贷款。

**Medium-term and Long-term Loans** loans with a long-term (usually beyond one year) maturity.

**外汇贷款** 境内金融机构对其他机构部门提供的外币贷款，以及国外对境内机构提供的贷款。

**Foreign exchange loans** loans in foreign currencies made by domestic financial institutions to non-financial residents and the rest of the world and loans to residents by the rest of the world.

**委托贷款** 由政府部门、企事业单位及个人等委托人提供资金，由贷款人（受托人）根据委托人确定的贷款对象、用途、金额、期限、利率等代为发放、监督使用并协助收回的贷款。

**Designated Loans** used and managed for specified target and goals by banking financial institutions entrusted by government, enterprises, households or other designators which offer the funds.

**其他贷款** 未包括在以上贷款中的其他贷款，如信托贷款、融资租赁、各项垫款等。

**Other Loans** loans which are not classified above, include trust loans, fianancial leasing, advances, etc..

**未贴现的银行承兑汇票** 指未贴现的银行承兑汇票，即企业签发的全部银行承兑汇票扣减已在银行表内贴现部分。

**Undiscounted Bankers' Acceptance Bills** bankers' acceptance bills which haven't been discounted in financial institutions, equals all the bankers' acceptance bills minus their discounted parts.

**保险准备金** 指社会保险和商业保险基金的净权益，保险费预付款和未结索赔准备金。

**Insurance Technical Reserves** consist of net equity of social insurance and commercial insurance funds reserves, prepayments of insurance premiums, and reserves for outstanding claims.

**金融机构往来** 指金融机构部门子部门之间发生的同业存放、同业拆借和债券回购等。

**Inter-financial Institutions Accounts** consist of nostro & vostro accounts, interbank lending and repo among the subsectors of financial institutions.

## 10 ◼ Concepts and Definitions for Major Indicators

**存款准备金** 指各金融机构在中央银行的存款及缴存中央银行的法定准备金。

**Required and Excessive Reserves** financial institutions deposits in the People's Bank of China.

**债券** 机构单位为筹措资金而发行，并且承诺按约定条件偿还的有价证券，包括政府债券、金融债券、中央银行债券、企业债券等。

**Bonds** securities issued by institutions to raise funds and repaid in line with stipulated terms and conditions, including government bonds, financial bonds, central bank bonds, corporate bonds, etc..

**政府债券** 是政府机构部门发行并承诺在一定期限内还本付息的有价证券。

**Government and Public Bonds** bonds issued and guaranteed by the government institutions with interest and principal repaid on dates as agreed.

**金融债券** 除中央银行以外的金融机构发行的债券。

**Financial Bonds** bonds issued by the financial institutions excluding the central bank.

**中央银行债券** 中央银行发行的债券。

**Central Bank Bonds** bonds issued by the central bank.

**企业债券** 非金融企业发行的各类债券。

**Corporate Bonds** bonds issued by the non-financial corporate businesses.

**股票**[1] 股份有限公司依照公司法的规定，为筹集公司资本所发行的、用于证明股东身份和权益并据以获得股息和红利的凭证。

**Shares**[1] documents which represent property rights on corporations and entitle the holders to a share in the profits of the corporations and to a share in their net assets.

**证券投资基金份额** 由证券投资基金发行的，证明投资人持有的基金单位数量的受益凭证。

**Securities Investment Funds Shares** issued by securities investment funds, indicate quantities of funds held by investors.

**库存现金** 银行机构为办理本币和外币现金业务而准备的现金业务库存。

**Cash in Vault** local and foreign cashes reserved for business by banks.

**中央银行贷款** 指中央银行向各金融机构的贷款。

**Central Bank Loans** loans to financial institutions by the central bank.

**直接投资** 外国对我国的直接投资及我国常住单位对外国的直接投资。

**Foreign Direct Investment** foreign direct investment from abroad and outward direct investments made by domestic residents.

① 目前仅含能在股票交易所进行交易的股票的发行筹资额。
① Only includes listed shares.

# 10 ■主要指标的概念及定义

**其他对外债权债务**　除储备资产、外汇存贷款和债券以外的国内与国外之间的债权债务。

**国际储备资产**　指我国中央银行的对外资产，包括外汇、货币黄金、特别提款权、在国际货币基金组织的储备头寸等。

**国际收支误差与遗漏**[1]　国际收支平衡表采用复式记账法。由于统计资料来源和时点不同等原因，形成经常账户与资本和金融账户不平衡的统计误差与遗漏。

**Other Foreign Assets and Liabilities**　the changes in foreign assets and liabilities other than reserve assets, foreign exchange deposits and loans, bonds.

**International Reserve Assets**　refer to external assets held by China's central bank, including foreign exchange, monetary gold, SDRs, reserve positions with the International Monetary Fund (IMF), and etc..

**Errors and Omissions in the BOP**[1]　arise from inconsistencies between current account and capital and financial account due to differences in source and point of time during the process of compiling the Balance of Payments through double-entry accounting.

## 5 ■5000 户企业景气调查

5000 户企业景气调查制度建于 1990 年。调查包括月度工业企业主要财务指标统计及季度工业景气状况问卷调查。调查企业以国有大中型工业生产企业为主，还包括一些具有相当经济规模，有代表性的集体工业生产企业及企业集团。1993 年以后增加了部分合资、外资及股份制工业生产企业。调查企业涉及 27 个行业，样本企业结构与中国工业的企业结构基本适应。调查结果大体上能反映中国工业的景气状况。

## 5 ■ Business Survey of 5000 Principal Enterprises

The system of business survey of 5000 principal enterprises was initiated in 1990. The business survey encompasses monthly statistics of financial indicators of industrial enterprises and quarterly conducted questionnaire research of business conditions of these enterprises. The state-owned large-size and medium-size industrial enterprises constitute the majority of surveyed enterprises with some representative collectively-owned enterprises and conglomerates of handsome economic scale also being included in the samples. Since 1993, some joint venture, foreign-funded and share-holding industrial enterprises have entered into the survey successively. The surveyed enterprises involve 27 industries and the structure of sample enterprises is commensurate with that of China's industrial enterprises. The outcome of the business survey can basically reflect the business conditions of China's industry.

---

[1] 由于无法区分国际收支误差与遗漏中经常项目和资本项目的金额，目前资金流量核算中将国际收支的全部误差与遗漏都记录在资金流量金融账户中。

[1] Because it is difficult to identify the amount of this item on the current account and on the capital account, all the Errors and Omissions in the BOP in the Balance of Payments are presented on the flow of funds accounts temporarily.

## 10 ■ Concepts and Definitions for Major Indicators

**货币资金占用系数** 为了实现一定量的产品销售需要占用的货币资金数量，即单位销售额占用的货币资金数。它可用于判断企业货币资金的松紧程度。

货币资金占用系数＝期末货币资金余额／（当年累计）产品销售收入额 ×12／月数

**Ratio of Monetary Funds Occupation** the amount of monetary funds required for realizing a certain amount of product sales, i.e. money required per unit sale. It is used for analyzing monetary situation of enterprises.

Ratio of monetary funds occupation=period-end balance of monetary funds/(current year accumulated)amount of product sales × 12/months

**流动比率** 指流动资产总额和流动负债总额之比。流动比率表示企业流动资产中在短期债务到期时变现用于偿还流动负债的能力。

流动比率＝流动资产合计／流动负债合计 ×100%

**Liquidity Ratio** ratio of liquid assets against liquid liabilities. It indicates an enterprise's capacity of liquidating assets to repay liquid liabilities when short-term debt becomes due.

Liquidity ratio=liquid assets/liquid liabilities × 100%

**资产负债率** 指一定时期内企业流动负债和长期负债与企业总资产的比率。该指标既反映企业经营风险的大小，又反映企业利用债权人提供的资金从事经营活动的能力。

资产负债率＝（流动负债＋长期负债）／资产总计 ×100%

**Liabilities / Assets Ratio** ratio of liquid and long-term liabilities to total assets of an enterprise during the fixed period. It not only indicates the riskness of an enterprise, but also the operational capacities of the enterprise in utilizing creditor's money.

Liabilities/Assets ratio=(liquid liabilities+long-term liabilities)/ total assets × 100%

**流动资产周转率** 指一定时期内流动资产平均占用额完成产品销售额的周转次数，反映流动资产周转速度和流动资产利用效果。

流动资产周转率＝（当年累计产品销售收入额 ×12／月数）／流动资产平均占用额

**Turn-over Ratio of Liquid Assets** number of times of average liquid assets' turn-over in a certain period for realizing products sales. It indicates the turn-over speed of liquid assets and effectiveness of the use of liquid assets.

Turn-over ratio of liquid assets=(accumulated sales of the current year × 12/months)/average liquid assets utilization

**工业产品销售率** 指一定时期内产品销售收入占工业产值的百分比，是反映工业产品生产已实现销售的程度，分析工业产销衔接状况的指标。

工业产品销售率＝产品销售收入额／工业总产值（现价）×100%

**Industrial Products Sales Ratio** ratio of product sales against total industrial production. It reflects the realized product sales in the industrial production enterprises and the links between production and sales.

Industrial production sales ratio=revenue of product sales/ value of industrial production(current price) × 100%

**销售成本利润率** 指一定时期内实现的利润额与耗费的销售成本总额之间的比率。

销售成本利润率＝利润总额／产品销售成本 ×100%

**Ratio of Profits to Sales Expenses** ratio of realized profits against sales expenses.

Ratio of profits to sales expenses=profits/product sales expenses × 100%

## 10 ■ 主要指标的概念及定义

6 ■ **零售价格指数**　由国家统计局编制，是反映城乡商品零售价格变动趋势的一种经济指数。零售物价的调整变动直接影响城乡居民的生活支出和国家的财政收入，影响居民购买力和市场供需平衡，影响消费与积累的比例。因此，计算零售价格指数，可以从一个侧面对上述经济活动进行观察和分析。

**居民消费价格总指数**　由国家统计局编制，是反映一定时期内城乡居民所购买的生活消费品和服务项目价格变动趋势及程度的相对数，是综合了城市居民消费价格指数和农民消费价格指数计算取得的。利用居民消费价格指数，可以观察和分析消费品的零售价格和服务价格变动对城乡居民实际生活费支出的影响程度。

**企业商品价格指数**　由中国人民银行编制，其前身是批发物价指数，始编于 1994 年。这是反映企业间商品交易价格变动趋势和程度的综合价格指数，其商品调查范围涵盖全社会物质产品，既包括投资品，也包括消费品。指数体系包括三种分类：一是按国家标准行业分类，二是按商品的生产过程分类，三是按商品用途（也称需求）分类。企业商品价格指数采用固定权数加权几何平均公式计算，所用权数根据投入产出表和工业普查资料、农业统计资料和其他补充调查资料测算。全国共有 220 多个调查城市，分布在除西藏以外的各省、自治区和直辖市。所选商品 791 种，规格品 1700 多种，报价企业 2500 户。

6 ■ **Retail Price Index (RPI)** reflects the general change in prices of retail commodities, which is compiled by State Statistics Bureau (SSB). The changes in retail prices directly affect living expenditure of urban and rural residents and government revenue, purchasing power of residents and equilibrium of market supply and demand, and the proportion of consumption and accumulation. Therefore, RPI can predict to certain extent the changes of the above economic activities.

**Consumer Price Index (CPI)** reflects the relative change in prices of consumer goods and services purchased by urban and rural residents, and is derived from urban CPI and rural CPI, which is compiled by SSB. CPI can be used to predict the impact of consumer price changes on living expenditure of urban and rural residents.

**Corporate Goods Price Index (CGPI)** compiled by the People's Bank of China and it was preceded by Wholesale Price Index (WPI), which had come into existence since 1994. CGPI is a comprehensive price index, which represents developments in the prices of goods provided in inter-enterprise transactions. The surveyed goods of CGPI covers all material products of the whole society, i.e. capital goods and consumer goods. And the Price Index System can be classified as three different categories: the first one classification is in line with the state standard industry classification, the second one is on the basis of different production process, and the third one is on the basis of commodity uses. The calculation of CGPI is based on the equation of fixed-weighted geometric mean with the weights calculated on the basis of the input-output table, industry general survey, agriculture statistics and other supplementary survey. There are more than 220 cities joining the survey, which covers all provinces, municipalities under direct jurisdiction of central government, and autonomous regions except Tibet. The CGPI covers 791 surveyed commodities, more than 1700 sample goods and 2500 outlets of enterprises.

责任编辑：贾　真
责任校对：李俊英
责任印制：裴　刚

**图书在版编目（CIP）数据**

中国人民银行统计季报．2020年第1期：总第97期／中国人民银行调查统计司编．—北京：
中国金融出版社，2020.3
ISBN 978-7-5220-0681-9

Ⅰ．①中…　Ⅱ．①中…　Ⅲ．①中国人民银行 — 统计资料—2020　Ⅳ．① F832.31-66

中国版本图书馆 CIP 数据核字（2020）第 117338 号

中国人民银行统计季报 2020-1
ZHONGGUO RENMIN YINHANG TONGJI JIBAO 2020-1

出　版
发　行　中国金融出版社

社　　址　北京市丰台区益泽路 2 号
市场开发部　（010）66024766，63805472，63439533（传真）
网 上 书 店　http：//www.chinafph.com
　　　　　　（010）66024766，63372837（传真）
读者服务部　（010）66070833，62568380
邮　编　100071
经　销　新华书店
印　刷　北京侨友印刷有限公司
装　订　平阳装订厂
尺　寸　210 毫米 ×285 毫米
印　张　7
字　数　212 千
版　次　2020 年 3 月第 1 版
印　次　2020 年 3 月第 1 次印刷
定　价　98.00 元
ISBN 978-7-5220-0681-9
如出现印装错误本社负责调换　联系电话（010）63263947